What
Sex Is a
Republican?

Works by the same author:

Innovative Leadership & Public Policy
Midwest Legislators Conference 2004

Women as Leaders
Women's Conference 2008

Inspiring Change from Within
2009

See
www.mccormickdawson.com

www.themccormickstandard.com

WHAT SEX IS A REPUBLICAN?

Stories from the Front Lines in American Politics
and How You Can Change
the Way Things Are

Former State Representative
Terri McCormick, MA

THE CAPITOL PRESS.

What Sex Is A Republican?
Copyright © 2023 Terri McCormick, M.A.

Photo insert design by Steve Russell

Library of Congress Control Number: 2023931417
             Paperback: 978-1-960362-02-5
             eBook: 978-1-960362-03-2

This book is dedicated to my faithful husband and family, who would never for a moment let me falter or fail in my mission to serve the people of Wisconsin.

I would also like to dedicate this book to my former legislative staff, campaign volunteers and supporters who understood that public service was not about us. Public service is about putting service over self for the expressed purpose of making a difference for the greater good.

Thank you all who gave me back my faith in democracy, in the power of people to move mountains and in our Republican form of government. All of my campaign supporters throughout the state— you forever have my gratitude.

To the veterans I hold in my heart, I know of your sacrifice. Thank you for your love and support.

Most assuredly, this book is dedicated to my "kindred spirits," Rep. Judy Krawczyk and Rep. Karl Van Roy ...

"All for one and one for all!"

*Now and then, an innocent man or woman
is sent to the legislature!*

**Frank McKinney Hubbard, 1868–1930,
American cartoonist, humorist, journalist**

CONTENTS

ACKNOWLEDGMENTS

Thank you, my husband, my best friend.

My sincere gratitude to Jared Guzman and Kristen Lease for their contributions in the writing of this book.

My sincere appreciation goes out to Tony Seton and Lori Widmer for their heartfelt patience through my several drafts of this work.

Thank you for the dedication and support of my work in public life to Jim Bartholomew, Dan O'Brien, Merry Wagner, Ellen Breithaupt, Dave Soulis, Oscar and Tom Boldt, Ralph Kennedy II, John and Rose Bykowski, Dr. Rick and Neelam Davison, Larry Bilotta, Susan Behm, Sharon Tornes, Julie Brickner, Brickner Family, Kerry Thomas, Karen Harkness, Jerry Stevens, B.J. and Carrie Johnson, Harold and Jean Grimes, Robert and Evelyn Kettner, Shawn Peter, Kittie Murray, Dan Davies, Steve Russell, Patrick Murray, Chad Kleist, Sarah Schneider, Robyn Gruner, Kyle Skidmore, Dawn Nowakowski, Steven Constine, Jerry and Louise Unmuth, Don Falk, Mark Ellis, Michael and Susan Edwards, Frank Krueger, Bill and Lois Yates, Vern Krawczyk, Bob Darrow, Michael Welhouse, Jennifer Streblow, Kelley Willett and citizen leaders who stood with us to make a difference.

A portion of the proceeds from this book will be donated to the Dawson Foundation.

The Dawson Foundation is dedicated to the education and development of leadership in government, business and the media with the fundamental principles of courage, integrity and citizenship.

FOREWORD

"We the People"

When we hear the word *politics*, our eyebrows rise in suspicion, as the corners of our mouths turn down in opprobrium. Sort of like how some people speak scathingly of environmentalists or even worse, liberals. Of course, those words have picked up such enormous baggage that it deafens most people to the facts. No wonder our country is so riven.

Is it the fault of right-wing talk radio? Or, for that matter, the two-party system? Perhaps it's that our civilization is still rather primitive, and we feel a need to separate ourselves from each other, and that comes down to pointing out that one of us is good and the other is bad.

If someone is trying to protect endangered species, he must be a wacko enviro, and we should ignore—nay, eschew!—his concerns about pollution. If some lib is seeking better education for her community, we should fight her, because being liberal must mean that she thinks everyone is entitled to everything, regardless of their willingness to work for it. Isn't that what liberal means?

No. Any more than politics means corruption, incompetence, and scandal.

Actually, the root of the word *politics* is fairly benign, but at the same time, its meaning is vital to our future. The word derives from the Greek, meaning "management of the community." Politics isn't bad or good; it is simply essential, whether applying the term to Appleton or the United States or the earth.

That's not to say that there aren't politicians inside the Beltway, in statehouses and city halls across the nation, who shouldn't be in prison. Politics attracts all too many people who find power an aphrodisiac. They're in it for the authority, the fawning treatment, the perks, the obsequious constituents.

Many—though not all—seem to want the title but aren't inclined to do the work. They become party loyalists, voting with or against proposals, based not on the merits of the issue but on the dicta of leadership. Or they do the bidding of special interests—read: "campaign contributors."

But let us not wallow in cynicism. It is important to remember that a large number of those in politics today are not ignorant, crooked, or venal. They are men and women who heard the clarion call of public service and who mortgaged their lives, in many cases, to do the work of the people. These good people can be found on both sides of the aisle, both downtown and on Capitol Hill.

Imagine their struggle with the power structure. They come in, fresh-faced, committed, and hopeful. Then they discover that the presumption of openness, integrity, and shared purpose has been rattled, kinked, and scorned in tomes on naivety. Instead of dedicated, hard-working bipartisanship, there's an entirely different mantra, one that compels supplication to those running the game. Sometimes, one party has control; sometimes, neither can own the shop, or they both find power-sharing more profitable than mutually assured destruction.

In some arenas, the novice is allowed to climb the political ladder, based on quality work as much as obeisance. Unfortunately, it seems that power does have a tendency to corrupt. Or maybe it is that we haven't evolved to a level of consciousness where the majority won't allow themselves to be swayed from the just cause and the right path.

I know, I know, dream on—but dreams are not enough, at least, not for those honest people in the trenches, those who won't waiver in their commitment to those who cast ballots for them. Probably, most political tyros arrive on the scene with intentions of honoring the wishes of their constituents, but they are told that to go along, they have to get along. (Or is it the other way?) They have to learn the art of compromise: the tenet that no proposed legislation makes it into law without the noblest author giving up some principles.

It's important that people in a country like ours understand this process so that they aren't discouraged by the reality of politics today, and so they can commit themselves to changing that reality. Our government is supposed to be of, by, and for the people; it should not be a tool of special interests to sate their gluttony.

Terri McCormick has seen these choices, up close and personal, in ways that would cow most observers and crush most players. Both at the state and federal levels, she's seen the evils of too much power in the hands of the depraved, either before their vesting or with the acquisition of power. Some were cheats, liars, and thieves before they arrived at the statehouse; others learned the trade from their party forbears.

In *What Sex Is a Republican?* Terri describes her experiences in very human terms, but she doesn't leave it there. Politics isn't a soap opera, after all; it is the legacy of our forefathers and the promise of our future. While she wrenches the moral gut with her description of the poisoned process, she holds her lens far enough from the crime scene to show us the vulnerability of those in control.

Ultimately—obviously, appropriately—it is we, the people, who can fix these problems and in a trice. We vote for most of these people every two years. That means that in half a decade, using the ballot box, we can send the rats scurrying for exits. That won't bring us to utopia in five years, of course, but it will certainly put us in the right direction.

Terri McCormick's journey and her concomitant and subsequent observations provide an important view of where we are, how we got here, where we want to go, and how we might get there. She elucidates rather than whines, encourages rather than cajoles. She reveals the facts with purpose, that we may heed her and take advantage of her struggles to bring reform to our political process. Using her ideas as a breakwater against further retreat, we can take up the baton and lead ourselves to a proper management of our community.

Tony Seton
Monterey, California
October 2008

Award-winning journalist Tony Seton produced coverage of Watergate, eight elections, Barbara Walters' news interviews, and business/economics news, primarily for ABC television. He also produced two public-television documentaries and wrote a television news textbook. Seton is a political consultant, whose clients have included former California Congressman and Director of the Bureau of Competition, at the Federal Trade Commission Tom Campbell (R), Former California U.S. Senate Candidate and current UC Board of Regent Ward Connerly (R) and Nancy Pelosi Speaker of the U.S. House of Representatives.

PURPOSE

The personal flaws of greed and corruption have ushered in an era of irresponsibility. The United States Constitution and an engaged citizenry will put an end to this era. Our Constitution contains the rules of the political game! It is high time we read this document and use it in our classrooms and homes across America. It guarantees our rights against an overzealous government run by the most dysfunctional leaders our nation has ever known. How else do we explain the present-day incompetence and gall of many tenured politicians to cast blame on others for the problems they themselves created?

As Charlie Reese, formally with the *Orlando Sentinel Star*, so aptly wrote in his last column, "Good-bye": "There are no insolvable government problems, instead the 545 individuals (435 house, 100 senate, one president, nine justices) running our government are the problem."

There is no question that many of the political class have lost their way, and we have lost faith in them. Under constitutional authority, Congress sets the budget, approves the budget and can veto or override a budget; it regulates our banks, and it has sustained unfair tax codes, chartered a federal bank regulating our currency and provided consent to our president to send our army, navy, air force and Marines to war in Iraq and Afghanistan.

Lobbyists don't hold a gun to the heads of lawmakers who choose to take bribes of money, home loans and other gifts in exchange for their votes. The people in our federal government and fifty legislatures in our state capitals choose or *do not choose* to be corrupt and unprincipled.

We need to support those courageous policy makers who put their constituents first and work from a core set of values.

Chuck Todd told the National Counties Association, assembled in Washington on March 9, 2009, "If you want to see corrupt, look inside the state capitols across this country." The stories to follow, from the front lines of American politics, show that former Illinois governor Rod Blagojevich—impeached in 2009 for allegedly selling President Obama's former U.S. Senate seat—has contemporaries. "We the people" are needed to make sure they have counterparts.

The political class, an "entitlement class," receives lobby-funded ski trips, golfing trips, free rides on corporate jets, and box seats for sporting events. What makes us think that education, health care, energy, jobs and the banking crisis will all be solved by those who could not solve these problems ten years ago? Could the special home loans from Countrywide or the contributions from Sallie Mae and AIG lobbyists have something to do with their inability to solve America's problems?

Do not be bamboozled into thinking that there is any difference between the elites in one political party and the elites in the other; they are all a part of the same club.

What Sex is a Republican? takes on the political class and provides us with the tools to change the way things are. Just when you thought it was all about elephants and donkeys, in walks the political class. Will the political class continue to con America? Or won't they?

It is all up to you!

The American republic will endure until the day Congress discovers that it can bribe the public with the public's money.

—Alexis De Tocqueville

ABOUT THE AUTHOR

What Sex is a Republican? presents a case for courage by a lawmaker who is uniquely qualified to do so. Terri McCormick is a former legislator and congressional candidate, who happens to be a woman. According to her friends and foes alike, "Terri has been battle-tested in state and federal politics." Both major political parties claim she can be trusted. An advocate for political and government reform and change, former Wisconsin state representative Terri McCormick has proven time and again that ideas trump career politicians and their trysts and turns.

Representative Terri McCormick made a career of defying the odds in fighting the status quo. As a private citizen she battled powerful special interests to write Wisconsin's first Charter School Law. In 2000 she was elected to the state legislature through a grassroots, door-to-door campaign that local newspaper reports gave little chance to win, yet she won over 70 percent of the vote in three contests. In the state legislature, Representative McCormick worked on both sides of the political aisle to pass groundbreaking laws for manufacturing, regulation reform, health-care cost reform and capital investment.

In 2006, State Representative Terri McCormick ran for the United States House of Representatives. Although outspent in a primary by over 20 to 1 (2.5 million dollars) and smeared by her own party's political machine, Terri defied the odds once again by running a positive grassroots campaign and winning a third of the vote. She captured the hearts and minds of the people she once served and will capture yours as well.

Come join her path to politics and chart one of your own. Terri encourages all of us to take the "honesty tour" to our own hearts and minds so that we may become the engaged citizens, voters, volunteers and candidates of integrity we need in government. Former representative Terri McCormick says, "It will take all of us to change the way things are."

PREFACE

FALLING OFF THE HORSE IS NOT AN OPTION!

Why do we fall?… So that we may learn how to pick ourselves up and stand on our own two feet.

—Jesse Boyle, 1944, Irish American businesswoman

"Power is distancing ... Politicians must know two languages and cultures—here and home. However, home soon becomes lost, forgotten by those who reach the seats of power." *Wall Street Journal* contributing editor Peggy Noonan writes that the GOP is losing confidence because of what she calls "detachment from the ground." It is clear to Noonan, a former President Reagan speechwriter and confidant, that career politicians soon forget who sent them into office and why they are there.[1]

Noonan points to what is obvious to me: that the theatre of public office, seldom resembles the reality of public office. Despite the talk of decreasing spending, it's skyrocketed under Republican rule. Promises of smaller government have long been forgotten, just as securing our nation's borders is a spoken priority, with little action backing it up.

The Democrats offer little more. Democrats are tagged as big spenders—big on ideas, short on delivery. Noonan contends—and I agree—that both parties are missing the boat. Party leadership has led both parties into dark, shadowy places with no light to see by.

The stories of American politics told in this book are based on fact. It is with the painstaking research and support of my former chief of staff, Jared Guzman, that specific dates and testimony have been cited. My home state will surprisingly resemble most states across this nation. The need for leadership and government reform is not a vacuous one. I have used personality types, rather than individuals in most of the stories from the front lines of politics, so that you may recognize the characters as your own.

Direct observations and empirical research was conducted for upwards of six years, so that the facts, actual events and testimony could provide a factual basis for this book. It is my aim to make an appeal to all Americans to become active and engaged in the political process, so that we may change the way things are.

The audience for this book is the American people—citizen, candidate and media alike—who represent the foundational trilogy needed to put our country right. I will take you behind the curtain of elective office into the belly of the beast of American politics for one purpose: to give you the tools to recognize the games of the political class. With this knowledge, it is possible to finally peel off the masks of virtuous deception and become better citizens and leaders. To the courageous idealists among us, it is time for a new "we the people" to step forward and change the way things are.

The political gender referred to in *What Sex Is a Republican?* has no biological or anatomical designation. Rather, it refers to a silent coup—a class warfare unlike any others. We may be familiar with the notion of class warfare between the upper class and the middle/lower class, Democrats and Republicans, conservatives and liberals. I can assure you that there is a class that transcends all of these boundaries in American politics. It is the political class made up of young and old, men and women, who believe they are entitled to their positions and endowed with an elite arrogance of self-service at the expense of the American people.

What Sex Is a Republican? could just as easily be written as *What Sex Is a Democrat?* Both major political parties have in them a political animus endemic to the political class. So embedded and institutionalized are these political animals that they have built around them political silos (extreme partisanship), paid for by unwitting fat cats fed on the emotional sound bites of well-trained political lackeys. So entrenched is the political class in the pursuit of self-preservation in public office that they would strangle the dreams and hopes of American ingenuity and innovation in its crib.

The political class' stronghold on my grassroots race for the United States Congress brought the revolution of class warfare to my door and to the doors of my constituents in northeast Wisconsin. It was during my primary race in 2006, within my own political party, that all of us—voters and candidates alike—realized that our free elections were not as free as we had once thought.

In my Republican primary I was asked routinely to appear before large audiences. Most of the crowds were independent conservatives of one political party or the other; neocon party loyalists were warned to step back and get behind the coronated candidate of choice—that wasn't me. On this particular afternoon in early summer, I was asked to speak before a large union group in Green Bay, Wisconsin. All of the candidates running for the Eighth Congressional seat were invited. The room was crowded and full of back-slapping union members of all political stripes. A handful of state legislative Republican candidates braved the room, and there were a few Republicans among the union ranks.

Ironically, the gathering came a few short days after then-president George W. Bush announced that he would be campaigning for my primary opponent—before the primary. It would mark the second event by the White House used to bolster the sagging polls of my Republican counterpart. Despite the millions of dollars slated to be thrown at this particular candidate, his negatives were proving him to be an "unwinnable" candidate. Much to my supporters' chagrin and outrage, the White House's spokesman cast me in a news article as an "irrelevant primary candidate." Despite my high polling numbers and popularity, the fact of the matter was that I was not a member of the political class.

The Green Bay Union Hall, to my surprise, was angry that the GOP president was interfering in a primary race for U.S. Congress. They believed, as did many voters in northeast Wisconsin, that primary elections should be decided on the ground, by the people. This power play to control the outcome of a vote designated for the people smacked of cronyism and disenfranchisement that didn't sit well across all party lines. As I walked past the aide of U.S. senator Herb Kohl (D), she expressed outrage on my behalf.

The behavior of the party elites flew in the face of the veterans in that room, who'd fought to defend the United States Constitution and our basic right to choose the outcome of our elections. Members of the various unions attending the Green Bay meeting approached me, one by one, and quietly cupped their hands over their mouths as they confided in me, "Don't tell anyone, but I am voting for you." The manipulation of the peoples' basic right to vote by any political elite blurred party lines and the ethics of straight-ticket voting. This action by the president of the United States to interfere, preprimary, was deemed "un-American."

I shook off the comments and the sympathy that the majority of the people in the room that day gave to me; I shook off any reaction to the rightness and wrongness of it all. I would have no part in a "pity party." That day, in a predominantly Democratic union hall in the city of Green Bay, I was an American who happened to be conservative. Green Bay is a city of great theatre, not the least of which is its political theatre. One never knows which political party is in play with any particular candidate—people there vote for the *person* more often than their union stewards would like to think.

As I took the podium in that union hall, I had a choice to make: I could frame my comments around the injustice of it all, or I could put the emphasis where it belonged—on the people. My record showed I could solve problems and serve the people of the Eighth Congressional District. It didn't matter whether I wore blue stripes or red stripes that day; it mattered that I chose to represent the needs of the people. I was not afraid of a good debate on the best way to solve problems through public policy; I was there that day for that debate.

If the people were to be served, someone needed to stand with them. As I looked out into the packed room, I paused, gently gripping my hands on either side of the podium. Today, I was allowed to speak to the people I had hoped to serve. That was an improvement. You see, I had been thrown out of rooms in this 2006 primary election before. I had been denied the right to speak by members of my own party. It had been only one month earlier that I was shown the door at a candidate forum in Vilas County. Kerry Thomas, a courageous supporter who couldn't believe the scene, wrote an article describing that odd event; as a result, "The GOP, Grand Old Patronage!" was printed in many newspapers across the state.

I asked myself what I had to lose. The support and respect growing in that room in Green Bay that day stood in stark contrast to the Vilas County picnic, where I had been invited to attend but prohibited from participating. It had nothing to do with political parties—Democrats and Republicans alike, many in the room, would be my opponents. Yet we all stood together that day. All of us honored something more sacred than political party. We honored the Constitution and the sacred right to vote and hold elective office—it was about being American.

In Green Bay that day, in a union hall, I was allowed to speak and lend my ideas, and I was given back my right to be heard. It was new territory, and its unpredictability made whatever notes I had with me useless. You see, my eighth congressional Republican primary opponent was faltering in the polls; as such, he just recently announced that he was bringing in the president of the United States—my party's president—to help him campaign … against me.

I took a breath, smiled—and then I began.

"Thank you all for your kind reception today. I wasn't quite sure what to expect as I drove up to the building. Thank you for your kindness, your condolences, and most of all, for not throwing me out—I have been thrown out of gatherings without the right to speak before, as I'm sure all of you have already heard. My name is Terri McCormick. I am a Republican, and I am running for the Eighth Congressional District against George W. Bush."

I dared to say out loud what the entire room was thinking—this was not a fair playing field. In fact, there wasn't a playing field at all. My primary opponent was being handed an open GOP seat by the political machine, against the will of the people. The people were denied a voice and a vote in this election as a result. My choices narrowed quickly, without my knowledge—they were to run away and hide, or keep my word to the people and stay in the race.

I was in this race to stay. "Falling off the horse is not an option!"

The thunderous applause was startling. I took another breath and then went on to thank the governor's representatives, who'd helped me to save taxpayers tens of millions of dollars in health insurance costs for prescription drugs. I smiled again and said, "That is right—a Democratic governor saw merit in my health-care reforms and wrote my competitive prescription-drug purchasing pool legislation into the budgets. ... We put people ahead of politics and saved taxpayer money in the process."

I also thanked Senator Kohl's representative for working with me on behalf of the court interpreter legislation that was given federal dollars. The legislation helps unclog our courts with cases left unheard because some defendants could not understand English, or because sign language experts were desperately needed.

To my surprise, everyone in the room that day treated me fairly. They were indignant and outraged at what appeared to be the manipulation of the political system, even if it was against a Republican. The larger point was this: ethics in politics is a much stronger desire of the people than which political party is being represented.

So what did I do differently? I didn't play the game. I could have taken the bait. I could have said "Poor me" and based my campaign on pity. Why? Why would anyone take that road? Isn't that admitting defeat from the start? My father's recitation of Notre Dame football coaches' and Vince Lombardi's speeches were too well engrained in my mind for me to take the low road. I wanted to win one for all people—but not at anyone's expense, including anyone who attacked me.

After spending six years in the legislature, there was only one course of action I could take. That time—amid some of the most backstabbing, ruthless behavior imaginable—strengthened my resolve to stand up, paste a big smile on my face and do my job.

My job, as I saw it, was to serve the people who had elected me. Those were the people who lived in my house assembly district and the congressional district that I was working to represent. In that union hall in Green Bay, Wisconsin, I did what needed to be done, what I continued to do throughout the U.S. congressional campaign. I raised up my chin so that I wasn't looking to the ground for answers, and I kept on going.

To stand against the corruption of lifelong politicos was one course of action. It appeared at this juncture that I also needed to erase the invisible barrier of stereotypes and personal smears flung against me as well. The lesson for all of us—candidates, citizens and media alike—is that when we stop feeling sorry for ourselves and begin to lead by example, from our hearts, minds and souls, we will be worthy of self-governing.

I was faced with a clear choice in the primary of 2006: I could stay on the ground with the wind knocked out of me, thrown off my horse. Or I could get back on my feet, snap the reins in my hands, and get back on the horse. I chose to take the reins and get back on the horse. Falling off the horse was not an option.

Shortly after my speech at the Green Bay Union Hall in 2006, the following appeared in the *Milwaukee Journal Sentinel* on September 6, 2006:

NODS TO MCCORMICK

The race for the Eighth Congressional District extends all the way to the White House.

President Bush thinks the best person for the job is the Republican house assembly speaker, and both he and Vice President Dick Cheney have visited Wisconsin this summer to stump for him. But while the speaker is clearly the front-runner in the primary because of his war chest and obvious party connections, the best GOP candidate is state Representative Terri McCormick.

Both are conservative and share similar views but McCormick has at times shown independence, refusing to toe the party leadership line on, for instance, the need for meaningful ethics reform. ... The speaker has been inclined to be overly partisan and punitive rather than pragmatic. On ethics reform, it was McCormick and four other Republican legislators who bucked the leadership in May and tried to do the right thing by attempting to bring Senate Bill 1 to the floor for a vote.

McCormick holds both bachelor's and master's degrees, taught school for a while, worked as an education consultant and was a key figure in the state's charter school movement before being elected to the assembly in 2000. Once in office she chaired a legislative task force to find ways to hold down governmental health-care costs, which led to a number of reforms, including a state purchasing pool for prescription drugs that has saved taxpayers millions of dollars annually.

From ethics reform to trying to get severely disabled veterans property tax relief to extending legal help for the poor, McCormick seems committed to her conscience, even at the expense of pleasing party honchos.

The death of democracy is not likely to be an assassination from ambush. It will be a slow extinction from apathy, indifference and undernourishment.

Robert Maynard Hutchins (1899–1977)

INTRODUCTION

A CASE
FOR COURAGE

*For the support of this Declaration … We mutually pledge …
our Lives, our Fortunes, and our sacred Honor.*

—the "courageous fifty-six," the signers of the
Declaration of Independence, 1776

It is our turn to put our government back on the right track. Whether you are a citizen leader, voter, political junkie, candidate or member of the press, this book lifts the curtain from the political stage and empowers all of us to change the way things are. Government is all of us, and together we are the "New We."

As I walked into the Committee Hearing Room on the second floor of the state capitol, I felt the eyes of senate leaders from both political parties dart around the room in panic. As though in a game of chicken, daring the opposing party to go faster, both political party leaders understood that there could be consequences if all of their actions were exposed to the light of day. Many leaders were offended and caught off guard by my bold attempt to support an ethics bill that had little chance of being brought up for a vote.

Little did they know that on January 25, 2005, the public was watching, the editorial boards were watching, and a brand new day was about to be born in American politics.

"Good morning," I began. "My name is Representative Terri McCormick, and I am here this morning to testify as the lead house author for Senate Bill 1; the Government Accountability Board and Ethics Reform legislation.

"Mr. Chairman, committee members of the Joint Committee on Finance: Thank you for allowing me to testify before you today on this very important piece of legislation. As you are no doubt well aware, legislators from both sides of the aisle have recently pled guilty to using their legislative offices as campaign headquarters, using taxpayer money to win reelection, and using positions of leadership to solicit campaign contributions from special-interest groups in exchange for action on legislation.

"The caucus scandal, combined with years of increased spending on pork projects and special-interest legislation has gradually eroded our state's reputation as a "clean government" state. In fact, $800 million was appropriated in road projects by both political parties, over and above the Department of Transportation requests in the most recent state budgets.

"Further, a survey from the Policy Research Institute in our state found that only 6 percent of our residents believe that their elected officials are putting their interests ahead of large special-interest groups. And that was before the public was made aware that dozens of U.S. representatives have received millions of dollars in illegal contributions and favors from lobbyists.

"I am honored to be the House Lead on Senate Bill 1, a bill that will merge the State Ethics and Elections Boards into a new Government Accountability Board. For the first time, this agency will have an enforcement division that is empowered to investigate violations and bring civil criminal actions to enforce the elections, ethics and lobbying regulation laws of this state.

"We must all be held accountable to the same legal standard as the citizens we represent."

My testimony before the Joint Committee on Finance put the business-as-usual crowd on notice that their legislative counterparts were not playing by the same rules. Rank-and-file politics and follow-the-leader intimidation tactics did not apply. Unfortunately, the business-as-usual crowd in the GOP were not paying attention to their hometown newspapers or to my testimony. They certainly were not listening to their constituents back home.

Newspaper editorials and headlines across the state and nation carried a unified voice and call for the end of corruption and the pay-to-play system that paralyzed the political process. The *Milwaukee Journal Sentinel* published an article on January 1, 2006, titled "To Play You Paid, Lobbyist Reveals," giving a detailed account of how the system worked with SBC/Ameritech personal checks of $40,000. Washington's *The Hill*, on January 11, 2006, disclosed an insider corruption story, "The Year of Abramoff," detailing a list of bipartisan corruption, naming political leaders and staff members who took bribes, used public monies for personal use and took illegal campaign contributions. A Gannett paper in Wisconsin at that time wrote a series of opinion pieces on the need for ethics reforms. One such article was "When Will We Get Reform in the Capitol?" Representative Stephen Freese was quoted in that opinion piece: "Felony convictions, emerging scandals and voter discontent are shaping up as the 'perfect storm.' We must do our best to improve the public perception of the legislature and Wisconsin government."

Roger Utnehmer, president and general manager of the *Door County Daily News* wrote: "Terri McCormick joins a small group of Republicans who understand Wisconsin voters deserve better than the partisan defense of the corrupt status quo you hear from leaders in her party like the Speaker. Members of the Republican Party would be wise to look to others who support clean government for leadership, men and women of conscience like Terri McCormick and others."

Another excerpt was written by a known GOP political insider who flippantly dismissed the right for "free elections" and the voters' right to choose its own candidates in a Love 'em or Leave 'em editorial comment. Unfortunately, his naïve words would begin a movement by the voters that would cost the GOP the general election in 2006:

> "When ostensibly Republican McCormick supporters attack the GOP leadership for interfering in the 2006 primary—President Bush, Vice President Cheney and others who have not been proven guilty of their charges—they don't seem happy with anyone. If they dislike the GOP leadership figures so much, perhaps their goals and agenda would be better served in another political party."

What Sex Is a Republican? Stories from the Front Lines of American Politics and How You Can Change the Way Things Are challenges and equips each of us—citizen, candidate and media alike—to stand up and change the way things are. "We the People" must ask ourselves, "What kind of nation have we become?" Then it is our collective responsibility to change it. I intend to make the case for a new kind of leadership and policy-maker to step forward to serve on all levels of government. In fact, all of us are needed to make our political processes and government work. All of us create a bold three-columned foundation for American integrity—first as citizens who must be more involved and better-informed voters, volunteers and consumers of the political process; second, as a responsible and ethical press, entrusted as truth-tellers within the fourth branch of government; third, as integrity candidates, who must earn the public trust and take to heart the responsibilities of public office under our nation's contract with our people, the U.S. Constitution.

Whether you live in Albany, New York, or Madison, Wisconsin, greed and corruption can be traced to the failings of individuals and a lust for power and control, the consequences of which are a failed political system that jeopardizes all Americans, their families, the national economy and our national security. We, as a people, cannot afford more of the same. The do-nothing Congresses of the past two decades represents the insanity of doing the same thing over and over again and expecting a different result. Evoking the names of politicians—Governor Rob Blagojevich, former Ways and Means Chairman Bob Ney, former congressman William Jefferson, former congressman Duke Cunningham, as well as Wall Street broker Bernard Madoff and lobbyist Jack Abramoff—creates dark and exploitive images that have led to the erosion of public trust in our economy and in our government.

There are two views of political leadership compared and contrasted throughout this book. Put simply, the leader who needs and uses politics for personal power (the political animal and member of the political class) is contrasted with the leader who needs neither politics nor power; rather, he/she is needed by the people to serve in public office (the integrity leader).

When asking "What sex is a Republican?" I could as well be asking, "What sex is a Democrat?" A political animal's survival depends on politics as a lifestyle, an entitlement and a business. The shadowy place in which this political animus thrives is the riddled world of fear and manipulation. They belie both political parties, creating a cycle of dysfunction and dysfunctional leadership. Corruption and deal-making follow the need for self-preservation, the result of which is a dysfunctional cycle of poor leadership, followed by the recruitment of bad candidates who can be controlled and kept in line by their respective party leaders, which breeds a continuum of dysfunctional leadership. "We the people" then inherit the fruits of their pay-for-play politics—an overtaxed and broken government.

In contrast, an integrity leader is the model for representative leadership, handed down to the American people by our founders in 1776. The "courageous fifty-six" sacrificed "their lives, fortunes and sacred honor" by signing the Declaration of Independence. They were educated people of independent means who sacrificed themselves and their families for the rights of freedom and self-government. The quiet confidence of these assured and independent innovators stands in stark contrast to the political class of today.

Integrity leaders will thrive in most environments, whether in business, industry or education, provided schemes of self-service and kingdom-building isn't part of the private sector landscape. Leaders with integrity stand by their word, operate in the light of day, and have a zero say/do ratio. (What they say is what they do.) It is in the shadowy places of greed and self-interest where integrity leaders fail. There is no honor for the integrity leader in self-service. Rather, there is only public service, making a difference and standing for ideals and principles. As with the "courageous fifty-six," the integrity leader will make self-sacrifices that will jeopardize his or her own future, income, career and family. Why? For the sake of serving the greater good.

Political opportunists wear shades of gray. Are there shades of gray between the political animus and the integrity leader? An emphatic *no*! The masks of virtue worn by the opportunists who play both sides against the middle may be the most deceptive of all.

How do we break the cycle of dysfunctional leadership within the political class? Keep reading …

In "Part One: A Call to Service for Each of Us," I discuss the dynamic and personal events that led to my path to public service. From the great influences in my life to the integrity principles learned as a child, I share stories that I hope will resonate and ring true for all Americans. Whether readers are interested in supporting quality candidates, becoming a more informed citizen, or exploring public service for themselves, I present a broad appeal for active citizenship.

As a state legislator, I quickly learned that the more successful I became, the more hostile my own political party front row became. Machiavellian-style antics ensued in the legislature, as tensions rose to a boiling point with my political adversaries within the GOP leadership. Lost opportunities of service continued as party bosses and their political animus remained out of touch with the people they were sent to office to serve.

To make sense of the political system, we will look beyond political party and ideology, revealing a political Ponzi scheme so well hidden that only the front-row players are allowed in on the joke—an empty Hollywood movie set has more substance. Beyond any reasonability. I expose the culture of the needy and the greedy in politics for what they are—an eco-system filled with political animals, a species of its own making. If you are an insider, if you are willing to pay, you are allowed to play. As a matter of fact, the elite in both political parties may act in concert against their own back rows.

Moving beyond the stereotypes of ethnicity and gender, I define problems for what they are—dysfunctional leadership in a flawed pay-for-play system. Cronyism and political favors monopolize the legislative agenda of the people's house. The only way past this kind of institutional corruption is to start over—a new "We the People" must call for new leaders and leadership to put the people's house right again. Changing political parties will only change the teams' jerseys on the field; the same institutional games will apply.

"Part Two: The Art of Political Power Games in a Vertical Silo" takes us inside the belly of the political beast, giving readers a front row seat that is rarely provided by politicians. From seating assignments to

controlled behavior by front-row elites, I call for political reform—
and I will show you how it can be done. The phrase "tipping the front
row" was coined to show how front-row politicians are tipped into the
backseat at the will of the people. From the Veterans Property Tax
Bill to competitive prescription cost pools, I will prove that the new
"We the People" doesn't sit in the front row of our state and federal
legislatures; they walk into the voting booths back home.

In looking at public service for the people and political self-service,
a comparison is made between modern-day politics and medieval
Machiavellian fear techniques. What are today's results and impact of
the do-nothing Congress that's prevailed over the last ten years? An
economy in distress, needing a trillion-dollar bailout; Wall Street greed
and corruption, fueled by an ineffective Federal Election Commission;
and job loss that rivals the Great Depression.

The techniques that are outlined in this section are not the only
answers, but they are a start. They will assist citizen leaders and
legislators alike to understand what an effective government office
should look like.

Intended to enlighten the voter and educate the government
student, the dark side of politics is presented with a humorous twist
in an unrelenting unveiling of dirty tricks and election engineering
schemes. From negative campaign smears to elitist tricks for
controlling the vote, you'll see the tricks of the trade in American
politics. A comparison of old-style politics to change leaders' tools is
provided for those who want to make a more informed choice in the
voting booth—to becoming an active citizen leader.

In "Part Three: Changing the Way Things Are," you'll see that
there is no greater measure of how a public servant will act in office
than how he or she runs a political campaign. From how much money a
candidate may need in public office to various strategies and techniques
in running a political campaign, readers will have the tools needed to
assist in building a framework for supporting a political candidate—or
being one. Regardless of your political or governmental desires, active

citizenship as an educated voter is an essential part of our republican form of government—and a critical one.

The public policy outlines provided in this section offer the voting public or the integrity candidate a reliable map for charting a course of public service. Using successful strategies that have proven effective, a case is made that anyone can serve in public office, if only he or she has a plan and the heart to do so.

The "mask of virtue" is addressed in the conclusion of the book. Senate Bill 1—and its promise of a more effective and ethical government—is stalled one more time, with fast and immediate consequences. An appeal is made to the American voter and citizen leader who, collectively, have the power to lift the mask of virtue through active citizenship. As voters, as campaign volunteers and as educated consumers of good government, there is no other option. Active involvement in the political process is our only path to integrity principles and self-government.

THE NEW WE

Integrity leadership requires that the American public is awake and involved. Deception and corruption is an equal-opportunity employer in political parties. Courageous leaders need courageous individuals to stand with them. That is why I ask all of us to get involved in our own political process and our own government. The business-usual crowd has mastered a bag of dirty tricks and retail politics. It is up to all of us to change the way things are.

The Danger that political factions and political interests pose to the American people is so grave that it requires the passage of the United States Constitution to protect them.

—James Madison, The Federalist Papers: No. 10

PART ONE

A CALL TO SERVICE
FOR
EACH OF US

Lincoln McCormick, Terri's
grandfather, and his father founded
the McCormick Farm Implement
Business with factories in Chicago
and Minneapolis.

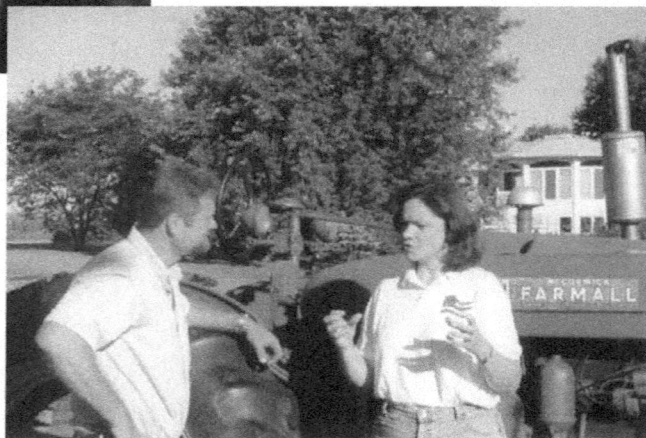

Terri, doing what she does best—listening to the
people in her district. Pictured with Terri is long
time friend and constituent, Jeff Griesbach of
Greenville, WI

CHAPTER ONE

THE HONESTY TOUR BEGINS WITH YOU

MYTH:

Politics is only a game—you can learn what
to say, what to think and how to act.

REALITY:

People of principle are needed to take the
games out of politics.

*I always did the very best I could with what I had. The only job offer
I received in the private sector on my graduation from
Stanford Law School was a job as a legal secretary,
so I started my own practice.*

—Sandra Day O'Connor

Our path to leadership in government and politics begins with an honesty tour within ourselves. It is a journey of self-examination of our heart's purpose, motivations and reasoning. The honesty tour underpins our personal challenges, self-doubts and dreams for the future. It leads us to define our core convictions, values and skills that we bring to the table of serving others. This tour takes us on one of two roads in public service—the road of endless irresponsibility and self-entitlement, which uses the public stage to "be somebody"; or the more difficult road that requires us to see government as much bigger than ourselves. It is the road of selfless service that requires the integrity principles of self-sacrifice, duty and honor in doing for others.

There is only one way to combat the corruption of closed-door politics—through having guts and using know-how.

Before I headed to the state capitol, my mother slipped a book called *Courage* into my briefcase. It gave me the gift of courage and confidence, and I hope to give you that same gift as you read this book.

BECOMING A BOOTSTRAPS REPUBLICAN

I am a Republican and a populist. At this moment in American history, that fact may not be easy to understand. My Irish and Scots-Irish American great-grandparents were Republicans with a strong belief in freedom, equality and the opportunities that exist in this great country of ours. You could say the GOP is in my DNA, which is why I ask the question, "What sex is a Republican?" I hold the same principles of free- and fair-market competition, limited government and a fair tax system as did our Founding Fathers. I believe in equal justice under the law, with no exceptions for relatives or for water carriers in either party. Sadly and ironically, it was my belief in and support of the United States Constitution and rule of law that set me apart from the front-row establishment of my own political party.

In fact, I believe it is the vertical party politics operating in silos (that is, exhibiting extreme partisanship), powered by turf wars and kingdom-building that has deteriorated the constitutional protections

24

and guarantees that founded this nation and led it to greatness. Because I am a populist, I believe in the vast strengths and talents of the people, more so than the party elites who operate behind closed doors in the shadows in our state and federal capitols. It is our people and our uncanny ability to stand up after we have been knocked down that separates Americans from other citizens around the world.

MY CENTER BECAME SELF-RELIANCE

As I turned the pages of the old family scrapbook, I couldn't help but notice the similarities in expression and attitude. The Irish and Scotch-Irish beginnings framed by the trimmed black corners edging each page shared a time continuum that I had never before recognized. Photographs and news clippings told a story of cross-generational values and themes. Among them were the construction of school buildings, homes and entire communities, carved out of the rugged wilderness of Minnesota's North Woods. Next were the photographs of soldiers with familiar faces and changing uniforms, from the Grand Old Army, to a doughboy in World War I, to my father's infantry uniform in World War II, all three of my brothers-in-law in Korea and Vietnam, to my brother in Beirut in his Marine khakis, and all of my nephews in all branches of service during Desert Storm, Desert Shield—they were all there.

Laughter, music and concertinas, accordions and violins filled a series of pages with the memories of family picnics held along the cold and frigid waters of Lake Superior, near the headwaters of the Mississippi in Itasca State Park. Familiar poses with pride-filled smiles echoed the laughter of the Boyle sisters, the McCormick sisters and my children. Love of family, love of country and dreams for the future embraced the yellowed pages that lived within that dark leather scrapbook that once had belonged to my grandmother, to my mother and now to me.

Family history and heritage is one of the most powerful cornerstones of a person's life; it certainly was in mine. Spanning the generations, looking across time, undeniably bridged my past to my present. I would use the strength and values of my heritage as a hitching post on which to nail the courage I would need throughout my life, but never was that strength needed more than during my time in public office.

ROOTS AND WINGS

The women in my family—my mother and my grandmothers—were my role models and gave me my roots and wings. They were straight-talking women who were well educated and savvy in the ways of the world. Grandma Jesse was the head of the grange and Grandmother McCormick was the first woman president of her regional Minnesota Farm Bureau. Above all, it was my mother and Grandma Jesse who gave me the courage to face down my fears. And it was the life of my grandparents on their small Minnesota farms that taught me the humility and character that would serve me well throughout my lifetime.

Growing up in a Scots-Irish family, I was challenged each and every day by my parents. At first, it was to learn the traditions of leadership, but then it was to offer up solutions that would change the human condition and the way things were. We were all taught to turn the page and begin again after we fell down—and when we succeeded. The lessons were brewed and steeped with pride as Americans—the opportunities we had in this country could only be dreamed of in Ireland and Scotland.

Through our hardships, challenges and opportunities, we were shown forgiveness and unconditional love when we failed in our own eyes. The joy and laughter of my childhood embraces my soul and provides me strength today. It is this foundation of family and ethnic spirit on which I pinned my children's hopes and dreams, as I taught them to embrace the opportunities that life had to offer. Family is the value I hold closest in my life. It is the core value from which I draw strength.

CHILDHOOD INFLUENCES

Among the many memories I have of my grandparents, those of my grandmother and her shotgun, and my grandfather and his horses are the most vivid. My grandparents, first-generation Americans, owned our family farms in northern Minnesota. During my childhood in the 1960s and early 1970s, Minnesota had not transformed itself into the lake-resort capital of the nation. At that time, farms were spread out; the land remaining rugged and remote. My grandpa Harry enjoyed working with his horses. He had tractors, but he still spent time training workhorses, especially Morgan racehorses.

It was around the date of my fifth birthday on an unusually warm day in October when we took the long trip to visit my grandparents on the farm. Grandpa was getting ready for a special Christmas that year, as he worked on a sleigh for the horses. We were sure that we would, at long last, be able to catch Santa Claus flying from house to house with that sleigh. As we got closer to the farm, I began to count the telephone poles to keep myself from getting restless. The evergreen trees seemed to tower over the country road, as if to emulate the size of Paul Bunyan.

Mom and Dad's hints about the new sleigh project this fall made that long car ride to Minnesota unbearable. Every small town, every road stop, every bump in the road was accompanied by the inevitable question, "How much farther is it?" Country-western music dominated the radio stations as we traveled.

As we finally drove up the long driveway to the farmhouse, I couldn't wait to get out and see what was happening. I didn't know which direction I would go first—Grandma's kitchen or Grandpa's barn! I bounced out of the car and headed into Grandma Jesse's house to announce our arrival. "We are here, Grandma! Grandpa, where are you?" I clamored to find them.

Noticing the bustle of energy inside the kitchen, it wasn't surprising to see Grandma at the wood-burning stove, which held several pots and pans, all boiling at once. It smelled so good in that house—a combination of scents from the fresh northern air outside and the cinnamon in the apple pie and the stew and dumplings on the stove. Everything tasted better at Grandma's house.

"Harry, would you please get some tomatoes from the garden so that I can finish lunch for everyone?" shouted Grandma, a bit impatiently.

There was no response. Grandpa Harry had just gotten back from the barn and hadn't finished getting his barn clothes off and his hands washed.

As I put on my apron, which I'd retrieved from my hook in the kitchen, I took my place next to Grandma at the cast-iron stove. I wasn't a real help in the kitchen, but Grandma made me feel that I was her assistant whenever we spent time together.

My grandmother seemed particularly impatient on this day. Evidently, Grandpa Harry had spent the greater part of the day in the barn, working on the new sleigh, and had forgotten to help with the garden.

I took over the stirring on top of the stove, as my grandmother lunged out the door to her vegetable garden, just outside the house. Within seconds, Grandma Jesse darted back inside the house without saying a word—she just opened the broom closet and pulled out the large double-barreled shotgun, then she stormed back outside, as though on a mission.

KA-BOOM!

I nearly lost my balance when I heard the sound.

Not less than fifty feet from the kitchen window, Grandma Jesse had fired at something in her vegetable garden—and no doubt hit it.

Now, with the tomatoes tucked carefully in the folds of her apron, Grandma put the shotgun back inside the broom closet.

"Harry! Harry!" she shouted. "I will not tell you again. Go into my vegetable garden with a pitchfork and get that rattlesnake out of my vegetable garden so that I can finish lunch."

That day was like any other on the farm. We all were expected to help as we could with the chores. A rattlesnake was something to be dealt with, and that was that. The garden was cared for and produced enough tomatoes for canning as well as for meals. The tools we needed were in the barn and in the broom closet inside the farmhouse. The rest was all up to us.

THE INFLUENCE OF FAMILY: MY FATHER'S ASSURANCE

As for most people who grew up during the Great Depression, my parents were impacted as children. Their hardships, now in the past, were nonetheless reminders to be thankful for the simple pleasures of life. That thankfulness and ability to stretch their savings was their gift to me throughout my life. My father, speaking in his melodic voice, told me stories in the form of fables—lessons that he passed down to me from his life and his childhood.

One of our evening rituals was for my father to walk me up the long staircase in our century-old French colonial home so that he could fully rid my room of monsters and goblins. The cheerfulness of my lavender-painted walls and freshly refurbished white furnishings did little to convince me that ghosts weren't lurking under my bed or in the hallway.

Father would carefully look inside my wardrobe and under my bed and then sit next to me in the chair that my mother had carefully reupholstered in white and lilac-colored blossoms.

As my eyes began to get heavy, I would insist on more and more stories about my father's boyhood days, growing up on the farm in northern Minnesota. One story marks his philosophy of life, as well as my own.

My father began, "You know I grew up in the Great Depression. Do you know what that means, Terri?"

"I don't know, Daddy. What does that mean?" I asked, seeming to begin my never-ending series of questions, for which I was dubbed Little Big Mouth by my well-meaning older sisters.

"It means that we were lucky that we grew up on a farm, with cattle and sheep and good soil to grow vegetables, when so many others had little to eat," Dad explained.

"Did your father tell you stories before you went to bed?" I asked.

"I don't remember a lot about my dad. You see, my father died when I was four years old," he said softly, with much hesitation in his voice.

I remember asking a battery of questions as I tried to understand how my father, who was the strongest, bravest man in the world, could grow up without his dad. "How did you buy things? How did you have food in the house? How did Grandmother manage with everything?"

"Terri, it wasn't easy for your grandmother," he went on. "I was the oldest, which meant that Grandmother needed to rely on me to walk into town for help or to take a sheep into town when we were low on cash and trade it for supplies."

As he continued, I couldn't help but feel sorry for him, and I missed not knowing my grandfather. I could feel my eyes well up with tears. We visited our grandparents and grandmother often, and so I understood the severity of the long, cold winters in Minnesota. The road was so long into town from the farm, I wondered how a child could manage to get there and back by himself.

As Dad caught the emotion in my eyes, he began to reshape his story with one of his parables. "Terri," he told me, "your heart will go through fire in this life. It will be up to you to choose whether your heart will turn to gold or turn to stone."

"*What?*" I asked urgently. "What does that mean, Daddy?"

My urgency to understand was met with silence for what seemed like several minutes. Then, my father made his final comment on his story: "You will know what that means when you need to."

I've often thought of that story. As a child, I was afraid I'd forget his words, but they are there. My father's voice, his patience and his laughter continue within all of us who were lucky enough to know him. And his stories continue to mark the wisdom of fables—to ask a question and empower the pursuit of the truth; it has a much longer legacy than would a command.

I smile, looking back at it all. And I'm thankful to have had a chance to say good-bye to both of my parents before they died.

THE COURAGE OF MY MOTHER

From my mother, my lesson learned was courage. As a young girl, Ardys Lorraine was told she needed to work harder in school. She was born with dyslexia, a learning difference that, in her case, flipped all letters on the page as if it appeared in a mirror. Today, researchers understand that dyslexia often accompanies a higher than average IQ and requires specific teaching and learning methods. Even today, dyslexia is often misunderstood. According to Harvard University neurologists, it exists when a greater than average number of brain cells appear on the right side of the brain, in the area responsible for creative thinking and complex problem-solving.

This should be a good thing, right? After all, Charles Schwab, Thomas Edison, Albert Einstein, even actress Sally Fields have had dyslexia. In addition to the common letter reversals, directionality difficulty and problems with reading retention are often symptomatic of dyslexia. Unfortunately, if educators aren't trained with specific methods for dyslexia's remediation, labels, such as "learning disabled," may follow, and this then becomes a self-fulfilling prophecy.

In the 1920s, the only research on dyslexia had been conducted by Dr. Samuel Orton, a neurosurgeon who himself had children with dyslexia. The teachers who worked with Dr. Orton were trained with multisensory methods to bridge the need for left-to-right directionality practice and letter-to-sound reinforcement. The teaching methods that came from the Orton classrooms became the difference between success and failure for many children. Fortunately, one such teacher trained with the Orton Method for reading moved to northern

Minnesota. It was this second-grade teacher who would change my mother's life forever, giving her the gift of literacy and learning.

My mother's courage came in her overcoming the fear of failure. It was not until her new teacher in second grade brought a mirror to school that my mother was able to put into words what she had been seeing on the page. Turning the letters over, one at a time, and placing them on the page as others saw them was the easy part for this little girl. Understanding and overcoming the fear of failure was the challenge. My mother inspired me with her courage—the courage to succeed through her willingness to risk failure.

MY PARENTS' LEGACY

I have been asked, "Why did you choose politics?" In truth, I didn't. Politics chose me. My parents both came from families that served in office and as citizen leaders. We were encouraged to talk about the issues of the day; the threat of nuclear war, the Vietnam War, and heroes coming home from the war and those who didn't make it home. Everything from UNICEF and world hunger to the price of gasoline and home-heating costs was shared in conversations at the dinner table; even as children, our own voices, convictions and solutions emerged.

My family was like most others in the 1970s. We coped as a family when my brother and father reached their maximums in their health-insurance coverage. We all knew the cost of out-of-pocket payments for physicians and hospital expenses. We just assumed that hard work and getting a good education would improve our lives and prospects for the future. It was this mindset that carried us forward as a family, generation after generation.

Sobering for me, at a very young age, was the realization that death was a part of life. It was the life-altering situations that I faced as a young girl that would frame my view and value of family. My father underwent a series of operations and illnesses before I finished grade school. Yet I don't remember a day that my father was without his contagious smile or kind words. His northern Minnesota accent carried a hint of an Irish flare when he would recite his stories and sing the ballads of Ireland—"Sweet Molly O'Grady" or "When Irish Eyes Are Smiling," all presented in an off-key voice, brazen with optimism and hope.

He and my mother were older than most parents in those days. Dad grew up in a single-parent household with his mother, a former schoolteacher. Grandpa McCormick made it home from WWI and built a business with his dad but died in the influenza epidemic four years later. Both of my parents were children during the Great Depression and came of age during World War II. My mother spoke of Churchill as her hero. As a young girl, she helped her mother with the farm and her sewing business. History unfolded on the radio for our greatest generation. "The only thing to fear is fear itself," Mom would recite to us when we paused or hesitated as children.

The reality of the effect of World War II hit home for me as my mother recounted the young men in her high school class who had gone off to war. One such story centered around the impact that the Lindbergh family had in northern Minnesota. Charles Lindbergh, the famous aviator, grew up down the road from my grandmother. It was a few years earlier when the world stood still for the first Atlantic flight of the *Spirit of St. Louis*. With the stories fresh in the minds of these young high school graduates and friends of my mother's, there was a clamor to join the fight early and sign up across the Canadian border with the Royal Air Force (RAF). My mother's voice often caught in her throat as she shared with me that none of them came home.

My mother's history unfolded around her memories of the Great Depression and World War II on the farm in northern Minnesota. It is with a sweet sense of poetry that the last gift I would receive from my mother was, in a literal sense, what she had given me all of my life. I was in my third year in the Wisconsin state legislature in 2003 and would return home with a full calendar of meetings with my constituents and groups back in the district. Meetings were scheduled over the course of weekend events—Friday, Saturday and Sunday that often floated into Mondays. This left very little time for my own family.

It was at our last breakfast together before my mother was diagnosed with aggressive cancer that she would be insistent on giving me her surprise.

"I have something for you, and I'd like to give it to you soon," she told me excitedly on the phone.

We met at a Perkins restaurant near her apartment in Kimberly, on the east side of Appleton. I could see that she wasn't feeling very well; her eyes were dim as she struggled to get up to hug me.

"Mom, are you doing all right? I am sorry that I haven't called. It has been so difficult to fit everything in these days."

"Never mind, Terri. I have more clippings for you from the newspapers. My neighbors at the apartment building are clipping them whenever they see your picture in the paper," she said with a smile.

After we finished our lunch and it was time to go, she pulled out a package from her large purse. "I mentioned that I have something for you," she said with a heartfelt smile.

"Mom, you really don't need to get me things," I told her. I worried about her ability to cover basic costs for rent, food and prescription drugs. Then I opened the package and found a book with a title so significant and meaningful, I cherished its significance—it was a book of quotes from my mother's hero, Winston Churchill, appropriately titled *Courage*.

"Carry it with you in your briefcase in the capitol," she said. "You never know when you will need it to bring light to the dark corners in that place."

This rich family history and the personal struggles of our family provided the backdrop for my interest in public service. It was Dad who encouraged me, early in my life, to get involved in a political campaign for his friend and neighbor, state assemblyman Rep. Earl McEssy. "We need good people in politics, Terri," he'd told me, "men and women who care about something bigger than themselves." And it was my mother who gave me a book about courage to strengthen my convictions while in public office.

Whether through tragedy or hardship, in fighting the Civil War, carving out a frontier, fighting in the Great War, overcoming the Great Depression, or making it home from the war, the tragedies and opportunities of this spirit have shaped me and my family. The joy and laughter of my childhood embraces my soul and provides me strength today. It is this foundation of family and ethnic spirit on which I pin my children's hopes and dreams.

THE CONVICTIONS THAT HOLD ME

Growing up with parents who were a generation older than my friends' parents was an advantage for me. I was a late-in-life baby, born to older parents. Maybe because of this, I never thought I had to fit in or follow the crowd. Quite the contrary, my mother, in her spirited moments, could slip into an Irish brogue, reminding me that she was raising eagles and not sheep in her household. My childhood in a middle-class household with two working parents in their fifties and sixties led me to think it my lot in life to fix the neighborhood problems and keep my younger brother out of trouble. It never occurred to me that I was "just a girl." Or that I was too young to do anything I set my mind on doing.

At age fourteen, I was chosen to lead a drum and bugle corps to the national championships in Boston, Massachusetts. The Marquis Drum and Bugle Corps would prove to be my first experience in learning about leadership. It wasn't easy for the older members of that drum corps to accept a fourteen-year-old girl as their leader. The only way I could think of proving myself was to work myself harder and smarter than anyone in the organization, and so I worked myself to the point of exhaustion. Not only did I win a few national awards, but I also scared off the competition—those who were not willing to work as hard as I was. Leading my peers on a highly competitive and demanding stage of national competition would prove to be one in a series of my leadership tests.

There was always the rumor or innuendo of why I was chosen to be the leader; teenagers can be cruel and unkind. My father was always first to listen and remind me, "Bad publicity is better than no publicity. Just please spell my name right." My parents were always there, cheering me on and coaching me to "reach for the stars." And so it went throughout my life, during the time that I had my father.

I soon learned that life was fragile and unpredictable when my father was diagnosed with heart disease. I knew by middle school that he would not be with me very long, as the hospital bed and the oxygen tanks rolled into what was once the dining room in our family home. I found that I began to appreciate every conversation I had with my father; I began to listen with my heart.

"Education is the great equalizer, Terri," I would hear him say. "I believe in you."

My father suffered with heart disease when I was in high school. He died soon after, yet I know I fulfilled what he would have wanted for me. Education was indeed my saving grace—and I would make a life for myself, based on my own abilities, talents and dreams.

With the death of my father, it became important for me to pull myself up that ladder of opportunity. Educational opportunities, competition based on merit, and equal justice under the law became the rungs up that ladder in American society. These rungs—these convictions—were to be my guiding principles throughout my life and career.

EDUCATION AS A CONVICTION

It was the frailty of my father's health and early death that led me to believe that education was the most important opportunity in the lives of children, whether rich or poor; black, white, Asian or Hispanic. As a young child I observed migrant families hunger to learn the English language and share in the opportunities that so many Americans take for granted. The caring nature of public school teachers in the 1960s provided the role models for many who relied on their teachers as examples of what could be and should be in their lives. The language of literacy in that small public school building became the language of opportunity for me. Even as a child, I knew that without an education I would have a difficult time supporting myself and securing my own future when the time came.

Perhaps it was because of this close connection I felt to education in my childhood that it came as no surprise when I was propelled into the hottest issue of the day: education reform. One Sunday morning, I opened the newspaper to an article about a crisis in the Milwaukee schools. In that article, the Milwaukee school superintendent announced his early retirement due to the frustration he felt in the position. No administrative tools or mechanisms were available to Superintendent Howard Fuller—there was no way for him to affect the lives of the tens of thousands of children who needed further educational options than traditional public education in urban Milwaukee.

Through a series of chance meetings and at the urging of a professor and mentor from Lawrence University's Education School in Appleton, Wisconsin, it would be my job to secure the statewide network and the legislation needed to initiate education reforms. Public education has always had the same struggles and challenges as the families who make up its student body, and in the 1980s, the Milwaukee Public Schools had reached a breaking point. In my heart of hearts, I knew this was an issue I would address.

FREE-MARKET COMPETITION AS A CONVICTION

Without the second rung on the ladder of opportunity—the ability to compete fairly in the marketplace of ideas—there would be no incentive to create or innovate ideas, solutions and products. Competition, when based on merit rather than privilege, can lead to social and economic opportunity and success. It is an ability to use talent and merit to rise to the top that levels the playing field, so that individuals can lift themselves up and make it on their own.

Competing on a level playing field has sharpened my ability to innovate and solve problems with public policy. It can create an entrepreneurial spirit within us all, as well as a willingness to compete, whether in government, business or industry. Many policy-makers have referred to this as the ability to think "outside the box." Some call it the ability to lead with vision. Maybe it is just a knack for new ideas and doing the impossible. Business and social entrepreneurs understand that if you are not looking to the future for new ideas, you will constantly be five seconds behind. The ability to compete and innovate makes the impossible possible—and solves the problems of today.

JUSTICE FOR ALL AS A CONVICTION

The third rung on the ladder toward economic and social success is equal treatment under the law, regardless of gender, ethnicity, religion or other differences. Justice must apply to all citizens equally, lest we break the spirit of a free people. Understanding the U.S. Constitution and its rights and responsibilities is an important place to begin in understanding the law of our land. Unfortunately, the American justice system is only as perfect as the men and women elected to serve as judges, and the attorneys who act as officers of the court.

The right to be treated equally under the law isn't just a conviction; it is a part of our nation's Bill of Rights. If the rules of the game, so to speak, were to apply differently to various Americans, it would be too easy to lose faith and hope in our judicial system.

As the vice chairperson of the State Legislative Judiciary Committee, I took this notion to heart. Front-row politics and political parties carried no weight with my belief in the Constitution. Thankfully, with the help of many individuals and constituents, we passed the Court Interpreter Program, providing deaf and language interpreters in our courts so that all of our citizens could realize their constitutional right to understand courtroom proceedings.[2] With the rule of law, a further commitment was made to ensure a basic right to counsel for all Americans.[3]

Finally, it was this conviction and core value of equal justice under the law that led me to take the role of House Lead on a bill designed to ensure that "all" lawmakers would be held accountable to ethics law violations under the Government Accountability Board.[4] Because of this conviction, I found offensive the alleged acts of former attorney general Alberto Gonzalez, during the George W. Bush administration. Not only did Gonzalez break with the U.S. Constitution, but he broke with the public trust in using federal prosecutors for political election purposes prior to the 2006 campaigns. Reportedly, federal prosecutors were dismissed from their positions for not swinging public opinion against Democrats before the 2006 elections.[5]

If you believe that justice should apply equally to all citizens and that the federal government should not abuse its authority in this regard, then it is time to put integrity back in the political process on all levels and in all branches of government.

IT IS YOUR TURN: THE HONESTY TOUR AND YOU! CITIZEN, MEDIA, CANDIDATES

Putting integrity back into public service will require all of us—citizens, the media and integrity candidates—to take our own honesty tours. According to the Merriam-Webster Dictionary online research, the most looked-up term in 2006 was integrity (a strict adherence to a core set of values and principles, an incorruptibility). At no greater time in American history is integrity leadership needed in our local, state and federal governments. How do voters find these integrity leaders? What are the ethical obligations of the press in ensuring our democracy? How is a candidate to find his/her center and act with integrity in the service of the public? Let's find out …

INTEGRITY CITIZENSHIP

Integrity citizenship requires a strict adherence to a core set of values and principles, as well as acting on behalf of the greater good. Our core values as a nation—according to President Barack Obama in his inaugural address on January 20, 2009—are honesty and hard work, courage and fair play, tolerance and curiosity, loyalty and patriotism. Further, our nation's principles, in letter and in spirit, were established with the Declaration of Independence and the United States Constitution.

It is our turn, as We the People, to put our collective American values and principles into action. As our government derives its power from the governed, it is the governed that must step up and be responsible for what our government becomes. Our sacred, civic duty begins with a solid education and civic literacy as to how our government works and then requires all of us to act. Volunteerism is a good place to start—from sharing ideas on the Internet to action in supporting a candidate or running for local, state or federal office.

Abraham Lincoln said the following about civic literacy and the Constitution:

> *Let every American, every lover of liberty, every well-wisher to his posterity swear by the blood of the Revolution never to violate in the least particular laws of this country, and never to tolerate their violation by others. As the patriots of the '76 did to the support of the Declaration of Independence, so to the support of the Constitution and laws let every American pledge his life, his property, and his sacred honor. Let every man remember that to violate the law is to trample on the blood of his father, and to tear the character of his own and his children's liberty ... Let it be taught in schools, in seminaries, and in colleges, let it be written in primers, in spelling books and in almanacs, let it be preached from the pulpit, proclaimed in legislative halls, and enforced in courts of justice. And, in short, let it become the political religion of the nation, and, in particular, a reverence for the Constitution.*

Integrity citizens not only educate themselves on the letter of the law with the United States Constitution, but they also act within the spirit of that document. From our beginnings as a nation, citizenship has been the responsibility of us all. Today, through the use of the Internet, mass media and social networking, we have the ability to create the kind of community that our Founding Fathers envisioned—

that is, a fully engaged citizenry involved in educating itself on the issues, providing private opinion and acting on behalf of the greater good. It is the act of public service and engagement in the greater good that determines an integrity citizen. Whether in the armed forces, Peace Corps, youth corps or other service to our nation, the core of integrity citizenship is to act.

The Constitution was written to protect citizens from abuse of power by our servants in the legislature or Congress. Elections and impeachment of lawmakers is one means of protection against those who would abuse their public offices. Jefferson believed in constitutional protections against overzealous men in public office. James Madison wrote in 1788: "Fear of the abuse of the power of political parties is as great as the abuses by kings. … Wherever there is an interest and power to do wrong, wrong will generally be done, and not less readily by a powerful and interested party than by a powerful and interested prince."

INTEGRITY JOURNALISM

A strict adherence to a core set of values and principles, incorruptibility is the standard for journalistic integrity of which the citizen/voter and candidate should be intimately aware. In today's society of instantaneous communications via blogs and the Internet, we must all guard against journalists who are tempted to forego the following values and principles by way of self-interest and greed.

According to the Society of Professional Journalists, the ethical standard of professionalism is to "seek truth and report it. … Journalists should be honest, fair and courageous in gathering reporting and interpreting information." Personal agendas and conflicts of interest are not only barriers to honesty and integrity in public office, but they also can be barriers to integrity-driven journalists as well. It is the citizen's right and responsibility to hold local newspapers, radio news journalists, television news journalists, and news agencies reporting on the Internet accountable for violating the public trust in this regard. Realize that bloggers represent their own interests and are not credible, reliable or subject to the ethics code below.

The Society of Professional Journalists' preamble and highlights from their Code of Ethics are below:

Members of the Society of Professional Journalists believe that public enlightenment is the forerunner of justice and the foundation of democracy. The duty of journalists is to further those ends by seeking truth and providing a fair and comprehensive account of events and issues. Journalists shall serve the public with thoroughness and honesty. Professional integrity is the cornerstone of a journalist's credibility. Members share a dedication to ethical behavior and adopt this code to declare the Society's principles and standards of practice.

1. **Seek Truth and Report It**. Journalists should be honest, fair and courageous in gathering, reporting and interpreting information. This includes tests for accuracy. Always question sources' motives before promising anonymity; never distort or mislead and avoid surreptitious methods of gathering information; distinguish between advocacy and news reporting; distinguish news from advertising and shun hybrids; recognize the special obligation to ensure the public's business is conducted in the open.

2. **Minimize Harm. Ethical journalists treat sources, subjects and colleagues as human beings deserving of respect.** Journalists should show compassion for those affected adversely by news coverage; pursuit of the news is not a license for arrogance. Private people have a greater right to control information about themselves than do public officials and those seeking office.

3. **Act Independently.** Journalists should be free of obligation to any interest other than the public's right to know. Journalists should avoid conflicts of interest, real or perceived; remain free of associations and activities that may compromise integrity or damage credibility; refuse gifts; disclose unavoidable conflicts; deny favored treatment to advertisers and special interests and resist their pressure

to influence news coverage; be wary of sources offering information for favors or money.

4. **Be Accountable**. Journalists should clarify and explain news coverage and invite dialogue with the public over journalistic conduct; encourage the public to voice grievances about the news media; admit mistakes and correct them promptly; expose unethical practices of journalists and the news media; abide by the same high standards to which they hold others.

Journalists, just as public officials, have a responsibility to the general public for ethical behavior. Integrity principles apply to all citizens, candidates and the media. Strict adherence to a core set of ethical principles, outlined above, provides the rules of engagement for the "fourth branch of government"—the press.

Citizen leaders—know your rights and responsibilities under the U.S. Constitution as they relate to freedom of the press and the first amendment, shield laws, and constitutional protections and the right to privacy, relative to the press. Tabloid journalists, bloggers and Internet voices—please know that constitutional rights and responsibilities apply to your form of media as well as to journalists.

At a time when competing sources for news and information is delivered in real time to Americans via the Internet, BlackBerries and iPhones, it is all too tempting to take shortcuts with the ethical standards listed above. It has been said that knowledge is power; it is hoped that ethical standards, as applied equally to citizens, candidates and the press, will ensure integrity leadership in getting our government back on track.

IT IS YOUR TURN: BECOME AN INTEGRITY CANDIDATE

Integrity leadership while in office can be more difficult to achieve than one might think. Before you run for political office, it is essential that you sit yourself down and define your belief system and core convictions. I have explained the process of sharing my honesty tour and journey that has shaped my core convictions; now it is time for you to do the same.

To begin, get a journal and write the answers to the following questions:

- What is your greatest source of inner strength? What is your center of gravity?
- What are the convictions that explain your decision making?
- How do you respond to people in need?
- Do you have the compassion necessary to care about your constituents?
- What is your motivation for running for public office?

If you've answered the last question with something like, "I want to be president of the United States" or "It is about my career path; it's an entitlement; it's for insurance and a pension," close this book and walk away. *I cannot help you.*

It is imperative that you understand yourself, your goals and your core convictions. Ask yourself the following question: "Why would I like to serve?"

If you frequently look at yourself in the mirror, and running for office becomes a part of your ego need, and you begin to use phrases like "It is best for me ..." then words such as integrity leadership, principles, and core values will seem like a foreign language to you. You can practice the words but they will have no meaning—you will be a *faker!* There are fakers who trick the public into thinking that they are compassionate problem solvers. These tricksters will participate in something called retail politics and become the best actors in the world in an attempt to fool you. These tricksters will have plenty of campaign cash poured in from Washington DC or a state capital in an attempt to buy the election. Do not be fooled by retail politics—the use of a lot of cash and campaign ads to fool and convince the public that someone is something that he or she is not.

Do not be fooled by these people, and do not become one, either.

In that land of gray opportunism filled with politicians who say what they need to say to be elected, elected officials can look and act like bobble-head dolls so that they can keep their jobs. I will not enable fakers; I will not be a part of deceiving the public by empowering those who wear masks of virtue when running for elective offices!

WHERE IS YOUR CENTER?

It is time for your honesty tour, so please ask yourself the following questions and answer as honestly as you can:

- What are the most important aspects of your life that money can't buy?
- What convictions hold you, rather than your holding them?
- As an elected official, for whom do you work?
- If you only had one year in office, what would your priorities be?

Think of stories that have impacted your life and made you think. Follow up with patterns of choices you have made, such as volunteering as a bell choir director, or Boys and Girls Club volunteer. What issues and topics light you on fire?

Citizen candidates—public service does not come with ticker-tape parades and throngs of adoring fans. Instead, it requires humility and personal, family and community sacrifice. Public service requires that you live and work by the values that hold you at your core. And it requires that your family share the most precious part of you—your time and attention—with the public.

It is the integrity principle that true leadership flows throughout your entire lifetime, from beginning to end. Someone may not always think of himself as "a leader" because he is too busy doing for others and making a difference where he stands. Those who never dream of running for public office often are the very best public servants.

If you have passion, purpose, spontaneity and sincerity—the "PPSS" of politics—you should consider running for public office. Passion, purpose, spontaneity and sincerity are characteristics of individuals who know who they are and why they hope to serve the public in office.

My core convictions hold every decision and every action I make, and they are threefold:

- Educational opportunities
- Equal justice under the law
- Fair-market competition

Without core convictions, the ideas and decisions I made during my tenure in the Wisconsin state legislature would have had no weight. I would not have been able to carry the strength of my convictions to the reform agendas that I led against the storms in the state capital. There is no question that I may have been swept up by the same winds of corruption that carried my front row in their 2001 and 2002 indictments and plea deals.

Those of you who base your judgment and leadership on your core convictions and values, and those of you who choose to make a difference in the lives of others, you are needed. You can make a difference.

INTEGRITY CANDIDATES AND THE PPSS RULE

Constituents whom I represented didn't often come to fund-raisers, nor did they arrive at my capitol office. They phoned when they had no place to go or when no one else would listen. Some called at a time of personal desperation, looking for an advocate and a little bit of hope. Small-business workers and owners told me of their struggles with health-insurance costs. Farm families choked back the tears when they were forced to give up the family farm. Veterans shared intimate stories about living with post-traumatic stress and the toll it took on their families. More and more veterans turned to me to make sense of what their country had become, and what their sacrifices in uniform bought this nation.

An integrity candidate will be an integrity public servant in office. There are four principles that true public servants have in common.

This is not an exhaustive list; it is a brief snapshot among so many snapshots that I have provided to make sense of a profession that I hold dear—that of a public servant.

First, people with integrity principles are people of purpose. They are often candidates who believe they can make a difference because of the skills and knowledge that they bring to the table on behalf of their constituents. They have a sense of a mission and a sense of purpose that comes from their heads and their hearts.

Second, people with integrity principles are people of passion who understand that time is of the essence. People who are struggling in today's economy and social environment cannot wait for someone to serve ten years to make decisions, when they have seniority. Passion to serve the public and make the world a better place is essential for candidates who hope to earn the trust of the people in their districts.

Third, people with integrity principles are people with sincerity in their hearts. They are not actors reciting the sound bites presented to them. Rather, they are sincere people who have earned their own way and often have blazed their own trails. They have compassion and empathy for those they wish to serve.

Fourth, people with integrity principles are people who are spontaneous. They do not need to rehearse someone else's platform. They can talk freely and off the cuff because they choose to serve others with principle, integrity and courage. What have you done? What can you do? The issues do not always break down upon partisan lines. You could be asked questions such as:

- What can you do about government overspending and my high taxes?
- How can you save my pension that has been taken by my employer (or my union)?
- How can I stop paying so much of my paycheck to my health-care program?
- How can I save my small business from overregulation by the government?

- How can you make sure I can hunt and fish and that the water will remain clean?

How do we know which politicians are deceptive and which ones are truthful? It is up to us, the citizens who vote, to make that determination. It may be an instinct of trustworthiness—or lack of it. It may be an intellectual discovery of inconsistent answers to questions. It may be the fact that the skill a candidate has does not match his or her résumé.

We need integrity-driven volunteers to step forward as citizen leaders. Without citizen leaders, retail politics—and its successor, pay-for-play politics—would dominate public policy, and the public would not be served.

CHAPTER SUMMARY

Currently, the state of politics focuses on retail politicians and pay-for-play strategies that do little to benefit the American citizen.

My core convictions on education, the free market, and justice for all inspired my political career.

The political system can change for the better with integrity citizenship, integrity journalism and integrity candidates.

*There is but one straight course, and that is to
seek truth and pursue it steadily.*

George Washington, letter to Edmund Randolph, July 31, 1795

CHAPTER TWO

PATH TO POLITICS

MYTH:

Politicians run for office in order to
serve the voters.

REALITY:

Mostly, they're going to serve their
own agendas.

*Great heart must have his sword and armour to guard
the pilgrims on their way.*

—Winston Churchill

CITIZEN LEADERS

It's funny how an idea can turn quickly into a passion. Throughout most of my professional and volunteer career, I have been hired because I have been considered a "change agent." I became comfortable with the term in 1996, when Bill O'Brien, the former executive director of an Appleton Catholic school district, suggested that I work with middle-school students. Creative and innovative, Bill O'Brien was looking for outside-the-box ideas in providing a curriculum for his financially strapped school district. More important, he had a class in one of his middle schools that had a reputation for chasing good teachers out of the teaching profession.

O'Brien recruited me, as he said, "because you just spent time getting the charter school law passed, and the teachers union is going to come after you like you cannot believe." (Charter schools operate with freedom from many of the regulations that apply to traditional public schools. The "charter" establishing each such school is a performance contract that details the school's mission, program, goals, students served, methods of assessment and ways to measure success.[6]) I knew O'Brien was right, as he went on, "We need you for these kids, and be honest—you need us right now."

With Appleton newspaper headlines such as "McCormick to Ruin Public Education with Controversial Charter School Law," I couldn't deny a word he was saying. Neither the teachers union, nor reporters with family members inside that union, was pleased with the change in the traditional education. A target was clearly on my back as the founder of public charter schools.

O'Brien went on, "If anyone can reach these kids, you can!" As he appealed to my need to make a difference, I couldn't say no. I had ideas—it seemed like I could think my way out of most challenges that life dropped on my doorstep. I would write a leadership curriculum to empower students, rather than simply talk at them. The ideas came one after the other—communications skills, speaking, decision making. I would give to those students a recipe for leadership. Through a series of leadership classes, I would find myself healing through my new career as a teacher and then a student of administration. It would take time to heal from the "charter wars," as they were called.

START WITH VOLUNTEERISM ON THE LOCAL LEVEL

In the early 1990s, I was recruited to chair a new Citizens Advisory Council for the Appleton Public School District. My children attended the public primary school down the street, so I believed it was my responsibility to give of my time to the public school district. Education, as luck would have it, became one of the hottest policy issues of the day. It attracted intense emotion and passion in our local community. Parents understood that the stakes were high; their children's futures were on the line. At the same time, the business community struggled with finding an adequate workforce—one that was literate. Community growth and livelihood hung in the balance.

Through the countless meetings, subcommittee meetings and phone calls, I began to find patterns in what parents, administrators and school board members were saying. That pattern was literacy; specifically, learning differences. Children with dyslexia, scotopic sensitivity (another visual perception issue) and other remedial learning differences were being left behind. Parents phoned me looking for help: "My child cannot read." It didn't matter the age or the IQ, these children were not learning to read and comprehend.

There were plenty of labels floating around to explain the phenomenon of nonliterate educated students. Some of those labels sent chills up my spine: learning disabled, emotionally disordered, troubled family, at risk, low socioeconomic background, divorced parents, trouble at home. It was fascinating to me that the phrase dyslexic or scotopic sensitivity or any other method-specific learning difference was not mentioned. It was as though my mother's teacher in that one-room schoolhouse in northern Minnesota was tapping me on the shoulder, saying, "What are you going to do about it?"

By 1992 I had been accepted into the education certificate program at Lawrence University. Encouraged by independent and gifted professor Ken Sager, I began what was to lead me to become one of the state's founders of the charter school movement. My background and credentials in public policy, international relations and foreign policy were meaningless. I now needed to start over. I would need education credentials if I were to be taken seriously as an educator and education researcher. Soon after finishing my education coursework and obtaining my credentials, I began tutoring children and adults with dyslexia, dysgraphia (deficiency in the ability to write) and scotopic sensitivity.

New patterns emerged through the research I was conducting through Educational Services, Inc., an educational research and developmental foundation. The findings were significant, and they were independently validated by neuropsychologists and special-education professionals. Dramatic improvement became measurable and confirmed with independent testing in the education community. Children and adults began to thrive with methods then not available in public schools. The overarching conclusion was this: the methodology and curriculum changes introduced to the students who had been referred to me meant the difference between success or failure in school.

By 1993, parents and school board members in both public and parochial school systems began to see me as someone in whom they could confide—or maybe someone who could at long last give them hope. Their stories were similar: "My son (or daughter) is smart, but he (or she) can't read." It didn't matter if the child was seven or seventeen with a high IQ. The notion of learning differences in a one-size-fits-all school system was going against the grain of accepted educational research in the traditional schoolhouse.

The public-school parents I encountered were increasingly concerned with not having a voice in choosing the right teacher and educational fit for their children's needs. I was asked to sit on educational assessment panels on all levels of K–12 education. One such instance provided a similar theme—a bright young man who tested at the top end of the intelligence quotient, with tremendous talent in music and art, was labeled as "difficult" by his high school teachers. My work with this gifted young man on the Woodcock Reading Mastery Test and phonemic awareness tests showed a cause for his being "difficult"—he was not only highly intelligent, but he was extremely dyslexic as well. (He was in good company: Albert Einstein, stock broker Charles Schwab, and Thomas Edison were all dyslexic.)

The new question became: "Is the traditional school system capable of change?" I was willing to hand over two years of research, study and materials that had been field-tested and pilot-tested to the public school system. For the sake of those children with learning differences who were underserved, I gathered my curriculum and research from Harvard, the Orton Foundation, the Neihaus Foundation, the Scottish Rite Hospital for Children and Learning Labs, and the International Irlen Centers for one purpose: I was determined to give away what I had learned so that children in the public schools could succeed.

I arranged a meeting with the area superintendent of schools, Tom Scullen. This man had retired from a similar position in Illinois but came out of retirement. He was either a man who had not had the ability to fulfill his dreams in his home state of Illinois, or he needed a second retirement plan; my guess was the former. He was a round-faced, white-haired fellow with a patient expression. He listened silently to my offer of giving the research and information I'd gathered, free of charge. Dr. Scullen agreed that the multisensory methods used at the Neihaus Education Center in Houston were classic methods from the Orton Foundation and would help tremendously in the remediation of learning differences.

"Terri, there is no doubt that what you have accomplished is accurate," Dr. Scullen affirmed. "But ... but ... the methods are too teacher-intensive, and I doubt that I can get them through the teachers union." He went on to say, "There is nothing I can do with that kind of resistance," and then, in order to try to placate me, Dr. Scullen added, "When I was in Illinois I tried everything from at-risk programs to talented and gifted programs—you name it. We will not be able to get these methods into the classrooms."

As I sat in shock and disbelief, I knew there was a way to provide more options for children and families who found themselves held captive by programs and methods that did not work well enough to teach children the fundamental skill of literacy.

DEFINING THE PROBLEMS IN EDUCATION

Two years of intensive research and volunteer hours resulted in the founding of a nonprofit foundation dedicated to the research and development of learning differences. I was determined that the thousands of children who could be helped in my home state of Wisconsin would not pay the price for a broken system that was unwilling to change course. I made a commitment that day to myself and to the families I had listened to as chair of the Citizens Advisory Council that I would change this system of public education. I would enlist my educational mentor, Ken Sager, of Lawrence University, and Dr. Tom Scullen himself, if I had to.

A public school system designed to help children reach their potential was not interested in using methods that were too difficult or too intensive for teachers to follow. The labels bantered about by professional educators began to appear more like excuses and alphabet soup than progressive steps toward student achievement. I knew it was now time for me to go back to my first educational interests, public policy and politics. Before I came home to raise a family, I was at graduate school in Canada in the field of international public policy and political theory. It was time to take a look at the barriers and obstacles to the families with children with learning differences and put this train wreck right.

EDUCATION REFORM IN AN UNYIELDING SYSTEM

Children were made to fit into a mold of traditional education that was controlled by social trends and issues, rather than scientific methods that worked for each child. Parents were made to believe that they were unwelcome intrusions in the classrooms that were neatly planned by professional educators, who knew best. It was time to change that paradigm. As I worked with groups like the Association for

Educators in Private Practice, I began to understand that there were teachers trapped within the traditional confines of public education, just as assuredly as there were students. The challenge, then, would be how to create the laws and administrative mechanisms, and build a coalition to pass those laws in a hostile political climate. It would take determination and the strength of my convictions to see it through—but it would be done.

My philosophy of education was emboldened by my core conviction that all children can learn; it is up to the adults in the room to find a way. My outside-the-box thinking was going to stir things up—but it was far easier to do that than to go against my heart of hearts. Challenging the educational establishment—the system—would have consequences. Still, my unshakable belief that all children can learn would not go away.

CHARTER SCHOOLS: THE NEW CIVIL RIGHT

A series of chance meetings led me down a leadership path as a school reformer and then pioneer of the charter school movement in the state of Wisconsin. In a literal sense, I threw the gauntlet down to one of the most powerful interest groups in the state: the Wisconsin Education Association Council (WEAC).

The graduation rate in Milwaukee is well documented at 45 percent[7]—less than half of the students in the system earn a high school diploma. I wasn't looking for educational initiatives; they were finding me. My work with students with learning differences spilled over into the need to provide public-educational choice and opportunity. Before I knew it, I was being invited to attend meetings held by known school reformers in Milwaukee and other Midwestern states. This new education movement soon began to resemble more of a civil rights movement than a simple PTA volunteer assignment. The winds of dramatic change were rising as a groundswell of parents from across the country were insisting their voices be heard.

My first set of credentials and background in economics and public policy, as a former student of international policy and politics, was about to resurface. It was time to sharpen my past knack for systems-thinking in policy that could affect the lives of the families in my state and many others. The conversation I had had with Dr. Scullen was a constant reminder that there would be no educational reforms unless I made it happen. I was dealing with an educational system so comfortable with the status quo that it was deaf to the public outcry for change and conscience. Inertia-driven education policies of the past would need market incentives and competition to snap its hamster wheels from their sprockets. What was needed was a new vehicle for change that placed parents, teachers and students on the same side of the negotiating table. Those new vehicles were public charter schools.

My reputation as someone who could help fix the educational system grew. In the fall of 1993, I was noticed by educational leaders throughout my state. It was at that time that I was introduced to two gentlemen with whom I would form an unbreakable alliance in education reform. They were the former Milwaukee Public Schools superintendent Howard Fuller, and Superintendent Bob Gilpatrick, a feisty and determined public-school leader in the Madison area. Together, we called ourselves the "mod squad," as it was the three of us who would usher in the grand experiment to be known as the public charter school movement.

Fuller had publicly resigned his position as superintendent of the Milwaukee school system. Out of frustration, he was quoted as saying he did not have the tools he needed to save Milwaukee's broken school system. He was angry, and I believed rightfully so. Superintendent Bob Gilpatrick was a man of conscience, who valued the quality of excellence in education. His frustration with the status-quo system was that nothing changed for the better; models of excellence should be rewarded and used to move the public school system forward.

Through a series of chance meetings and referrals, I began to meet with Lt. Governor McCallum's chief of staff, Jim Bartholomew. It would be through our efforts that the charter school law would be drafted by the legislative reference bureau attorneys. We studied outlines of laws from other states that were blocked by their counterparts. I listened to the obstacles and patterns of barriers discussed by dozens of school organizers across the state in order to address and remedy every bump in the road.

It would be the "mod squad"—Howard, Bob and me—that would create the impetus for the coalition needed to lobby for the new law. In the small town of Verona, near Madison, the three of us would meet to discuss the strategy that we would need to get our charter school law passed. Howard's frustration level and impatience was at peak level that day as we sat at a small round table in one of Verona's public schools.

"We need to move ahead with the legislation and get it passed," I began. "I am almost finished with the bill draft with the lieutenant governor's policy staff."

Howard's response was brusque: "You cannot get the charter school bill passed through *your* state senator!" His frustration stemmed from years of trying to affect change, only to be stonewalled by politicians who didn't like to take political risks with their own careers in public office.

It had been rumored that my state senator was too close to the teachers union to be objective about public charter school reform.

Maybe I was naïve, or maybe I just didn't take no for an answer. I found myself saying, "Howard, give me six months!"

He looked at me in disbelief. I repeated my statement with more resolve—and I could feel the conviction coming up out of my heart this time—"Give me six months!"

Howard exploded with passion. "Okay! You can be the president of the Wisconsin Charter School Association. You get that bill passed!"

I didn't know it then, but this volunteer assignment, president of the Wisconsin Charter School Association, would be as rough-and-tumble as it could get in state politics. There was no pay or big promotion involved; I was only a citizen leader, trying to do what I thought was right, stemming from a passion that some would consider fate. I simply believed that all children deserved an opportunity to an education that would lift them up into a better life. In this passion for education reform for all children, I would be tested every step of the way by the forces of the status quo. Yet nothing could have prepared me for the gamesmanship required in the world of retail politics.

CITIZEN LEADERSHIP MEETS THE WORLD OF RETAIL POLITICS

In the March 9, 2008, edition of *New York Magazine*, actor and political activist George Clooney defines retail politics and where it began. "Since the Kennedy and Nixon debate, presidential campaigns have been Hollywood. You're never going to vote for a candidate who has a high, squeaky voice. They consult on everything now: part your hair on the left because it's more soothing, wear blue because it inspires confidence. Rather than win over the masses, they are trying to pick off demographics. That happens everywhere—in news, in movies and with candidates. It's all the same."

Staying in public office requires that candidates win elections. Retail politics tilts the scale in winning elections—balloons, bumper stickers, buttons, radio and television ads, yard signs, and campaign literature all require money to create, produce and deliver. What is the link between getting public policy passed and retail politics? Can voters be lured and fooled into voting for political candidates through the gimmicks of retail politics? You decide.

Looking back on my first political fund-raising reception, I was provided a glimpse in the window of retail politics and its successor, pay-for-play government. I was attending as a citizen leader, volunteer, and president of the Wisconsin Charter School Association. The cold hard reality was that if I wanted to get a public charter school law passed, I would need to get the support of legislative leaders.

I soon came to realize that politics is like a Hollywood movie set. Some movie sets include only one or two rooms of a house, yet the staging is such that it looks like a real home. It is rare that a movie set includes the entire home, complete with a family and all the furnishings. Likewise, it is rare that voters have the opportunity to see the "real deal" when they view the candidates. Integrity candidates and legislators who have heart, soul and enough intellectual firepower to solve the problems for people can be drowned out by the Hollywood staging of well-financed candidates and party machines.

Such was the case in my attempt to garner support for public charter school law. My job, as I saw it at this political fund-raiser, was to find the legislators I could count on to put principle over politics. The inner city families, children with learning differences, and school and community organizers counting on me to get this law passed had no money to donate. They could not help these politicians, with their retail-politics funds, to buy balloons and buttons. I was counting on integrity leadership to surface in the faces of the elected officials attending that reception. It would take courage to stand with me and the Wisconsin Charter School Association and vote for education reform.

It would be a few months before the legislative session ended in 1994; I had a few months left to keep my promise to Howard Fuller, to get the Charter School Law passed. Senator Mike Ellis was then the majority leader in the state senate and the man who could schedule a vote on my bill. I was his constituent, which was one reason why I attended his political fund-raiser. The other reason was that the lobbyist from the Wisconsin School Board Association, Senn Brown, insisted that my attending this event would improve our visibility as "players." I didn't know what a player was, but I was about to find out.

I drove past the perfect shrubs and down the winding road to the country club and up to a red brick building resembling a scene from the Great Gatsby. Entering the grand building, I took the long staircase up to the right and found a room surrounded by windows. There, the buffet-lined room was filled with people who had gathered to meet the senator.

I rehearsed my lines prior to approaching him: "Hi, I'm Terri McCormick, the president of the Wisconsin Charter School Association, and I would like to thank you for your support for my groundbreaking charter school law."

I knew I was stretching the truth—the senator hadn't yet agreed to support the law—but I was determined to use positive energy to encourage him to "do the right thing." How else could the Wisconsin Charter School Association, a group of integrity citizens with *no money*, gain enough political clout to pass a controversial reform package through the Wisconsin State Senate?

I was about to pull off one of the grandest political perception schemes of all time—I was about to flip not only the state senate leader's position but also change the minds of a majority of legislators to vote for a piece of education reform that would rile the largest Democratic union in the state.

I don't remember what the price tag was for my attending the reception, but I know it appeared to be more of a debutante's birthday party than a serious attempt to influence public policy. As I approached another legislator who was pointed out to me, he seemed to be trying to avoid me—his eyes leaped everywhere around the room but toward me.

"Representative Green?" I inquired as I approached him.

"Yes?" he replied, somewhat sheepishly.

"I'm Terri McCormick, the president of the Wisconsin Charter School Association."

His gaze searched the floor, avoiding direct eye contact.

I pressed on. "I hope that you will be able to support our bill creating charter schools in the state." I wasn't surprised at this man's hesitation and apparent discomfort. I'd expected it; he didn't appear to be any different than any other politician on this issue. I tried to find some common ground. "All public schools in the state of Wisconsin should be public charter schools." That must have provided a logic with which he couldn't argue.

This novice legislator finally grinned and said, "Yes, they all should be public charter schools."

In 1993 and 1994, I simply believed in the abilities of all children to learn. Passion and purpose led me to create the opportunities to prove it. As the founder and president of the Wisconsin Charter School Association and author of the Wisconsin Charter School Law, I was a volunteer and citizen leader.

Ten years later, national education reform groups would spend large amounts of campaign cash to further influence the decisions of lawmakers on the topic of charter schools and educational choice.

Integrity leadership—what a novel concept!

CHINESE CHARACTER FOR CHANGE
'DANGER AND OPPORTUNITY'

荣誉

The source of resistance to change is human emotion.
In the political environment, reaction and perception are reality.

COALITION BUILDING

Since the Charter School Association had no money, it was time to build a broad statewide coalition of integrity-driven citizen leaders. With uncertain support from politicians, we would need a multifront strategy. My motivation was twofold: my passion to help children caught in ineffective educational systems, and the fact that time was running out on my commitment to Howard Fuller—six months was up at the end of the 1994 legislative session.

WASB

We managed to create a strong alliance from an unlikely source: the Wisconsin Association of School Boards (WASB). Admittedly, the WASB was a reluctant ally in the process of defining and writing laws for self-governing public charter schools. Due to the power of the teachers union, however, the WASB found itself at a crossroads. Parents and administrators alike voiced the need for more public school options to meet the needs of their diverse school communities. It was this convergence of voices from all constituencies within school districts that empowered the superintendent's ranks, which began to see public charter schools as a part of their arsenal in educating children who were underserved and struggling.

The support of public charter schools, however, came with a hefty personal and professional price. Back in 1994, the radical idea of "public charter schools" was a political hot potato. The Wisconsin Association of School Boards magazine told the story in an article titled "The Ten Who Dared."[8] This denoted the ten superintendents who dared to step forward to support the public charter school alternative for their schools. Those ten superintendents would soon become the seven … and then the five … and then, ultimately, the three who dared, due to the overwhelming pressure and hard-ball politics played by the state's largest teachers union.

The teachers union was a powerful lobby, garnering the support of legislators in my state who were motivated by fear and were then moved to inaction. Any attempt to effect change within the public school system was quickly quashed because the union itself had other ideas. Members didn't want to, as they put it, "lose power and control" by adopting a charter school program. There was so much political angst from union stewards that those teachers who dared to teach in a public charter school were punished. The common penalty was to lose all seniority within the public school system, and with that, they forfeited their pensions and benefits. Soon, teachers unions forced charter school teachers out of their retirement and benefits packages altogether. This was the price they paid for stepping outside the ranks of union protection. It was an overt attempt to strangle the public charter school movement.

In one case, a school administrator who had moved to Wisconsin from Colorado confided in me as a member of the Wisconsin Charter School Association. With more emotion than I usually heard from a grown man, he told me, "I can't lose my job. I need to be able to feed my family."

My response consisted of two words: "I understand." As difficult as it was to see him go, I did understand, on a personal level, what he was going through.

"I am sorry," he continued. "I have to drop out of the charter school movement." He sounded tired and beaten.

This was my first taste of the politics of fear and intimidation. This was the price a public school teacher or administrator would pay for supporting something as "radical" as public charter schools.

A PERSONAL PRICE

My children were subject to pressure and added criticism in their public elementary schools. Worse, I received a warning on my home phone, telling me, "Stop supporting these charters—or else."

Unshaken, I asked, "Or else what?"

The voice on the other end of the phone pushed further. "Check underneath your car before strapping your children in their car seats."

That is the price one pays for being a "change agent," a "reformer." It was a personal price, one that tested my convictions and my ability to see past the smokescreens and the fear tactics, even those introduced to my own children. I had a choice to make—curl up in a ball and be a victim, or stand tall and continue to do the right thing. This was a difficult decision for me. Any number of fears ran through my mind as a parent of young children—guilt, panic, anger, indignation, remorse.

Incidents of intimidation were reported at my daughter Kellie's elementary school. One such report occurred in the form of a personal phone call to me from another parent, who was volunteering at the front desk at Kellie's school. This parent was so disturbed by the treatment my daughter received that she phoned me at home.

My immediate response was to get the principal on the phone—he clearly loved children, and I trusted him to verify for me what was happening in my daughter's fifth-grade classroom.

The principal's response was as follows: "Yes, Terri, Kellie's desk has been pulled out of the row and pushed to the far back corner of the room."

"Would you tell me if there are boxes on it and a plant, so that she may not even have a seat in her classroom?" I asked, wanting clarification of the report I had received.

"Yes," he admitted, "there were boxes on her desk, and I removed them so she has a place to sit." If the principal thought to pacify me with that statement, didn't work.

"I am leaving my meeting, and I am driving directly to school so that we may chat," I declared.

Later, the principal and I discussed the options that lay before me: pull my children out of public school, confront the teacher, see to it that Kellie was not singled out for no reason again. This was a stupid act by a teacher who was either told to intimidate the child of the president of the Wisconsin Charter School Association, or it was a thoughtless act of a teacher who needed help.

After that incident, I consulted a close friend and colleague, who gave me the words that I needed to hear: "Intimidation by those who do not want change will continue, Terri. Are you willing to back away from what you know is important to so many children and let this continue?"

My children needed to know that they would be protected. And at the same time, they needed to know that we, as a family, would not back down to fear. Undaunted, I continued to lead the charter school movement through the passage of the public charter school bill, signed in 1996. More determined than before, I set out to impress upon the politicians that public charter schools had widespread support. I appealed directly to the people of the state through editorial boards, letters to the editor and, most important, through the statewide network of faith-filled, heart-filled parents and families who were fighting for the survival of their children, students and communities.

Building a strong grassroots base of support was critical if we were to take on what was feared to be an unmoving union. The Wisconsin Charter School Association and its members met monthly and spoke via the Internet and on the telephone frequently, as challenges and crises intervened. Listening to the concerns and feedback of the charter school organizers from around the state, we created communication strategies that kept our organization energized and filled with hope.

THE STRATEGIES OF DAVID

We have heard the stories of David and Goliath. David's strategy was to aim at Goliath's one point of weakness, the spot on the giant that wasn't armored. The American school system was such a Goliath, heavily armored in layers of bureaucracy that resisted the calls for change. An education reformer and former New York City teacher said it best: "The American education system is broken, failing too many children," according to John Taylor Gatto. Impersonal bureaucracies and cookie-cutter approaches left far too many children behind, particularly in America's largest cities.

Gatto wrote that reform would take nothing less than "blowing up the system." Fortunately, it didn't come to that. It instead took the slingshots of passionate individuals driven with a singular purpose, "to provide educational opportunities for all children." The proverbial stone in David's sling was an idea so powerful that it built a nationwide network for educational change.

BIPARTISAN STRENGTH AND SINGULAR FOCUS

The Wisconsin Charter School Association represented every area of the state, every political faction and every network concerned with children and education. What gave this unfunded charter school movement strength at a time when there was no cash to buy political influence was simple: *courage.*

The sheer number of grandparents, parents, teachers, administrators, community groups and individuals together, all determined to put children's lives first, made that difference.

Our phone calling trees, faxes, and routine visits to state legislators' offices made that difference. We didn't need to be paid to do the right thing. It was simply the right thing to do!

Those of us in the charter school movement in the early 1990s raised our voices with such clarity of purpose and passion that lawmakers had no choice but to listen. We spoke with one voice and gave one message that was easy to understand: children in impossible educational systems deserved a way out.

Technology would create an opportunity to reach all legislators and leaders in a position to call for a vote on our legislation. The automatic fax dial-ups on our computers made hundreds, of supporters appear to be thousands of supporters, which then grew into tens of thousands of supporters overnight. The political muscle of the people (more specifically, parents and community leaders) was unwavering in the fight for the rights of children to have quality education.

The sincerity of parents who were fighting for the survival of their families could not be denied. No political need for power or control, no position of power or control, and no heavily funded union, association or political machine could stand up to the conviction of a family's right to fight for its own survival. Education equates to survival for families whose children have fallen through the cracks of public schoolhouses.

State constitutions across this country guarantee every child's "right to an education." This political and legal argument became so powerful that it indeed swayed even the most reluctant politicians. Even those who dreaded the recourse from the union's political action committee monies that would rain down against them, come election time.

And, as they say, "The rest is history." Today, Wisconsin has well over thirty thousand students in public charter schools—many of them in my own backyard.[9]

Senn Brown, a lobbyist of the school board association, confirmed the importance of the vote and the changes in education law, as he whispered in my ear the day of the vote, "Terri, look what you have done! The charter school law is one of the most significant public school reforms in Wisconsin's history."

I had the honor of leading and being a part of one of the most important movements in the history of the state of Wisconsin—a civil rights movement to many, and my core conviction as a citizen leader. *We had done it!* Zero dollars to lobby politicians, and the results were priceless; we would touch countless families and future generations, even though we would never meet.

JOINING THE FRAY

It would take a four-year hiatus from the political spotlight before I would finally agree to run for public office. Speaking as a panelist for the S. C. Johnson Wingspread Conference on the importance of education reform, I gained statewide recognition once again as a citizen leader. My sincerity on the issue reinforced that I was the real deal and deserved notice. There were many phone calls and meeting requests from outgoing members of the Republican caucus. They all saw me as someone who was needed in politics or who could serve ... or more to the point, might be able to win an election.

I had had enough of politics after this charter school war ... so I thought. It wasn't enough for me to be asked to run for public office; I needed to know in my heart that I could make a difference in that position. Was I worthy enough to run?

MY ROLE MODEL IN PUBLIC OFFICE

Soul-searching took me to my first inspiration and role model in political office, Representative Earl McEssy. It was this man's act of kindness after my father had died that lingers with me still. "Go to Representative McEssy if you or Mom need me after I am gone," Dad told me when he knew that his death was certain.

I remember standing in the hallway of Rep. McEssy's large home on Forest Avenue, just down the block from ours. It was there that I would find the help my mother needed. It appeared there was a problem with Dad's medical insurance coverage at the end of his life. The medical evacuation helicopter was not covered, and my father's life insurance policy was being held up for that reason. Widowed, with only me to help, my mother could not find a way to pay for my father's funeral.

Our family sorrows became Rep. McEssy's sorrows. My mother cradled her head in her hands in grief as she tried to work her way through the medical and ambulance bills on her desk. It was time for me to turn to my father's friend for help.

I quietly phoned him from the next room. "Representative McEssy? I am George McCormick's daughter. My father died last week, and we are running into some pretty difficult problems. I am sorry to bother you …"

The need to help my mother gave me the distance I needed to block my own grief and sorrow.

I went on, "Rep. McEssy, my mother needs help working through the requirements of the insurance company—they need proof that my father was on Medicare insurance in Minnesota before his death.

"You see, Rep McEssy, we don't know how to get the paperwork from Minnesota to the Social Security office in Washington," I managed to finish before a sense of hopelessness felt its way down my face in the form of a tear.

McEssy's voice was kind, steadfast and reassuring. "Terri, tell Ardys that she is not to worry about anything. Tell her that I will take care of this and it is not a problem." He went on in soft tones, "Terri, don't be afraid. I will help you."

I managed to say the words "Oh, thank you … thank you so much" before I hung up the phone.

It was this memory that has acted as a pivotal moment for me, that shapes the way I view the responsibility of an elected official. It was Earl McEssy. our trusted family friend and state representative. who cared for us and carried us through a difficult time with his integrity.

AN HONESTY TOUR CAMPAIGN

My campaign resembled more of a ragtag volunteer army than a well-oiled political machine. We had heart, a passion to serve and a sincerity that was welcomed, quite literally, into the homes and minds of the people who lived in the Fifty-sixth House Assembly District in Wisconsin. For me, it has not been easy. I've always wanted to make a difference but haven't always wanted to be in the limelight. For that, I needed to believe and be convinced to run for elective office.

The voices of former students visiting my office encouraged me. "Stop talking about how things can change and how to change them, Ms. McCormick, and get out there and run for public office."

Before I knew it, "we" were running for the Fifty-sixth House Assembly seat in the Wisconsin legislature. Joining forces with me to form the best grassroots campaign the state had ever seen were Susan Menge, Jenny Vosters, Lauren Breithaupt, Jared Guzman, Michael Welhouse, Jeff Dercks, and Dan Brellenthin—and my own daughters and son. Ellen Breithaupt led our voter-list brigade, and Evie and Bob Kettner, the owners of Mr. and Mrs. K's Restaurant, held countless town meetings in Greenville.

In the summer of 2000, I went door-to-door, asking the people for their confidence and trust to represent them in the state legislature. I was battle-tested, as they say, from my pioneering days with charter schools.

My old "pals" at the teachers union would be there, too, ready to "reward" me for passing that landmark legislation for public charter school reform—they would spend forty thousand dollars *against* me in my own Republican primary, and countless more dollars against me in the general election.

As luck would have it, my constituents were looking for something different, rather than the same old politics. The voters of the Fifty-sixth House Assembly District would stand with me in 2000, proving that it wasn't about the money. Our band of citizen leaders and volunteers would carry us to victory.

I became a state legislator at my swearing-in in January 2001. Now, it was my turn to represent the people who elected me.

CHAPTER SUMMARY

- A political career can often be jump-started by volunteering at the local level.
- By trying to solve problems at the local level, one gets experience in the current political system.

- Retail politics and pay-to-play issues even affect small local elections.
- Citizen leadership often uses the strategies of David to help defeat a political Goliath.

I believe that the law was made for man and not man for the law; that government is the servant of the people and not their master.

John D Rockefeller, Jr., Inscription at the Rockefeller Building, New York City

.

CHAPTER THREE

COURAGE IS A PREREQUISITE

MYTH:

You cannot fight City Hall!
Political party bosses and wealthy people
own the political system!

REALITY:

It only takes one voice—your voice—
to make a difference!

Courage is resistance to fear, mastery of fear,
not the absence of fear.

—Mark Twain

Integrity candidates and elected representatives must possess courage and poise under fire if they are to serve their own constituents. And voters and citizen leaders must have the courage to stand with integrity-driven representatives.

Greater than any one political party, greed and its dysfunctional quest for power is not about Republican, Democrat or Independent; it goes far deeper than that. The battle for the control of the legislative agenda is a battle over the purse—he (or she) who controls the purse, in a business-as-usual government, rules. When dysfunctional leaders are allowed to rule on behalf of their respective party elites, they hold court, collect fund-raising cash and then grant legislation accordingly.

It matters not what the impact is on the American public.

There are two forms of political leadership: leaders who run for office as a way to "be somebody," and populist leaders who run for office to serve the people and effect change through public policy. When our republic works, the "public" remains in public policy. When elite-run party machines are left unchecked by the American people and the press, they buy elections and throw populists out of public office.

THE LOSS OF A REPUBLICAN GOVERNOR

I was about to be provided a front-row seat in a legislative production called "How to Defeat Your Own Sitting Governor," by the little-people production company in the front row.

Little did I know that the Republican Party of my state, along with house assembly "leaders," would take out its own sitting governor. These same leaders would be investigated and indicted within the same month for felony misuse of public office. This was more than simple "sibling rivalry"—it was something far more brutal. It involved Republican leaders smearing the reputation of their own political party's governor and then ruining any future career he might have in public office. I was beginning to realize that the beautiful marble hallways, majestic paintings and ornately designed dome in the state capitol far outclassed many of its inhabitants.

It was 2001, just a month after my swearing-in as a freshman state legislator. I was about to receive my first official call from the press. No policy briefing, no amount of study of public policy options could have prepared me for what I was about to hear.

The reporter on the other end of the telephone began, "Your house Chairman of Joint Finance held a press conference earlier in the day. He blasted your party's governor as not being a 'real Republican' and then he said that the governor's budget was a sham!"

I shook off the statement, at first thinking it was a joke. After I processed the question in my mind, I had a few questions of my own for the reporter. "Okay, back up the tape. What did my Joint Finance chair do?"

He repeated the same story. The Joint Finance chair, a young kid from Marinette, had held a television news conference and discredited his own sitting governor, right after Governor McCallum had announced his 2001 state budget to the press. I was at that budget announcement in Green Bay, with most of my Republican colleagues; I supported his budget. This was the most fiscally conservative governor the GOP had in a long time.

I responded, off the record, "That's impossible. Governor McCallum is an innovator. He has brilliant ideas on economic development and technology. I know this governor; I worked with him four years prior as a private citizen. He is the reason our state has a charter school law."

As shocking as that phone conversation was, nothing prepared me for what I saw when I pulled into my driveway. The television cameras were rolling. They wanted to know if I was willing to speak on camera.

I'd been in public office for a mere month, and I'd never dealt with the press. I began to ask them if any one of my esteemed colleagues would go on film. After they assured me that "none of them" was willing to give a comment, I agreed.

There was only one course of action to take: tell the truth.

"I have all the respect in the world for all of my Republican Party colleagues. However, I have a far different opinion of Governor Scott McCallum. I believe him to be a fiscal conservative and a solid head of the Republican Party in Wisconsin."

Whew. That wasn't so hard.

As I watched the news later that evening, I began to put the puzzle pieces together. This childish attack on the governor had been staged. There were maybe two people in the room with the television cameras. The immature young man, who somehow had enough years under his belt to be appointed as the chair of Joint Finance, was trying to take out his own party's governor. He was finagling behind the scenes to take over the GOP house speaker slot, knowing his boss would be indicted on felony counts for misuse of public office. This soon-to-be junior speaker of the house assembly was on television, taking out the only Republican in his way—the sitting Governor.

What I couldn't understand as a freshman legislator was why this attack was occurring at all. Little did I know that this was a tactic used by the GOP, my party, all too often to separate the chosen few of the political machine from the noisemakers—those people who were actually trying to effect real change for the people of our state.

The next Republican caucus in the house assembly was scheduled for the next week. It coincidently overlapped with Take Your Daughter to Work Day, a tradition in my home. My then-fifteen-year-old daughter, Kristen, accompanied me to the legislative session. Sadly, she was the most mature one in the room, for there were grown men threatening each other and her mom during those meetings.

We have rules that prohibit sharing of information of what occurs in closed caucuses, so I will just share with you the actions that my daughter saw from the people we elected to guard principles and ethics and to provide leadership.

Kristen viewed what could only be described as staged political theatre.

The first lines were given by the chair of Joint Finance. With a pitiful look on his face, as though he were the wronged party, he began, "I don't know why Terri got up on television and trashed me, but I don't think that was right."

He looked in my direction expecting a response; I didn't provide it. I remembered what I carefully had told the television crew: "I respect all my Republican colleagues, but I reject any of those statements about our governor." If anything, this kid should have been apologizing to us.

Next, his sidekick—a six-foot-ten guy with a Herman Munster appearance and a brutish temperament—raised his voice to the level of eardrum-shattering on a boom box in his attempt to create a smokescreen for his "wronged" friend. As he pointed his finger in my direction, I continued to tune him out. I saw no need to respond to the theatre; it was not amusing.

Maintaining his booming and thunderous roar, pushing his voice further toward me, he demanded my attention by asking, *"Do you know who this man is?"*

Racing through my mind were the retorts, "Who? That inexperienced child?" and "You mean this monkey at a circus?" But that wouldn't do for this august body, the Wisconsin state legislature; I wouldn't be disrespectful.

Still, I had had enough of the histrionics of the soon-to-be junior speaker and his sidekick. And it looked like no one else was going to say anything to pull this outrageous behavior in line. It was as though they were handing their school lunch boxes to the schoolyard bullies.

As everyone else in Fourth Floor North in the state capitol slid down in their chairs, I realized that it was up to me … again. At least, I thought someone should say something in defense of our governor.

I began, "I do not know who you both think you are. The fifty-six thousand people who elected me to this body did not elect someone who would sit like a lemming and watch as her own party trashes its sitting governor. Unless you would like to start referring to Attorney General Doyle as "Governor Doyle" right now, I suggest we begin to start working with Governor Scott McCallum."

My comments drew applause from the majority of my caucus, but the damage was done. Standing up for what was right that day would cost me dearly. From that day forward, our party's next speaker would see me as competition—an upstart and someone who was in his way. Never mind the fact that the "team" was tearing apart one of its own—the governor. I was trouble, and they weren't going to rest until they taught me how to fall in line.

Impossible? As you read this book you will begin to understand that the politics of governance is not about political party and ideology as much as it is about obedience to the "front row"—to those party bosses who pay for political elections and who dictate the front row's actions. Politics is all about the party elites who hold the purse strings and command obedience—if you let them.

There is only one way to change things: we the people need to vote for leaders who will represent us. And I do mean *vote*. Without citizen leaders who are elected to serve the people back home, we will continue as a pseudo-democracy resembling monkeys playing in circus tents. What we the people need to remember is how to restore the great experiment of democracy that was once placed in that shining city on the hill.

ABSENCE OF OUTRAGE

None of this may surprise you. You may be thinking this is just one more story of politics gone badly. You've heard it all before, and it's getting to be a bit boring.

Have we all forgotten how to blush? Have we forgotten what it is to be American, or have we forgotten how to be courageous? Do we understand what we have? Do we, as a nation of individuals bound by the U.S. Constitution, too often forget that the document enumerates the freedoms of all men and women in this great nation under God? Or are we all too comfortable sitting in our armchairs, letting someone else make decisions, vote, and lull us into giving away our freedoms one at a time?

Courage is not found in just those who ride out into battle or face down mortal enemies. Living each day well takes courage. Before I began writing this book, I was afraid—it is important that I admit that to you and to myself. I was afraid that speaking out would deliver problems to my door, problems that I could easily avoid by being quiet. The larger problem, though, is that I was raised to face down my fears. In fact, it is now more important than ever that we all come together, to change the politics of the schoolyard bullies into what the courageous fifty-six signers of the Declaration of Independence gave their lives and sacred honor to create.

We need the press become the truth-seekers they can be, shining candles in the corners of dark rooms. We the people need to take our place as citizen leaders who vote, support integrity candidates or run for office ourselves. Who knows? One day we just may get the government we deserve.

LEADERS AND LEADERSHIP

During the George W. Bush presidency, speaking out against GOP policies or against decisions made by the administration or GOP state leaders was quickly re-spun. The Republican political pundits were quick to label those who didn't agree as unpatriotic, and they smeared individuals and representatives who got in the machine's way. Yet here's the thing: silence is not patriotism and neither is it party loyalty.

I was elected in 2000 and took the oath of office in January 2001, the same year that lifelong politicians were being indicted of felonies. As a result, I have learned much about the political process—far more than any textbook from which I have taught or lectured.

HEADLINES WELCOMED FRESHMEN LEGISLATORS TO PUBLIC OFFICE

The Sunday *Milwaukee Journal Sentinel* article, "To Play You Paid," on January 1, 2001, detailed the indictments of my party's speaker and majority leader and the Democrats' majority leader and chair of Joint Finance. The culture of paying for legislation, rather than solving problems for the people, was the culture I walked into on those marble hallways of the state capitol. The question remains: have we learned from the indictments and later convictions, or is it still going on?

I have learned that for government to be representative of the people (by, for and of the people), we need inherent change in the way government does business. When elected politicians are confronted with ethical dilemmas, should they follow their party leader? Should they look the other way to protect themselves? It's time to ask ourselves if we are putting the results of the next election cycle ahead of the needs of the people we were elected to represent. For me, the answer has always been an easy one, but for a number of public officials, the power that comes with public office can cloud judgment.

How can we be lawmakers if we are finding new and unusual ways to skirt and to spin the law? The continued chatter about "war chests" and "money needed to secure elections" must be secondary and doing the people's business, primary. A return to open and honest debate is now possible due to the technology of the Internet. The question is, when did we the people, as citizen leaders, take a backseat to war chests? Most political researchers will tell you that it all changed in the 1960s, when large amounts of monies poured into political campaigns to buy airtime and advertising messages.

What responsibility do lobbyists and associations have, in this culture of corruption, that pays for campaign propaganda? If dysfunctional leaders weren't being paid off with bribes, wouldn't they stop stuffing the budget and legislation with pork? And if these leaders stopped extorting money from lobbyists, wouldn't they be free to focus on educating lawmakers on the merits of public policy? There are plenty of good actors sitting in the middle of this culture of corruption that either get fed up and quit, or are driven out by their respective party machines.

How can we the people do our part to make sure the good actors who represent us get a fair shake in government service? The answer, at least in part, lies with an engaged, free and appropriate press—and an engaged "we the people." The alternative to our active involvement is allowing schoolyard bullies, who can never get enough power or enough money. American people certainly know the face of one such player on the national stage—former governor Rod Blagojevich of Illinois, who allegedly attempted to sell President Obama's former U.S. Senate seat in 2008. Is this sort of power play happening in other states? You might be surprised.

SECOND VERSE, SAME AS THE FIRST

It has been several years since the summer of 2006 and my congressional race in Wisconsin. It has taken that amount of time for the people of northeast Wisconsin to gain the perspective and understand my experiences; it's taken that for me, too, as well as to then frame my experiences on these pages. The story to follow is one of an enduring struggle in every democracy around the world—populism versus elitism in an ongoing struggle for independence and self-rule.

The story of one party elite or another that supports a chosen one is not new. What is new is the interest and control shown by the political class in an era of corruption and irresponsibility—not seen since the beginning of the twentieth century. The White House itself was pulled into what should have been a wide-open race for U.S. Congress. Together, all of these factors created the "perfect storm." With it, a magnitude and force would shift the ground under the feet of an embedded political class. In its place would stand an engaged citizenry, with the power of one vote.

THE LOSS OF A GOP U.S. HOUSE SEAT: SETTING THE SCENE FOR A RUN FOR CONGRESS

Some would call the notion of preprimary electioneering a stereotype of a political bygone era of cronyism and backroom deals reminiscent of the late 1800s and turn of the twentieth century. The image is clear—party bosses and career politicians, sitting in leather chairs in dark rooms, with the shades pulled down, smoking cigars, handpicking their candidate. Yet this scenario, one hundred years later, appears to be part of a cycle that repeats itself when "we the people" are not engaged in our own government.

As a candidate for the United States Congress in January 2006, I began the usual exploratory committee comprising community leaders, veterans, friends, business leaders and education leaders. As the founder of the charter school movement in Wisconsin twelve years earlier, I decided to make the historic announcement of my bid for Congress at a charter school. Once I had thrown my hat into the congressional race, I planned a trip to visit with party leaders in Washington DC, meeting with the National Republican Campaign Committee (NRCC) to seek their help and advice on the process.

Yet when I arrived in Washington, things were already decided. In an unusual twist, I was given one story by the NRCC and another story by a Washington news correspondent.

I had arranged for a lunch meeting with Brian Tumulty a Washington news correspondent for Gannett, a leading news and information company that publishes, among many newspapers, *USA TODAY*. Our conversation spanned the topics of my views on public policy, past record and family life. He asked me what my schedule was in Washington. I mentioned that later in the day I would be meeting with the National Republican Campaign Committee to see what kind of assistance they offered candidates in Republican primaries.

After our luncheon, Mr. Tumulty offered to give me a tour through the *USA TODAY* offices in Washington. Amid rows of awards, I found row after row after row of newspaper desks for Gannett newspapers across the country. It reminded me of the newspaper bullpen at the Wisconsin state capitol but much larger.

"Here are the offices of the Gannett newspapers for Duluth, Minnesota … Dubuque, Iowa … and on this side of the building are the *USA TODAY* offices," he said, showing great care and consideration for the importance of his work. "This is where the guardians of democracy do their work," he added.

A sigh and feeling of relief came over me as I spoke out loud, "Thank goodness we have the press." Tumulty turned for an instant and looked surprised at the sincerity in my voice. The press was my backstop at the state capitol. I relied on the transparency that journalists provided to keep some of my political colleagues honest—or at least on notice. Those front-row game players who believed "politics is only a game" were trouble for any of us who were there to serve the public.

As we finished the tour, my belief in our government had grown. Not only did this seem to be a good first meeting, but I had the sense that this man would treat me fairly throughout the campaign. I walked away feeling as though I could trust him.

Next, I hurried to catch the subway to the capitol square stop, where I was about to meet with leaders from the National Republican Campaign Committee (NRCC). The Republican Headquarters was next to the Capitol Hill Club, adjacent to Congress. There, I would find staffers from the NRCC who were assigned to brief me and help me navigate through the press and process of running for the U.S. Congress.

The meeting seemed brief. The staff we met with appeared to be in their twenties. Aside from the security check going up and down from the elevators, the only memorable comment I was given by one staffer was: "We treat all primary candidates equally. Whatever information we give to one candidate, we give to all primary candidates so that the races are fair and the people get to decide on the local level."

The flight to Washington DC, running to catch subways and the variety of meetings had worn me out. I headed back to my hotel room to freshen up and take a nap before my husband and I planned to go out for dinner. It was at this time that my hotel phone rang with an unexpected caller.

"Hello," I answered, still tired from the activities of the day.

"Terri, this is Brian Tumulty with Gannett newspapers. I have been doing some checking on the recently released financial reports from House Speaker Hastert, and he has given a maximum contribution to your Republican primary opponent."

As I scrambled to grasp what that could have meant, I listened further to his questions.

"Terri, did you meet with the NRCC? And if you did, what did they say?"

"Yes, I met with the NRCC," I responded, "and they assured me that this would be a fair race; that they would give all information and resources equally to all candidates in the republican primary."

"So the NRCC did not tell you that they were doing a preprimary endorsement of your primary candidate?" Brian asked. "Do you have anything to comment?"

I was stunned. I was speechless. The NRCC had led me to believe just forty-five minutes earlier that this primary was an open primary for an open seat in the U.S. House of Representatives, and they would treat everyone fairly.

This was a reporter whom I had only met that day over lunch ... yet I believed him.

Tumulty interrupted the silence. "Let me do some more research, and I will get back to you. Will you be at this phone number?"

Betrayal and utter disappointment swept over me all at once. The whole idea of my own party leader's deception was as though all of the air went out of me. *Who would do such a thing?* I thought.

When Brian Tumulty phoned back a short time later, he admitted that he had gotten Hastert's staff on the phone, "What about this Rule No. 11? The RNC and the NRCC said that they have permission to do anything they can to get your opponent in, because of your party's leadership in Wisconsin."

"Rule No. 11?" I questioned back. "I have never heard of Rule No. 11." *How could a party rule take the right of an American citizen to run for office and to vote?* I wondered. So there I was, facing an unprecedented situation, one that left me with a choice: back out of the race now, or go back against my words in my announcement for Congress. Once the initial shock wore off, I made a statement to the press. My words were from the heart, and they were quoted accurately by Gannett's Washington news:

> "Call me old-fashioned, but I believe the voters should decide who represents them in Washington. The preprimary pick of Hastert and the state party elites is nothing more than electioneering."

Perhaps it was because I was considered a reformer, beginning with the charter school movement as a private citizen, and then with capital investment innovations as chair of Economic Development. The competitive bidding models I proposed put Wisconsin on the map for saving tens of millions of dollars for prescription drugs, not to mention the national models for support for manufacturers and the small-business regulation reform.

How could this be a merit-based decision? Whatever the reason, it was clear that the GOP elites from outside my congressional district were reaching into the Eighth Congressional District in Wisconsin to help throw the election.

ENEMY OF THE STATE AND A CLANDESTINE MEETING

Shortly after my Washington trip, I received a phone call from an individual whom I had met in one of my national committeeman's offices. Nick had served many years in the GOP and risked much by meeting with me ... or so I was told.

When Nick requested a meeting, I suggested a well-known public restaurant near my home. I believed that whatever this man wanted, I would be more comfortable if our meeting was in the open. After all, I had just had the rug pulled out from under me in Washington. I was both reluctant and relieved that someone in the GOP upper echelon seemed to be having second thoughts about what had transpired.

As I walked into the restaurant, the manager of the restaurant greeted me with familiar cordiality. Nick had arrived earlier and was already seated at a table. As I walked up to him, I saw the sympathetic eyes of a father figure.

"Hi, Terri, how are you?" Nick inquired.

"I have had better days," I responded cautiously.

At this juncture, I wasn't sure what had happened. The Washington Gannett correspondent welcomed me warmly, but an hour later, he was telling me that my own congressional delegation had lowered the boom on any political future I thought was possible. Then he added, "Terri, I'm here because I don't agree with what was done to you by the party. I know you. I know you to be the leader we need in Washington."

Somewhat frustrated, I asked, "What happened? Why did these people do this?"

Nick took control of the conversation, telling me that he would not give me details on what was done and why. Then he said something that I never would have believed if I hadn't heard it with my own ears: "You have made powerful enemies." As I sat with my mouth agape, Nick said, "I don't agree with any of it."

I responded in astonishment and dismay, "How can that be?"

"Powerful enemies!" he replied. The seriousness on his face was unmistakable.

"How can that be?" I repeated. "I have been serving my people. I have acted in the best interests of the voters in northeast Wisconsin. There is nothing but solid public policy and the awards to prove it."

Nick shrugged. "Look, I like you. You are smart, you have a lot to offer … and all I can say is that I made it known that I didn't agree with any of this, and that is all I can do." Nick would say nothing further on that topic.

Nick did confirm that for the past six months in the Wisconsin state legislature, when my bills had been blocked, my ideas stolen, and threats were flung against me, I had gone against the political class of the party political machine that pays for elections and puts house assembly speakers in place.

What I was experiencing was a push to oust me and to remove any threat I might pose to the GOP establishment from choosing the candidate that they wanted in the Eighth Congressional seat. The establishment had ordained that it was someone else's turn.

Questions raced through my mind all at once: Wasn't it an open seat? Didn't we live in the United States of America? Wasn't I a part of a political party that embraced competition? How did I make these enemies?

It dawned on me that it was the SB1 Government Accountability Board and Ethics Bill that sealed my fate. A letter, written on GOP stationery, made it perfectly clear that I needed to back away from the issue of ethics in government. This letter warned me not to "meddle with the finance system of our elections." Ironically, I had never taken up that issue. The memory of this letter was ironic—I did not support the Washington-based Campaign Finance Reform Act, known as the McCain-Feingold Act, Public Law 107-155, November 6, 2002. It was a bipartisan boondoggle that did little to reform anything it claimed, such as soft money financing, issue ads and curtailing contributions from government contractors. There were loopholes written for contributors that were large enough for a truck to drive through. Worse, the McCain-Feingold Act created the nefarious "527's," a new political entity that the American people can thank for those "hate-filled attack ads" on television, produced under the dark veil of anonymity.

I had made "powerful enemies"? He had to be kidding. The antics, five years earlier, when the sitting Republican governor was taken down in his reelection bid, were repeating themselves over again. The same players were involved. This time, however, they were caught. The intricate plan was blown. The GOP party elites sitting on the Wisconsin Congressional Committee, who had made the decision to steal the election from the voters, were, in fact, "outed"! Gannett's Washington news correspondent Brian Tumulty had been right—in the *USA TODAY* offices. The press was the only guardian of freedom and democracy—when it did its job as "truth seekers."

The indictments and convictions of the GOP and Democratic Party leaders have done little to curb the dysfunctional elite leaders in the political class and their need for power and control. Worse, many of these politicians have been rewarded with jobs and placements as lobbyists or consultants that guarantee higher-paying salaries. The only remorse these players seem to have is they were caught.

Virtue, principle, ethics and integrity must be restored *internally* in order to return our state houses and our nation's Capitol back to the people in the cities, farmlands and hills across this country. Once we discover that choices in our own behaviors and in our principles are in our hands, we can get back to the business of serving others and strengthening the democracy envisioned by our forefathers.

Maybe that seems like our conclusion. Maybe it seems as though restoring order internally will serve as our final act to put things right again. But in reality, this is merely our beginning.

CHAPTER SUMMARY

- In-party politics can have just as much impact as intra-party politics.
- Going against one's party leaders and the political class may have devastating effects on a political career.

Nearly all men can stand adversity, but
if you want to test a man's character, give him power.

—Abraham Lincoln

CHAPTER FOUR

POLITICAL GENDER HIERARCHY

MYTH:

Political talent will naturally
rise to the top.

REALITY:

There is a pecking order in politics.
To change the way things are, you will need
to be able to swim against the current of the status quo!

*They will say you are on the wrong road
if it is your own.*

—Antonio Porchia

Who swims in the political stream of politics? Is there a specific gender or personality stereotype that best fits the job of politician? Amid Associated Press reporters and citizen accounts, there is a public gauge of politics and politicians that does not favor the status-quo party structures of either party. In March 2006, Max Bowen, a citizen of Neenah, Wisconsin, wrote an opinion column for the *Appleton Post Crescent* newspaper: "The GOP's Top-Down_Style Is Unfit for Democracy!"

Bowen observed:

> "Since 2000, the GOP has been run like a street gang. All power is vested in the leaders, and others are to follow with unquestioning loyalty. Talking points are sent from above, and loyal followers are expected to stay on message. Dissent from the ranks is not tolerated."

Bowen goes on to say that "this approach belongs in a monarchy or dictatorship; it is a poor fit for a democracy. We have all paid a price. In a democracy, the rule is let the people decide."

Washington DC Associated Press reporter Larry Margasak wrote on May 21, 2006:

> "The public increasingly disapproves of the ways legislators behave. For the first time since the Abscam scandal a quarter-century ago, multiple lawmakers face criminal and ethics investigations that are tarnishing Congress. Already, public views of Congress are low, with bribery, conspiracy, corruption, misuse of public office and other scandals mounting in Republican leadership ranks."

New York University professor Paul Light, quoted in Margasak's article, noted, "It's like members of Congress don't have any shame! ... It is as though an entire generation of Americans have grown up viewing congressmen in orange jumpsuits."

WHAT'S LIFE LIKE IN THE POLITICAL ECOSYSTEM?

We have all heard the term "living in a fishbowl" as it refers to politicians living under the watchful eye of the public and the press, but there is a hierarchy to living in the political ecosystem as well. The front rows in both political parties have a pecking order and a spoils system that determine who is rewarded and who is punished. Party leaders who sit in the front rows of Congress and in our state legislatures determine which ideas get heard in the form of a bill, which ones go to committee and which ideas ultimately are voted on and become law.

It is the use of this front-row system, on each side of the political aisle, that the pecking order is decided. The humans living in the political ecosystem have one main objective: to be reelected. If the party in charge is not reelected, it changes which leaders can sit in the front row, which interest groups will be partners in writing legislation, and which political groups will be called upon to donate to the majority party in power.

THE POLITICAL ECOSYSTEM

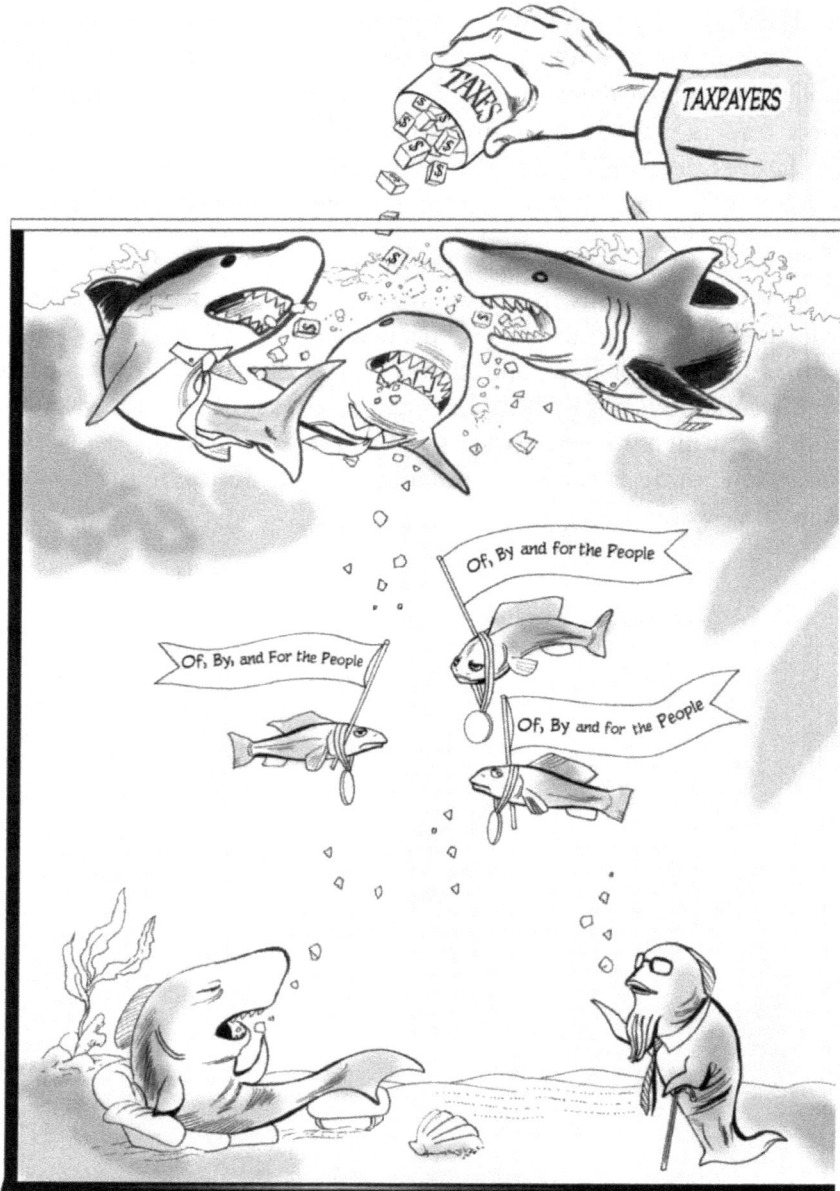

THE POLITICAL ANIMUS AND ITS ECOSYSTEM

A political animus (political animal) has little to do with gender, ethnicity or religion. In fact, gender is indeterminable. Far beyond any differences in anatomy or stereotypes of male or female; black, white, Asian, Latino, or Native American; or religion is a psyche that can only be attributed to the political class. All we need do is study the proverbial political fish tank to cast some light on what is meant by "political animus."

Those thriving as politicians swimming in their proverbial "schools" often do so as the beneficiaries of their respective sharks in their front rows. With the self-purported generosity of individuals and groups paying homage to the sharks in the front row, cash for campaigns is assured. The term leadership, in the context of front-row politics, has spawned what I will refer to as "pisci-humus," a political animal all its own. As you look at the political fish tank, there are the sharks on the top (closest to the fish food); the swimmers in the middle, who remain close to their constituents; and the bottom-dwellers, who catch the droppings from the top.

There are political outsiders who have not been brought into the inner circle and the intimate deal-making and trading that goes on to ensure that the top feeders (the front row) remain in power. But decisions are not made for the greater good or even on behalf of the ideology of one political party over the other. It is all about keeping the front row in power—or it was, up until the majority shake-ups in the 2006 midyear elections.

There are visionaries, or "idea people," who make up the swimming class. These individuals are usually swimming against the current, unless they are brought up into a holding tank and judged as to just how hungry they are for a seat near the front. Often, the swimmers are thrown to the back row because they raise questions of ethics or refuse to fall in line when orders from the front row violate the rule of law. Unfortunately, these swimmers are destined for failure—they just can't stop doing what they believe is right.

Somewhere in between, we have combinations of all types of candidates and legislators. It is in this gray pool of water that the "go-along-to-get-along" politicians live. If they connect with the sharks on the top of the tank, they soon believe that they, too, must become predatory to get along in the world of politics. At times, this go-along-to-get-along group can include over 70 percent of the legislative body.

Meantime, the wannabes are jockeying for position continually. They are not a part of the top feeders in the front rows of either political party, and they are not a part of the middle swimming class. The wannabes support the power of the status quo in the hope that they will be promoted up. They will do anything to support the people who are making deals in the front (on the top of the tank). They are often swayed by and join forces with the predatory fish on the top of the tank. Their hope is that some of the crumbs will fall their way.

The front row makes the rules and skews the game of politics to their own interests. Consider campaign cash as fish food—it is a wise shark that guards the food for itself. In direct conflict with this political-gender swimming on the top are those who work for change and believe in citizen-led legislatures. It takes much more effort to swim against the current of the status quo of self-interest than it does to generate new ideas and call for reform on behalf of the people. What is the result of this fish-tank politic? There are many more politicians who are coerced or are comfortable with the old-style politic of falling in line than with the new politic of swimming upstream.

My favorite minority class of political fish is the up-and-coming outsiders! This class in the political ecosystem represents those who are waiting for an opportunity to lead and have their ideas heard. Often, this group doesn't have an opportunity to present their ideas because of the nastiness of the predatory top feeders, but this group of swimmers simply cannot be bossed or bought—and they are infuriating to the front row. Despite the obstacles and games played, it is this group of swimmers to whom the American people's hopes and dreams are entrusted.

Consider the following example: If you are a citizen voter, you use the say/do ratio in your thinking—determining the ratio of what a politician says to what he or she actually does. The political class says many things while proclaiming beliefs and party platforms. Republicans, for example, are often associated with the idea that we should tax less and spend less of the public's money.

Take a look at the following spending issue as it relates to the say/do ratio:

THE BUSH/OBAMA EXPERIENCE WITH CONGRESSIONAL LEADERS

As you may recall, President George W. Bush's final days in office in 2008 were marked by a burgeoning banking crisis, caused in large part by the collapse of the real estate and housing market, which led to record foreclosures and bankruptcies, which further broke the banking industry, which had overleveraged and overvalued homes, and gave what some consider unethical home loans on balloon payments to people who could not afford them. This led to the collapse of Wall Street, due to the fact that stocks and bonds were tied to home values and the housing markets. The inflated valuations of homes that led to the silent hyperinflation of prices and relative commissions would all come back to bite the banking industry and Wall Street as they depended on home sales, home builds and the values of homes to continue to go up and up, despite people's inability to pay for these things.

The banking industry, as of this writing, has tightened all capital (paying only its own debts) to the point that small businesses and manufacturers in America don't have access to the capital they need to run their businesses, which then collapsed many small businesses as well as hitting large businesses wired into the same supply chain in the American economy. There were 71,400 job losses reported on one day: January 26, 2009.

What is the impact of this domino effect? Take a look at the policies below.

PRESIDENT GEORGE W. BUSH'S 2008 ECONOMIC STIMULUS POLICY

The policy answers that the Bush administration presented were denial, silence and then a $700 billion blind stimulus package, with no details provided to the U.S. Congress. Congress was given just days to pass this package for fear that the collapse of Wall Street was imminent. Half of the monies—$350 billion—was released to members of the banking community. No explanation, no transparency and no discussion or debate was offered on this massive stimulus. In fact, the stimulus package proposal appeared in the middle of the 2008 presidential campaign in October.

CONGRESSIONAL LEADERSHIP RESPONSE

John McCain, 2008 Republican candidate for president, halted his campaign to fly back to Washington, pledging that he would get the votes needed to get the $700 billion Republican stimulus passed. The Republican leadership, now in the minority, continued to support their president's policies. Republican leaders, while in the majority from 1996 to 2006, had a history of record spending and record earmarks. Democrats in 2008 and 2009 became the guardians of the purse, calling for transparency and accountability for the 2008 President Bush stimulus package.

The monies went to AIG, Citicorp, Wells Fargo and others in the banking industry. The American people were increasingly dissatisfied with this "taxpayer bailout," due to the fact that people were losing their jobs, losing their homes and still didn't see an end to the economic crisis. To make matters even more controversial, scandals broke that exposed excesses within the very industry being bailed out. AIG was caught using its bailout money on a luxury getaway for its executives. Citicorp was ready to buy a $50 million corporate jet, the exact amount of its bailout check. "Where is my bailout money?" was the response from middle America. Demonstrations broke out from Republican-leaning constituents in the form of "Taxpayer Tea Party" revolts.

Now turn the dial forward on the clock one month.

PRESIDENT BARACK OBAMA'S STIMULUS POLICY

President Obama's 2009 American Recovery and Reinvestment Plan stimulus package was focused on $819 billion worth of investment spending and tax cuts. The spending portion passed by the House included $550 billion in renewable energy, science and technology; infrastructure projects, such as roads and bridges; education and health care. It also included $259 billion in tax cuts for the middle-class and poor. Yale economists are concerned that the stimulus package is too small, given the impending economic depression.

CONGRESSIONAL LEADERSHIP RESPONSE

Republican leaders sent a memo to their caucus mandating that they all vote no. It was reported that very few of the congressmen had a chance to read the stimulus package proposal. President Obama had scheduled to meet with the Republican caucus to listen to their ideas, yet the memo by Republican leader John Boehner had already been sent. It said, "Vote no." Speculation by Republican radio talk-show hosts the week before was that Republicans in Congress must vote no, or they would lose more seats in Congress in 2010. With this logic the following talking points were presented to the press by Republican leaders: "You cannot spend yourself out of trouble with taxpayer money. What we need are more tax cuts."

The vote on January 28, 2009, in the U.S. House was split along party lines. The House members in the Republican ranks voted as a block against additional spending. The American public, on the verge of one of its worst economic crisis and job losses since the Great Depression, waited on the vote.

Republicans in the U.S. Congress during the months of January, February, March and April 2009 began to shift back toward more conservative voting habits (voting against spending and against taxes), with the exception of one erratic vote on March 19, 2009. The vote on HR1586 was one for the record books. The backdrop for this vote was the historic number of recently unemployed Americans (5.8 million), the loss of 60–70 percent of Americans' retirement monies and finally, the recurring public outcry in the form of Taxpayer Tea Party protests held in every major city across the country. To make matters more interesting, the Associated Press was about to break the connection between AIG (the insurance corporation receiving record bailout money) and its pension and retirement client the U.S. Congress and federal employees. Eighty-five House Republicans broke ranks with their party leadership and their party ideology by voting for a 90 percent tax on bonuses for AIG executives with HR1586.

This scene described above—taxing the elite executives and calling for their heads—would be the populist tea party thing to do and almost was believable, had it not been for the fact that the current AIG CEO and president was only receiving one dollar as his compensation. In addition, there was another inconvenient truth—that AIG had spent $9.6 million for congressional reelection campaigns in 2008 alone. This campaign booty was paid out at the same time that AIG was going bankrupt and the nation was teetering on the verge of the worst banking and economic crisis since the Depression.

This AIG debacle, if not carefully documented, would overlook the price that the people of this country are paying for electing the political class, over and over again, into public office. An Olympic-style swimmer in this ecosystem could have made all the difference in finding real solutions to the problems that face America. To further punctuate the hypocrisy of would-be conservative ideology, only three Republican senators opted out of earmarks in the Obama stimulus package. The say/do ratio is an important citizen-voter scorecard to keep in mind, provided voters can distinguish between the theatre and the reality.

To perpetuate the problems that face our nation and to preserve the silo politics of the political class in both parties, then the minority party tactic of obstruction at all costs—in order to shut down the majority party in power—would be the way to do it. This is the answer under the old-style politic. What has been the result of this kind of government? Think of it this way: The elephant team may have a turn on the field, and the donkey team may return to the field from time to time, and the jerseys may change, but the same game will be played with the same game rules.

STEREOTYPES IN POLITICS

In the world of political manipulation, stereotypes of ethnicity, gender and religion pose would-be barriers in the minds of some of the voting public. When these stereotypes are used in conjunction with insider political class/fish-tank politics or "food for favors," corruption becomes the culture. Simply, the partisan bickering and rancor creates an illusion to most of us in the general public, clouding the reality of ego and power needs of the front row. Politics presents an equal party opportunity for greed, corruption and power mongering—call it tom-fishery in the ecosystem.

When we oust one political party from the power to distribute scarce resources to their respective constituencies, all we are doing is bringing onto the scene another political machine that will call the same political plays. The net gain in this change is zero. Social and economic issues are bantered about, creating an ideological illusion for Republican and Democratic followers—the outcome appears to be the same. What's more, unless we break this perpetual cycle of changing one political machine for another, there is no hope for change. One front row alternative to this status-quo political ecosystem is the same as the other. The kind of change we need can be brought about by electing people more willing to swim upstream, against the front rows.

BARRIERS OF ETHNICITY AND GENDER

Our 2008 presidential race created an opportunity for all of us to examine not only gender but ethnicity with the highest level of politics. We were having serious and frank discussions for the first time in American history, facing our fears and misperceptions of race, gender and leadership. Senator Barack Obama didn't appear to meet the mark of any of this nation's preconceived notions of what a presidential candidate should be. Governor Sarah Palin didn't appear to meet the nation's notion of what a vice-presidential candidate should be.

Obama was characterized as inexperienced and too young to hold the position of president of the United States. Attack ads in his Democratic primary were "soft" ads, asking "Who is best suited to pick up the telephone?" Barack Obama's childhood was a challenging one, with an admission of some youthful drug use. Due to his admissions in a biography, Obama has faced stereotypes in the form of personal smears and rumors that did not stick. Perhaps the most potentially damaging stereotype was that his father was a Muslim and his pastor was a radical against whites. His high-road strategy, however, staying away from the fight, served him well.

Sarah Palin was characterized as inexperienced and too young to hold the position of vice president of the United States. Smear campaigns by the Democratic party were aggressive and gender-focused. "Who is taking care of her small children at home?" ads asked, and noted "She does not have a passport." Initial polling suggested that Governor Palin saved the McCain presidential ticket. The only certainty about this historic election year was that the pundits have been wrong in both primaries, and they were wrong about the mass support a woman could garner on the GOP ticket.

The 2008 campaign marked the first time in American presidential campaign history that a major political party chose an African-American man and the second time in history that a woman was placed on the ticket as vice president. Both candidates confronted our fears and stereotypes of race and gender. The election of 2008 offered an opportunity for all African Americans to see themselves in the face of Barack Obama. And to a great extent, the selection of a woman by the GOP broke an even more profound gender barrier. The gauntlet was thrown, challenging all of us to move past the stereotypes of the past.

It is only then that we may have one nation, looking to the future of our United States of America.

POLITICAL PERSONALITIES AND MALE STEREOTYPES

There are several theories and stereotypes of men in politics, just as there are with their women counterparts. Consider the following:

THE NAPOLEON COMPLEX

One could argue that the Napoleon complex, an insecurity born out of being "vertically challenged," is a relevant political archetype that affects men—and perhaps some women—who serve in government. Napoleon, who was reported to have been five foot seven, was of average height in France in his day, but he was short when compared to his bodyguards, who towered over him.

The current research (2008) conducted in the Netherlands reveals that there is a correlation between short-statured individuals and the need to control and dominate others with aggressive behaviors. The Napoleon complex, or "short-man syndrome" as it is also called, reveals a historical archetype for leaders throughout history that includes Napoleon, Mussolini and Attila the Hun, all of whom are reported to have been shorter than average height.

LESSONS FROM MACHIAVELLI

Machiavelli (1496–1527), rightfully or wrongfully, has been given the dubious honor of being called the founder of modern political and social thought. Up until Machiavelli there was no double meaning in terms like virtue, social goodness and the heavens. Machiavelli is attributed with inventing the concept of propaganda, stating that power needs but two tools: the pen and the sword. As propaganda goes, Machiavelli invented the term hypocrisy as well. He believed that fear and control of others was always justified to hold onto power. Power at any cost was virtuous. Machiavelli abolished moral standards—he didn't believe in them, nor did he believe in the moral essence of leadership. He did not believe in looking to the heavens for guidance; rather, he believed in what he could control—the greed and selfishness of man.

BEYOND THE STEREOTYPES AND ARCHETYPES OF GENDER

The notion of women as leaders has long been misrepresented by the use of stereotypes and classic gender-based archetypes. Incompetence, emotionalism, instability and vindictiveness are genderless personality traits that have no place in any professional office, let alone a seat in government. I will admit that my patience was tested by individuals who were more focused on self-service than public service, each and every day when I walked into my legislative office.

It was not my intention to go into politics as a "woman"; I simply ran for politics to make a difference and get things done. I did what I always did—worked harder and (hopefully) smarter than those legislators who couldn't see their way to the solutions needed. For this reason, I was considered a problem. Surrounding myself with journalists and other talented and capable staff became not only a good idea but a savvy one. In addition to a professional staff from outside politics, we drew on key private-sector policy advisors, who became a part of my team and who focused on solving problems through key policies ,which soon became national models. Among the major reforms recognized nationally by the Small Business Administration in Washington was the small-business regulation reform, competitive prescription drug purchasing pools and the capital investment corporation model, which created transparency in government tax credits.

We simply wanted to work on policy that would help the people I represented. Some would call that leadership; others would call that something else. If I broke stereotypes, personally and professionally, that was not my intent. The fact was, I was an elected official who simply happened to be a woman. My advice to all women is to not take on other people's labels. The femme fatale who is always breaking a nail and crying out for help; the woman who takes an office poll before every decision; the woman who wears inappropriate clothing into a business meeting and is not prepared to conduct the business of the organization—all these are stereotypes of women who aren't ready for leadership or public office. The greater challenge for many women serving in politics is this: we must learn to trust our own core values, as well as our own personal sense of purpose.

GENDER BLOCKING IN 2006? YOU DECIDE!

Admittedly, political blocking has been and is currently a part of the landscape. Competition knows no gender or ethnicity, but a series of campaigns and a pattern of White House interference with federal campaigns seem to have focused on women. I was one, as were two others, which begs the question, what sex is a Republican?

As Brian Tumulty of the Gannett Washington bureau reported in August 2006, "Party officials traditionally stay neutral when there is an open seat or multiple challengers seeking the right to run against an incumbent." But Hastings Wyman, editor of the *Southern Political Report*, admitted, "McCormick was not alone in the GOP primary snub. What happened to McCormick happened also to Republican candidates in Colorado, Illinois, Ohio, South Carolina, Texas and Vermont. They were just pulling out the stops to make sure their guy wins."

On January 11, 2006, in Washington DC's *The Hill*, two related stories broke within days of my being blocked by the GOP machine from running for U.S. Congress. Interestingly, these are only two of several stories in which women happened to have been the candidates blocked. The first story broke on Deborah Pryce (R-Ohio), the only woman leader in the U.S. House of Representatives. Her colleagues accused her of "not being aggressive enough in supporting Majority Leader DeLay when his indictments were brought down." As the conference chairwoman, Rep. Deborah Pryce was in the mix for a chairmanship of the Rules Committee. This was due, in large part, to the reshuffling of GOP leaders as they were ousted or demoted during the Jack Abramoff bribery indictments. GOP Majority Leader Tom DeLay (Tex.) made this statement as his staff and he himself were under investigation at the time: "Pryce did not respond forcefully enough to ethics charges Democrats leveled against me."

As proof that Rep. Pryce had the ability to win leadership seats, she trounced two Republican men to gain her current leadership position as conference chairwoman. But several lawmakers, including Rep. Mike Rogers (R-Mich.), now a candidate for Majority Whip, and her vice chairman, Jack Kingston (R-Ga.), as well as her conference secretary, John Doolittle (R-Calif.), were considering challenging Pryce.

Another interesting example is the Florida primary for U.S. Senate. Rep. Katherine Harris's 2006 bid for U.S. Senate came about after Harris came on the political scene as the darling of the George W. Bush 2000 chad ballot-counting controversy. Harris had drawn understandable attention from the Democratic base in the state as a political hot potato. She was viewed as capable, yet incapable of ridding herself of the 2000 presidential election baggage, meaning that as Florida's Secretary of State, she helped George W Bush. Harris became the target of media reports as to her inability to win the Senate race, despite her decided victory two years earlier in the U.S. House of Representatives.

This was puzzling, in that she not only was a member of the House of Representatives as a member of the GOP, but she also had proven that she could win elections. In fact, the polling showed that Harris was the clear front runner in the Republican primary. A different set of "facts" were circulated to the press, however, by her fellow Republicans. Reports indicated that she was funding her own campaign. "So what?" you might say. What's more, GOP veterans were speaking out anonymously against her supposed "dwindling" supply of campaign cash and alleged staff problems.

The GOP reaction to Harris's report on using inheritance money for her campaign provided more inner-party sabotage when staffers gave anonymous "expert" advice that they wanted an alternative GOP candidate.[10] No such contender surfaced, as polling continued to show that Rep. Harris was the stronger GOP candidate. Perhaps the most flagrant attempt to block Rep. Harris, despite her polling and despite her own money used to fund the race, came at a campaign rally for Florida candidates held by then-governor Jeb Bush and President George W Bush. Not only was Rep. Katherine Harris not recognized as being in the room as a party snub, but she was not allowed to participate as a candidate for U.S. Senate. Gender blocking? Possibly.

The point is this: whether or not it was gender-based, a party snub smacks of election engineering and collusion at the highest levels of

POLITICAL GENDER HIERARCHY

GOP leadership. It violates the United States Constitution and our most basic right to vote as American citizens.

"MY TURN" POLITICS: A STORY OF BLOCKING

In the two years prior to my congressional run, I was focused on creating solid public policy for the constituents in my legislative district. I was honored to represent the Fifty-sixth House Assembly District, and I was focused on just doing my job. Many accolades in a variety of media sources were offered on the reforms I had led since I took office in 2001. In fact, the Small Business Administration in Washington DC wrote a letter to my legislative office, telling me that without my leadership, the regulation bill would not have passed. I didn't use that letter, on the advice of the National Federation of Independent Business president, because it may have angered my party's leader, speaker and primary opponent.

It was my practice to read constituent letters, e-mails and trends from my district in the state legislature. Books such as the *World is Flat* and *Manufacturing Trends and Reports* from authors who wrote ahead of the business and economic curve became important, so that I could anticipate the competitive needs of major employers in my state. I believed then, as I believe now, that if you are busy doing something for someone else, you are not swept up with the pretense of "being somebody." More important, if you earn your own way, you cannot be bossed or bought.

In spring 2003, just two years before my first conversations about running for U.S. Congress, a story ran in the state's largest newspaper that riled political rivals in my own political party. The *Milwaukee Journal Sentinel* published "One of Four—Up and Coming Leaders in the Republican Party." The four rising stars identified were Paul Ryan, a young congressman; Mark Green, another congressman with ambitions to become governor; Scott Walker, who had recently become Milwaukee County Executive; and me. I was described as the "mother of all education and health-care reform." The chatter about my early reform initiatives created a buzz that went through the editorial boards and the lobby corps alike.

I was too busy working to notice, but my competition noticed. It wasn't until an attorney with Foley and Lardner and former GOP political director spoke to me privately in my office that I began to realize the stir that article created. He said, "One day soon you are going to have a competitive race and you will move up where you belong." I was taken aback by his statement for the moment but continued my path of working for major solutions to major problems of the day. I was already someone, I thought, but I was too busy "doing things" to care or to notice. I never saw the angst and anger brewing in my political party's front row or the curve ball that was to be thrown at me in 2006.

THE CURVE BALL

What I didn't anticipate was the jealousy and pettiness that would surface from my own political party in 2006. I had met and discussed my race with Wisconsin's congressional chairman, the dean of the congressional delegation in Washington and the state's GOP chairman. All three individuals assured me that my race for Congress would be a fair one. In fact, all three men were enthusiastic about my bid for Congress … at first. At least, they were enthusiastic in our face-to-face discussions. The congressional dean told me that my party's speaker was running for governor, not Congress. He was a bit mistaken, unfortunately. All three gentlemen, in private face-to-face meetings, confirmed that the GOP would not meddle in my congressional primary race, and there would be an even playing field.

That all changed when I traveled to Washington DC to meet with the National Republican Campaign Committee (NRCC) in January 2006, just after my formal announcement to run. In the meeting with congressional staffers, I was assured that my Republican primary for Congress would be fair and open. I was told that all resources of information and support would be shared equally between me and my primary opponent (my party's junior speaker). In fact, I remember walking away from that meeting feeling great about my government and my party and thankful that I lived in the United States, a country that honored free and open elections.

What was the magic rule that changed everything? Rule No. 11!

The Rule 11, cited by the GOP political class January 2006, was a made-up rule, according to former GOP state party chair and state coordinator for President Reagan and now publisher of the *Wisconsin Conservative Digest*, Bob Dohnal. This bold and sage leader not only stood with me during the Republican primary, but he took on the elitist wing in the party to do so. Mr. Dohnal looked at the credentials and the merit of the two candidates and made an independent decision. The problem for Republican elitists was that Dohnal thought all Republicans in the state should do the same. Later, on March 19, 2006, as quoted by the *Green Bay Press Gazette*, NRCC chairman Tom Reynolds denied any knowledge of Rule No. 11, saying, "The NRCC had no choice in the preprimary meddling. It was a state party decision, not mine."

The Wisconsin GOP political class made its decision and passed it to Washington without a call to anyone—and now it was too late for me to do anything but honor my word to stay in the race and give the people the best I had. Never mind the polls from the Terrence Group, which declared that my primary opponent's negatives were too insurmountable to win either a primary or a general without the help of the president himself. The deal was done.

Was this gender-based? I doubt it. I'd like to think that this political deal was cut without my party leaders' knowledge, but that would be naive. One of the junior congressmen from southeast Wisconsin was a part of the boondoggle that would eventually remove my congressional race from the hands of the voters in my district. I learned of his involvement in an earlier visit to Washington in 2005, when I was urgently requested to come out and meet with the National Republican Campaign Committee (NRCC) director. The then-director of the NRCC explained that there were deals being thrown around, and I looked like a better candidate.

I had assumed that Paul Ryan would be helpful in showing me the ropes, giving me some pointers and introducing me to people in Washington. After all, it was in 2003 that Ryan drove from southeast

Wisconsin to my district in Appleton in a torrential downpour to be my guest speaker at what could have been my announcement to run for U.S. Senate.

I presumed that young congressman Ryan had read the article and understood that people in our home state acknowledged what I could do in public office. I was wrong; merit and accomplishment would have nothing to do with our meeting. Ryan would take quite a different tack. Instead of a tour of the congressional offices and introductions to party leadership, I was ushered over to the Capitol Hill Club, just steps away from the NRCC offices. It became clear that Ryan didn't want me to meet anyone in Washington. At the Capitol Hill Club, this awkwardly tall man in his thirties met me just outside the door. Within moments Ryan had demanded the names of the two young men (and their bosses' names) who'd accompanied me to the meeting with him in Washington. His shakedown skills were reminiscent of the guttural scenes from the movie *Gangs of New York*.

Ryan aimed his questions in a young-gun accusatory fashion: "Who are ya? Why are you here? Who do you work for? Vito? Hah— the congressman from New York? I'm going to give him a call."

That day in 2005 Ryan appeared to be a brash political animal, operating out of fear and survival. Something was motivating him and I was about to find out what it was. Ryan was a member of the political class, a typical insider, a young staffer right out of college, working for Senator Brownback, then transported after one term to Wisconsin to run for a newly redistricted GOP congressional seat. As we moved up the steps toward the dining room at the Capitol Hill Club, I spotted someone I had met at a state convention, Congressman J.D. Hayworth from Arizona. I waved in his direction but was abruptly interrupted and told to take a seat in the far corner of the dining room. The two young staffers with me were visibly shaken.

Ryan controlled every detail to follow, including where I would sit—at that far corner table. I was told to sit with my back to the wall, facing outward to those in the dining room. Ryan's chair was immediately across from mine, with his back to the dining room. The two young staffers with me began to sit motionless, with nothing to offer at this point and nothing to say. White pressed table linens and fine china with a congressional seal presented an elegant and stark contrast to the conversation that would follow.

"Would you like something for lunch? I am not hungry," Ryan aggressively started.

Picking up his lead I said, "No, I don't care for lunch either. The water is fine."

As Ryan leaned in to tell me what the orchestrated meeting was about, he looked like a snake, uncoiling just before it bit his victim. "I have to tell you that I will be supporting your primary opponent." His comment was not surprising, given the tone and accusatory questions at the front door of the Capitol Hill Club. He went on, "Your opponent's wife is my friend. I have known her for a long time."

Okay, I thought, *this is a first*. My opponent's wife was a former appointee of a GOP governor. She evidently had enough authority to give orders to Congressman Ryan.

Realizing the game this guy was playing, I leaned forward, put a large smile on my face and softened my tone as I said, "It is nice to have friends. Everyone should have friends."

Ryan seemed perplexed that I wasn't shaken or concerned with his blatant attempt to intimidate me out of the race.

I went on, "I have no intention of getting out of the primary for Congress. Who are you to take an election away from the voters?"

Ryan openly laughed and acted as though he was holding all the cards.

"You should know," I continued, "that I come from an Irish family that does not quit when the going gets tough. We were farmers, business owners and fighters."

Ryan dismissed my last remarks with a chuckle. "Well, we were just potato-pickers from Ireland. I don't know anything about what you just said."

I calmly and quietly whispered, "I have no intention of getting out of this race."

Ryan grinned and boasted, "Well, then, I will be watching from the ground. I will be doing everything I can to see that your opponent is elected."

On January 14, 2006, in the local Gannett newspaper, Rule No. 11—the made-up rule that made it all right for the political elites to reach into a congressional district and take an election away from the people—came alive with the headline: "GOP Takes Stance Early and McCormick Finds National Support Building for her Opponent." The article noted, "This goes beyond the boys' club, and this goes to engineering an election and electioneering, trying to fix an election before the primary."

The second headline, published by the *Green Bay* (Wisconsin) *Press-Gazette* on March 19, 2006, read: *"McCormick Not Alone in Party Snub, People Not GOP, Should Choose Candidate, She Says."* The article that accompanied that headline found it best to get behind a candidate who the people want. ... It is best to trust in the democratic process that the people will decide who will best represent them."

The powerful lesson learned in the GOP primary race would take quite a different turn from the intentions of those "watching from the field" in 2006. The people would have the final say in this safe GOP seat in Wisconsin. ...The results? The *political class* would lose—despite the $2.5 million spent to buy the seat. The Democrat candidate was awarded the "safe GOP seat," and Congress itself would change hands. Several GOP convictions that same year would prove to the public that the "Era of Irresponsibility" needed to end. The Hollywood movie set was exposed for what it was.

MOVING FORWARD WITH GENDERLESS MUSCLE

Don't think for a minute that I believe that only men are capable of this type of unethical behavior—far from it. Women follow just like men follow. The point is this: we don't need followers! We need heavy lifters. We need those who aren't afraid to engage in intellectual battle and who have poise under fire. And we need people who can provide one or more of the following attributes:

- *Inspiration and communication*—these are the necessary skills for getting things done. If people cannot inspire, move ideas forward and get others to be on board, then they cannot lead.

- *Ideas and solutions*—people need problem-solving skills. They must have the ability to see the world differently. They must be able to see the whole picture, not just a linear view. And they need mental toughness. When others are jealous or petty enough to quash their idea rather than solve a problem for the entire state, these people have to step ahead of that roadblock and find a solution.

- *Impatience*—these people must be impatient enough to push for something they want done. Thinking and planning are useless skills if they don't have the fire under them to jump into action.

Women and men are both capable of unethical behavior, but we hear about the men more often. Why? The only logical explanation is that there are more men in politics. I would take that one step farther and say that women aren't necessarily as willing to play Fishbowl Predatory Politics. I base that statement on the following:

RESEARCH ON WOMEN AS LEADERS

In my own home state of Wisconsin, we have seen a steady decline in women Republicans elected to the state legislature. A direct correlation can be drawn with this sharp decline of Republican women in the state legislature to that of a more dictatorial, fall-in-line approach to leadership within the GOP ranks itself. The Wisconsin state house lost two-thirds of its women representation in GOP-held seats in the state house alone, during a six-year period, 2001 to 2007. The U.S. House of Representatives in Washington DC also has steadily lost women-held seats throughout the tenure of GOP majorities on the federal level.

Research has not been conducted as of this writing to determine the cause for this sharp decline in GOP seats held by women, but it was reported in March of 2008 by MSNBC that the Republican National Committee has conducted polling on the topic of gender and race. It would appear that the GOP is polling negative campaign material to determine how far negative they can go against a potential woman or minority candidate for president.[11]

If I were to ask if it were more likely, statistically, to find women in the role of governor or the United States Congress, you might be more likely to say Congress. Research reports, however, that both political parties have had a sharp decline in women serving in the United States Congress. Are women being squeezed out? Or are they opting against party machine politics? Even with small numbers, women can leave an indelible mark in politics, given the tools and the right approach. Waging intellectual battles and displaying poise under fire are skills that can be learned.

Women, if provided an opportunity to run in independent-leaning districts, tend to better connect to the needs of their constituency back home in their districts. "Voters give female governors significantly higher marks than their male counterparts on such qualities as honesty, cooperation and caring—as well as toughness," reports an article in *Newsweek* in 2007. *Newsweek*'s descriptions of women governors showed that women governors were "pragmatic, post-partisan and focused on solving problems." Further, it was reported that women as governors work especially well with high numbers of independent voters in their states.

This appears to be a welcome change from the partisan rancor that has described state and federal government, as mired in finger pointing and territorial posturing. Indeed the last 108th Congress in

2006 was described as the greatest "do nothing" Congress in American history. The Wisconsin legislature, too, has closed its 2008 session with a similar reputation.

BARRIERS TO WOMEN RUNNING FOR AND SERVING IN PUBLIC OFFICE

According to the research conducted by the Barbara Lee Family Foundation, there are six identifiable barriers to women who aspire to serve in public office. From their publication *Cracking the Code*, "Political Intelligence for Women Running for Governor" (2004), these barriers are:

1. Executive Leadership: Given the few examples of women chief executives in the public and private sectors, women candidates for governor must be able to demonstrate successful executive experience in order to win voter confidence.
2. Preparation: Women need to provide more evidence than men of their financial and crisis-management skills to persuade voters they are as "qualified" or "ready to serve."
3. Outsiders with Insider Connections: Women are presumed to be "outside" the harsh push and pull of politics, but they must have inside connections to mount statewide campaigns.
4. Outsiders with Insider Know-How: Women are expected to be "honest," but in voter's minds that raises the question: Can they make the necessary deals?
5. Management Style—Tough but Caring: Women must walk the line between seeming "tough enough" but not "too tough," and compassionate but not weak.
6. Family Matters: Voters are curious and make assumptions about women candidates and their families. They wonder who will come first—the candidate's family or the public, and how she will juggle both.

RESEARCH ON WOMEN AS GOVERNORS

Research on women governors has described them as being willing to take on the corruption in their states. Republican governor

Sarah Palin of Alaska was quoted on October 15, 2007, as stating, "It's time for Alaska to grow up and end its reliance on pork-barrel spending." Shortly after taking office, Palin canceled funding for the "Bridge to Nowhere," a $330 million project that Senator Ted Stevens (R) championed in Congress. The bridge, which would have linked the town of Ketchikan to an island airport, had come to symbolize Alaska's dependence on federal handouts, as it would serve fifty people. Governor Palin, instead, would rather prove that Alaska can pay its own way, developing its huge energy wealth in ways that are "politically and environmentally clean."

Governor Palin meets with Rep. Terri McCormick
and others in Green Bay in 2008

Governor Palin recognized that "if we had the same good old boys serving, nothing would change. We needed some new blood. [She] also recognized that you had to be the top dog to make those changes."[12] Palin was seen as a golden girl of the Republican Party, a hardworking, pro-business politician whose friendly demeanor (evidenced by that Palin smile) made her palatable to the typical pickup-driving Alaskan man.

Governor Kathleen Sebelius (D) of Kansas further proves the research right on women leaders. She blurs the partisan divide by describing herself as a post-partisan who is focused more on solving problems than pointing fingers. Named as one of the nation's five best governors by *Time* magazine in 2005, Sebelius is described as someone who "really loves studying policy." She is a self-proclaimed risk-taker who has learned from her father. "You have to be willing to fight for something and risk taking the loss."[13]

WOMEN AS POLITICAL LEADERS

This phenomenon of women being able to cross party lines and being more prone to solving problems is, ironically, at odds with the front-row mentalities in rancorous fall-in-line party politics. The predatory fall-in-line politics is dependent on turf wars and silo building. Further, the survival of the front-row leadership ranks is often dependent on maintaining the same old ideological battles between the two political parties. It is not in either party machine's interests to solve problems. Political donations and campaign cash is a direct result of creating fear and angering their respective voting bases.

The very nature of serving the people, or populist thinking, may hinge on the need for increasing the numbers of independent voters, who demand change in our political system. Independent voters formed a show-me aspect of politics in the 2006 and 2008 elections. They insisted on information and research on all candidates across the political spectrum. And it was then that they cast their votes and encouraged their social networks to cast their votes for candidates of integrity and ideas.

Women as leaders in politics, specifically in the governor's seat, may prove one way to break the back of the current rank-and-file clubs that seem to have bolstered political intrigue and partisan politics. If American citizens hope to find policy makers interested in solving problems, rather than those resembling schoolyard thugs or bullies at recess, we might learn a lesson from citizen leaders who do their homework and keep an open mind before casting their ballots in political elections. In fact, the research shows that the growing numbers of independent voters—35 percent at this writing—makes post-partisan thinking and problem solving possible.

The challenges we have today cannot be solved with backward thinking. It requires forward thinkers who have the capacity to envision new paths that have not yet been created. This will require all Americans to participate in the political process.

CHAPTER SUMMARY

- The political ecosystem is composed of the "sharks," who are all about self-serving in office; the "feeder fish," who attach themselves to the sharks; and the "outsiders" who aim to serve their constituents.
- Stereotypes about male and female politicians abound.
- Research about women as leaders show that women have made significant strides in the past few decades.

Being powerful is like being a lady.
If you have to tell people you are, you aren't.

—Margaret Thatcher

PART TWO

THE ART
OF
POLITICAL
POWER GAMES
IN
VERTICAL SILOS

Representatives Krawczyk and McCormick ...
Leading from the Back Row.

CHAPTER FIVE

LEADING FROM THE BACK ROW

MYTH:

Insider politics is the stuff of
Hollywood imagination.

REALITY:

Insider politics is alive and well
in your capitol.

In reality there is perhaps no one of our natural passions so hard to subdue as pride. Disguise it, struggle with it, beat it down, stifle it, mortify it as much as one pleases; it is still alive and will now and then peek out and show itself.

—Benjamin Franklin

Upon entering the state and federal capitols across the United States and walking the hallowed chambers of the legislative bodies, you may see formal seating assignments that determines who someone is, what that person will be, and what he or she will be allowed to accomplish. Those who wield power in their respective front rows make these decisions.

THE FRONT ROW AND ITS IMPORTANCE

There is a physical front row that faces the lecterns of power, separating the lieutenants and generals from the main body of both political parties. There is also an aisle that divides the two major political parties, the Democrats and the Republicans. The lines drawn between the political insiders (the front row) and the political outsiders (middle and back rows) are much less known but far more important. The caveat is dysfunctional leadership. Front row division from members in the middle and back rows is far more divisive when led by dysfunctional leaders than any political party differences.

When the House was in session, and we were called to caucus on Fourth Floor North, I would sit in the back row. The real debates were hidden from public view, and they were held in our party caucus rooms. I chose the back remembering an old family lesson dating back to the Civil War: "Keep your back to the wall"—a saying handed down to me from my great-grandfather.

Sitting alongside me was a woman who was to become my colleague and closest ally, Judith Ann Krawczyk. We were both "freshmen legislators" in 2001, a term used to keep wide-eyed new legislators in line. I was a fresh-faced politician, full of big ideas and an even stronger sense of purpose, given the fact that I was the state's original charter school law author as a private citizen. My sense was that I could make a larger impact now that I was an actual member of the state legislature. Little did I realize how very naïve that thought was.

Representative Judy Krawczyk was sixty years young and full of street smarts and common sense. She often told me, "I have a nose for people and I can smell trouble." The day we met, we were both sensing the building tension and political posturing. At the moment that we were to be introduced to our party's caucus on the fourth floor, both of us looked around the room. It resembled a high school auditorium on the first day of fall classes. "Let's sit in the back," we both said at the same time.

Sitting in the front row is a subconscious clue to the aspirations of those occupying those seats. They're there for power, control, to be heard and to lead their own agendas. Yet little do they realize that leaders are all around them in that room—some of us are sitting behind the white pillars in our state and federal capitols, watching and listening. When the time is right, we'll lead right from where we sit. Unfortunately for the front, many of us lead very well from the back row.

From the back I could see the entire political class, the orchestrated moves in our caucus from the lieutenants who were instructed to agitate votes during our discussions. I could easily see the cupped hands and silent whispers of instruction given to the whips who paced about at the end of the aisles. There were more times than I'd like to admit when I saw talented legislators ostracized and used as "examples" by the leaders in the political class. These legislators were verbally browbeaten and torn down in front of the body. A few of us stood up to intervene; Representative Krawczyk and I were such bold ones. Unfortunately, the damage had already been done, as many of these individuals would resign shortly thereafter. The games played by those sitting in the front row were brutal. Many colleagues had short-lived political careers at the hands of the front-row elite, whose jealousy and petty games were aimed at weeding them out and driving them away from government service. Little did I know that my choice to sit in the back had afforded me a label of someone who would be quiet and submit to the rules of the front row.

Before we get too far into the dysfunctional aspects of lawmaking, perhaps it is time to show you a chart of "How a Bill Actually Becomes a Law." You may be surprised to learn about the contrast between the ideal on paper and the reality of the political game, as it is played today.

The following chart focuses on the legislative body, the lawmakers. On paper, there are three readings of the bill—first, when it is introduced and referred to committee; second, when the bill comes up before either body (Senate or House); and third, when the bill is read for its last time before it is voted on by the body. A conference committee follows, if both houses pass a different version of the same bill, to work out the differences between the Senate and the House. The final product is then enrolled and sent to the governor's desk for his/her signature.

How a Bill Becomes a Law
"IN THEORY"

House Assembly	Senate
Representative	***Receive House Message 1st Reading***
Introduction and 1st Reading	Senate Standing Committee
House Standing Committee	Public Hearing
Public Hearing	Committee Amendments
Committee Amendments, Executive Action, Committee Recommendation	Executive Action, Committee Recommendation
House Rules Committee	Senate Organization Committee
Calendar and 2nd Reading	***Calendar 2nd Reading***
Debate and Amendments	Debate and Amendments
Calendar Engrossment and 3rd Reading Passage House Message to Senate	***Calendar 3rd Reading*** Concurrence Senate Message to House

Enrolling	***Law without Signature***		
Governor	***Approval with Signature***	Secretary of State	Publication
	VETO, whole or part	Calendar House/Senate	Passage, Notwithstanding Gov's Objections

The question becomes, what does the political class in the front rows, either Republican or Democrat, do with political adversaries who stand in the way of their own agenda? The answer: they set out to overcome them in Machiavellian fashion, watching their every move through staffers and lieutenants, reporting back to the front-row elites.

This information is used as spin and often is used to discredit the member in the eyes of the caucus—or worse, in the eyes of the public. Political knives often are sharpest in one's own political party. One such example was state Senator Tom Reynolds.

In 2004, Senator Reynolds was chastised in the *Milwaukee Journal Sentinel* by anonymous staffers. You see, Reynolds openly condemned overspending and pandering to special interests, calling it "self-serving and corrupt." He was a favorite of the *Conservative Digest* publication for his courage to stand against needless spending. Unfortunately, there was a price to pay for his criticisms against his Senate majority front row. Reynolds was smeared maliciously by GOP bloggers, and these blogs were picked up by the *Milwaukee Journal-Sentinel*.

The quick exit of a senator or a representative requires their own party leadership to control their offices through their staffers. Such was the case with Senator Reynolds. A "loyal" staff was put in his office, one that would report directly to the Assembly House Speaker and the Senate Majority Leader. As a result, Reynolds fired his disloyal employees. What happened next was no doubt actionable. Front-row leaders began to create rumors and innuendo that Senator Reynolds was "crazy." Keep in mind this was his own political party, his own leadership, who saw Reynolds as some type of threat to their front-row operation and schemes.

The need to control the message and members was more important than honoring the ideologies of the Republican Party, such as lowering taxes through less spending. It was more important than honoring Senator Reynolds's free speech to change the corruption he witnessed in his party's caucus. GOP staffers moved very quickly to discredit Senator Reynolds and today, they claim it was justified because he "threw his party under the bus." This man's reputation and career in the legislature was ruined by those in the front who didn't want a noisemaker telling the public that "Republicans needed to stop overspending and taking corrupt fund-raising monies." The rest of the story? Republicans lost Senator Reynolds's seat to the Democrat candidate.

The key difference between those in the front and those of us in the middle and back is our motivation. Back-row leaders are motivated by doing for the public, for the voters we represent. For us, glory and power are just a waste of time unless we bring results for the people back home. Quite literally, those who run for office to *do something* are frequently at odds with those who run for office to *be somebody*! Those of us who earned our own way didn't have to be paid to do the right thing in office.

How does one get around the control games of the front row? We move over, under, around and through, bypassing the very power and control that the front-row occupants use to push their agendas. Instead, we build coalitions where we can find them. We tend to be much more horizontal in our thinking, focused on solutions rather than ultimatums. It is the front rows in both political parties who continue to live in the vertical silos created by the standoff win/lose politics of the past.

The trick is to stay away from the front-row loyalists. One of my closest colleagues, when first elected to public office, was handed a bluebook directory of legislators. Notes were carefully written under every photo and name of our caucus. The notes included references such as "straight shooter," "water boy," "self-absorbed," "watch your back," and so on. This road map of the characters serving in public office etched out an invaluable lesson in the culture of personality politics. It separated those who were more likely to fall in line and pass along our thoughts and ideas, from those who could stand on their own two feet and be trusted allies and friends.

This massive spying game against members of one's own political caucus members is nothing new. Open the book titled *The Prince*, written in 1513 by Niccolo Machiavelli. This is the book responsible for the "anything goes" approach to modern-day politics. Based on spying, games and building networks of fear, Machiavelli describes the bipartisan dysfunction in politics today. For those of us who run for office and wish to make a difference, we have no time for these games. For us, this network of spies, made up of staffers and weak colleagues, were easily exposed and easily overcome. Legislative life proved to be a lesson in dysfunctional leadership and how to stay away from it. Unfortunately, there were those who became drunk with their own status and title, and they entered a life of no return, playing a game of Machiavellian power and control.

First-term legislators are called junior senators or freshmen. The term is supposed to describe the number of years a legislator has served. Yet it's used as a label meant to segment those who have not paid their dues or who haven't spent enough years carrying water for the front row. The more senior a member of the house is, the greater the entitlement philosophy ("I am owed my seat"). The length of time served in our state and federal capitols has become far more important than the solutions and results we have created for our constituents back home. The free exchange of ideas on a stage of open and honest debate is a goal worth fighting for. It is not, however, the reality of the political landscape of government today.

STORIES FROM THE FRONT LINES

I worked on two very important pieces of public policy during my first session in the Wisconsin legislature. One, I fell in to quite accidentally; the other was no doubt intended to keep me out of trouble and busy. My strength in politics lies in the fact that I dislike the injustice of politics. Instead, I am wired to solve problems and look at the system as a whole. Dollars and cents do not factor into my judgments, unless it has to do with cost analysis and fiscal impact on families and on jobs. All decisions and actions that integrity-driven legislators make are based on values and convictions. Some people call this a moral compass; some a center of gravity. I'd like to refer to it as simply having heart.

When an individual in public service has heart, he or she feels compassion and empathy for others. More important, there is a direct and intentional focus on others. Solving problems and making a difference for others is a common core value among legislators with heart. In contrast, the politician or political hack is consumed with the "me" game of politics, which translates to the need for power and control.

THE CRANDON MINE AMENDMENT

There are not too many people's instincts that I would take over facts and logic, but my own instincts are one exception, and that colleague sitting in the back row with me is another. I was drawn into a crisis situation that was about as popular as a fart in church. Rep. Krawczyk was not just a legislative colleague; she was a kindred spirit. My house district and hers had one common denominator: water, and lots of it. She represented the Bay of Green Bay; I represented the Wolf River Basin, Fox River and Lake Winnebago.

The Crandon Mine issue had been debated for years and was on schedule by my party's front row to be pushed through for a vote.

My involvement seemed innocent enough—make sure the methods used to carry the tailings (residue from the mining expedition) were safe and that they were being disposed of in an appropriate manner. Rep, Krawczyk insisted that her nose smelled trouble, and the ground water itself was in jeopardy. The Crandon Mine sat at the head of all of the water that both of us represented in our districts. A misstep with the Crandon Mine could mean that pollution would literally be flushed throughout the Wolf River Basin like a toilet, impacting 40 percent of all surface water in the state.

Krawczyk and I had only been in office for a few months when her instincts kicked in and her hand pulled on my sleeve. She urged me to find a way to check on the mining operation and its potential impact on the surface water. Krawczyk could cook; I could research and write public policy. It was not long before the two of us made a nightly ritual of eating at her apartment and studying alternatives to burying mining waste at the top of the water basin.

Both of us were conservatives in the tradition of Teddy Roosevelt, which meant natural resources had value and needed conserving. Such was the case in the attempt to reopen a mine in Crandon, Wisconsin. The best interests of the general public were bantered about, with the topic of jobs versus water; and then jobs versus tourism jobs. Most important to this discussion was Rep. Judy Krawczyk's smell test—the issue just didn't smell right.

A formidable mining project—backed by party elites in both front rows in both political parties—was being pushed through for a vote after several years of heated debate and stalls. Who was I? I was only a freshman and worse, I was listening to another freshman's instincts. My problem was that I didn't vote on things until I read the fine print and did the research the best I could. Sometimes the facts and impacts were not easily discernable. At other times, the facts and research were hidden from our view and replaced with marketing spin.

One point became increasingly clear: it was time I began to do independent research on the mining company and its history. Graduate coursework I had conducted in the early 1980s in Windsor, Ontario, led me to some professional contacts. My first call was to an urban planner and colleague in the Canadian government. Canada had long led the United States in conservation issues; their economy depends on tourism.

In my years of graduate study in Windsor, I grew familiar with Great Lakes issues and water issues in particular. The Great Lakes Commission and its influence on city planning commissions throughout Canada led me to the provincial government. Through the years I had maintained contact with a knowledgeable and well-connected city planner in the province of Ontario, Dennis Gratton. Gratton was in the Ottawa office when he took my call.

"Dennis, have you heard of the Australian Mining Company?" I asked.

"That company is working inordinately hard to influence Wisconsin legislators on the Crandon Mine project in my state," Dennis responded in a supportive tone. "Let me look into things on this end and see if they come up on any of our government radar screens."

It didn't take long before Dennis Gratton got back to me with his response. "Terri, that mining company left the province of Ontario with $1.5 billion in cleanup costs."

I asked him to fax all of the supporting documents he had, as well as contacts he used, so that I could verify all the documents independently.

It appeared that my concern was justified. The potential impact of the mining company could affect water quality for the state of Wisconsin and the Wolf River Basin for generations to come. The political argument before the legislature favoring the mining operation was that it would create jobs in an area of the state that was badly in need of jobs: Crandon, Wisconsin.

As I began to research a bit further, I found that tens of thousands of tourism jobs could be placed in jeopardy if the pollution levels in Wisconsin came anywhere close to the impact made by the same mining company in Ontario. As a pro-business legislator I needed to make sure that the potential costs to the tourism industry did not outweigh the jobs the mining operation would create in Crandon. The numbers didn't add up. I found that the number of Crandon mining jobs ranged between forty and sixty. Further, these jobs would be short-lived and phased out after the mine was depleted.

The thousands of tourism jobs, weighed against the forty to sixty new mining jobs, made no sense. As we began to find political influence peppered in both Republican and Democratic parties, I knew that the issue was far greater than I could handle with a full frontal assault. I didn't have the horses in the lobby core, nor the time to rally a citizen coalition against it. Besides, this would mean a direct confrontation with my own party leaders; I didn't want that.

Instead, I gathered all of the data I could to present facts and evidence in the committee hearings. Rep. Krawczyk and I would study data, letters and editorials as well as the evidence from the provincial government in Ontario. The purpose was to track the actual costs in jobs to allowing the mining operation through. We had only one political strategy—to use facts and logic to add on to the existing legislation. Instead of rallying votes against the bill, we instead argued for daylight in how the tailings, or shavings, from the mine would be tested before they were to be dumped into the landfills. This was the middle ground that both sides could not argue against. Testing the tailings would ease the minds of those most concerned about the environment. At the same time, testing the tailings could not be opposed by those who insisted that the forty to sixty new jobs in Crandon could mean an economic boom. Before I knew it, my party leaders and the legislators were in a box with no place to move.

The McCormick-Krawczyk Amendment was simple and to the point:

> *All tailings, or shaving residue, taken from the mining process shall be tested, with the results made public before they are to be dumped in the impermeable landfills. If Republicans and Democrats in favor of the Crandon Mine agree to the testing of these tailings (shavings) from the mine, then the mining operation could proceed as planned.*

The game of Battleship, played by guessing where your opponent's ships are hidden on the game board and then sinking them, was the only strategy we had at our disposal. We were not political insiders; we were new to the caucus and we had absolutely no clout. Facts on the issues wouldn't be enough. We began to look for the battleships that were able to be sunk. Were these tailings normally tested? No. No one had considered that option. Did I know what the testing of the tailings would find? No. What I knew was this: this mining issue had lasted over two years, confirming that a level of hazardous pollution was plausible. The facts revealed hazardous pollution from the same

Australian mining company creating 1.5 billion dollars' worth of damage in Ontario, Canada. "Battleship found."

Lobbyists for the landfills made face-to-face contact with me, assuring me that nothing could leak out of their landfill. Common sense told me otherwise. I just wanted to know what they would be pouring into those landfills. The result was twofold: first, Krawczyk was threatened on the floor of the legislature by some front-row nervous Nellies for delaying the vote on the Crandon Mine. She was told, "If you don't back down from the mine, then I will go after your paper companies in Green Bay." I was standing right behind the then-state representative who threatened Rep. Judy Krawczyk. I'm not sure why I didn't get threatened in this … but my time would come.

Second, Krawczyk and I held our ground. We would not be intimidated. The amendment I crafted served its purpose and the mining operation stood down. I didn't need to know if the landfills were secure—no one could guarantee that. I needed to know what they would be dumping in there. And if it was a public hazard, as it was in Ontario, we could have cross-checked the mining debris and residue from the tailings that caused the devastation in Ontario. I can only guess and speculate as to why the well-paid lobbyists and Australian mining operation walked away.

THE COMPETITIVE PRESCRIPTION DRUG PURCHASING POOL

Looking back on things, there is no doubt in my mind that my freshman year chairmanship of the speaker's Task Force on Health Insurance Partnerships for Local Governments was designed to keep me out of trouble. After the Crandon Mine fiasco, it was a wise appointment by Speaker Scott Jensen to keep me busy, studying what was perceived as an impossible issue, that of health-care costs. It was well known that the skyrocketing costs of local government health insurance was steadily rifling up the costs of property taxes. The issue was sticky and it would boil over with testimony from school board members around the state, who would echo the concerns of counties, municipalities and townships.

"Health insurance costs" for public employees was a traceable escalation of costs that impacted taxpayers' wallets directly. Unlike the business sector, health-care costs for local governments could be made transparent and accountable. As the task force chairwoman, I shaped the issue by working with my three attorneys to draft legislation that would provide mechanisms for health-cost sharing that didn't exist before. The politics were basic, old-style politics; poised to pit public employee unions against the taxpayer. As a result, this issue of local government insurance costs created a political time bomb. I'm quite sure that my front-row leadership thought that I would pull the pin and go up and smoke with the issue. I saw things differently: my focus would be to create listening groups statewide and then find the common ground to solve the problem. Workable solutions would need to provide market forces to lower health insurance costs and thereby put more money into employees' paychecks as a result.

The only problem with using market forces was with the state's largest teachers union, the Wisconsin Education Association Council (WEAC). The WEAC and its insurance company, WEA Trust, are one in the same. The union owned its own insurance company and therefore didn't want to compete with other insurance companies. In fact, WEAC's argument remains the same today—they have the Cadillac of insurance policies for their members and the public should just pay more, be taxed more and spend more to pay for it.

Does the term "conflict of interest" come to mind? The fact is that countless teachers were requesting help from my office to reduce their health insurance costs so that they would have more money left in their paychecks. Further, the testimony my committee heard from school board members across the state confirmed that WEA Trust not only didn't like competition, but they also were willing to intimidate school board members to maintain their corner on the insurance market. This "Cadillac" health insurance company not only had a conflict of interest in bleeding income away from school teachers, but it also held their school boards hostage with their rates. Sadly, high health insurance costs are not in the interests of teachers, nor are they in the interests of school boards and taxpayers struggling with decreasing budgets for basic classroom materials for students.

As I held a series of committee hearings, information sessions and statewide forums on the topic of reducing health insurance costs for local governments, I heard many recurring themes. School board members, in testimony, recounted the burden of health-care insurance costs on ever shrinking school budgets. Despite this, accounts of intimidation and scare tactics were mounting, aimed at school board members who supported alternate insurance coverage.

The proposals centered around the solution of a transparent bidding process, which would require local governments to take a minimum of three health insurance bids and then post those bids on the Internet for the press and the public to see. After weeks of testimony and statewide listening sessions, my proposals for health-care insurance costs became crystallized. The State Association of Administrators, the League of Municipalities, the Alliance of Cities, and the Counties Association all came together to lobby on behalf of my proposals. Unfortunately, with what should have been a slam-dunk initiative to save dollars in local government employees' paychecks became a ping-pong ball, with my party as one of the main detractors.

When I called for the vote, it was not surprising that the WEAC would control the votes of all the Democrats. What was amazing to me in 2003 was the roadblock put in place by my own party members. The highest ranking member of my Health Care Cost Committee was also second in command on the House Assembly Joint Finance Committee, Mike Huebsch. Rep. Huebsch was a former staffer, young, slick, connected and ambitious. It was the odd conversation with Rep. Huebsch that made me aware that my party's front-row leadership didn't necessarily want to solve the health-care cost crisis for local units of government.

We were near the close of our long months of work on a package of reforms that would break ground in using large prescription drug purchasing pools to leverage down the costs of prescription drugs.

After a final break in discussions, I called for a break before the final vote on the package.

That is when Rep. Huebsch confronted me in the hallway, just outside our hearing room. "I don't know if I can vote on your health care package," he said.

I gave him a puzzled look and said, "What? You sat in on all the proceedings, you watched me author and write all the initiatives, you heard all of the testimony and pleas for help. Why wouldn't you vote for the competitive bid package?"

He retorted, "We won't underestimate you again."

His statement spoke volumes. I did not choose this battle, but I would not run from it.

Now, here is where the story gets more interesting. The speaker of the Republican house, who appointed me to the post of task force chairwoman, left his seat due to felony indictments. But he remained in the legislature, acting as a shadow speaker.

Here's the interesting part. The new speaker, a junior speaker, was the same young man who sabotaged Governor McCallum in the press conference just a few months earlier. As luck would have it, he would also be my primary opponent for U.S. Congress.

The new junior speaker stalled the vote on the competitive prescription drug purchasing pool and other measures in the health insurance package, despite the fact that every city, town, village, county and school board association demanded that it be passed. Full court press lobby efforts were waged on leaders in both the state senate and house. This groundbreaking health-care cost package was seen as a way to save local government budgets without raising taxes. With no result, the junior speaker wanted to hang on to it.

I appealed to the past speaker, the shadow speaker. After all, the shadow speaker was still the brains behind the operation, and he and I had similar views on the need for competition and market economies.

Unfortunately, there appeared to be nothing that he could do. The new guy, who came to power out of someone else's misery, buried the health-care package. He no doubt would manipulate the dates and bring my work up at a later date, to attempt to pass it off as his own. This was a typical move by the political class who clearly had few ideas of their own. The very fact that in 2002, the press and local government associations, across the board, valued my work on the health-care reforms and competitive prescription drug cost reforms created a problem for that idea-less political class.

The new junior speaker saw me as competition, especially in the 2003 and 2004 session. It was at that time that one of my former task force members visited me, someone who evidently was quite pleased with his recent appointment by the junior speaker to the powerful Joint Finance Committee. This man was a former mayor of a small town in northern Wisconsin and now was a second-term legislator, as I was at that time. Rep. Meyer should have understood the gravity of the health-care cost issue to local governments, as he had been a stickler against state government and its impact on local property taxes in his small town.

Rep. Meyer's questions at our meeting in my office at the beginning of the 2003/2004 session were poignant and appeared to be politically motivated. "So now that you passed that health-care package out of committee, what are you going to do with it?" The grin on his face should have given him away, but I assumed he was serious.

My response was naïve. "I thought we would pass it and begin to give local governments and employees the needed relief on their health insurance costs."

This is only part of the story. Every member of my task force committee who watched me craft the reform package was appointed to the "powerful Joint Finance Committee" by the junior speaker; I was not given such an appointment. Further, my bill to reduce health insurance costs as well as other initiatives would be stalled by my own political party. Okay, it was about doing the job. But what about the several months of work I put in writing the health-care cost control package? Well ... the junior speaker erased my name from my work and, to quote an insurance lobbyist who was shocked at the gall of the man, "cut and pasted it into a fix for the 2003/2004 state budget crisis."

A win/win for the front row—erase the author and talent behind the idea and claim credit! How did I find out about the tactics used against me by the front row? A lobbyist passed by my office to thank me for my work on the health insurance task force and to congratulate me for the whole thing being used in the upcoming state budget. And then he said, "You must be so proud they are using your ideas to fix the budget."

I said, "What? I wasn't told!"

"Oh, I'm sorry. They cut and pasted the entire reform package you wrote and stuck it into the budget to resolve the state employee cost crisis."

The "get it done for the people" part of me said *Great!* The ethical, public servant part of me felt her gut wrench. This childish move to steal my ideas left me shaking my head in disbelief.

So what happened to competitive bids that reduced health insurance costs? In 2005, my fifth year in the legislature, the dynamics of personal politics from the front row used my work again. I believed I had seen it all. And then the phone rang in my legislative office, with someone from the governor's office on the line. I was a bit surprised, but not more surprised than my chief of staff, Jared, who took the phone call.

"The governor has the numbers in on your prescription drug purchasing pool for state employees," said the governor's representative, "and they prove that we are saving thirty million dollars the first year."

The Democratic Governor had recognized my ideas and policies on health care as important—his office called my office to give us credit for our own work. This was something new—our own party leadership, conversely, lied to us, cheated and kicked us around for solving problems, but this—being given credit for my own work—was a political tactic for which I was not ready. The governor was calling to ask us if we wanted to issue our press release first, before his went out. My office felt vindicated; ideas mattered and they were valued.

I finally understood—it was about a flawed personality in politics. It wasn't about Democrat versus Republican. It was about an individual who was desperate to "be somebody," putting himself continually above the people he was supposed to serve. And in contrast, it was about a governor who seized an opportunity to use my health-care reforms to solve the budget crisis. He'd reached across the ideological aisle, so that we could put solutions above partisan rancor. It was about "doing the right thing"!

State Representative Terri McCormick, Chairwoman
Jennifer Streblow, Committee Clerk

The Wisconsin State Legislature. Committee Hearing, 2002
The Health Care Sub Committee, Local Government
Health Cost Partnerships

THE BALANCED BUDGET VS. FRONT-ROW POLITICS

I will never forget the late-night budget standoff in 2003, shortly after my second oath of office, in the Wisconsin state legislature. My committee appointments were as the chair of the Economic Development Committee and vice chair for a second term in office on the House Judiciary Committee. The "budget crisis," as it was identified by county after county and municipality after municipality, was caused by a ripple effect from state unfunded mandates, escalating costs of health insurance, and poor collaboration and planning between local, county and state government.

State budgets are always in crisis in Wisconsin in that we make budget decisions based on getting our majorities back in office. The ripple effect is the pork stuffed into legislation that was promised by the front-row leaders in setting the house legislative agendas. Notice I did not mention "public policy agendas"—there is little of that. The power for setting the agenda and moving the legislation to be voted on rests in the hands of the house assembly speaker. Any checks and balances thereafter are in the hands of the governor's line-item veto. Without a need to have money in the budget before you spend it, or "pay as you go," you may as well give an open checkbook to a teenager at holiday time. And therein lies the problem: there is no accountability for state-level spending if the political will is stronger than the public policy will. It's truly a case of "Who is watching the hen house?"

One vivid recollection I have of this front row versus back row dynamic happened during the 2003/2004 budget debate. The conservative arm of our GOP party had done the math, and the current tax levels in no way could afford the massive giveaway programs that were being carved out by the front row in the Republican leadership ranks. It was 1:00 a.m., and both political party front-row benches were meeting privately behind the scenes to work out a "deal," as their private discussions were so often called. The body, as a whole, had very little idea of what was happening in these private meetings. That's not to say they weren't paying attention. It's that the front row plays a "leadership game" that gives off an illusion of power that few feel able—or willing—to criticize or challenge.

A first-year legislator on my side of the aisle was glued to the discussion in the front of the chamber at 1:30 a.m. Her eyes were wide open, almost in a state of desperation, despite the late hour. I asked, "Are you all right? It's late. Do you need to lie down on one of the couches in the back and get called to take your votes?"

The freshman legislator said, "Absolutely not. I have to keep an eye on them in the front so that I can make sure they don't do something stupid."

She was right. The deals worked out with the front rows of both political parties were not provided to committees for consideration and public scrutiny. The real deals happening in the budget were based on a couple of giveaways to the minority party, in exchange for their votes to pass a law or to suppress the minority party from bringing up issues that would embarrass vulnerable members in the majority party—the party that controlled the budget process.

– Good Old Power and Control – State Budget

THE VETERANS PROPERTY TAX BILL

Sometimes the most difficult part of my job was being able to do my job. The year was 2006, and I was receiving more push back than usual on a veterans property tax bill that I wrote, with the help of Harold Grimes, a highly active and distinguished Vietnam veteran. The bill would have provided property tax relief for our returning veterans from Afghanistan and Iraq, as well as other veterans, with a 100 percent combat disability. The subject was clearly property tax relief, yet in a matter of a few hours after the bill's introduction, the focus changed.

The junior speaker shifted the focus of the Veterans Property Tax Relief to protocol—the newer protocol—and worse, the debate unraveled to its core. The real issue again was who would get the credit for writing my bill? This bill had—and still has—the support of veterans, as well as a number of political figures. Yet the leadership clique appeared to be creating excuses in an effort to block what would be an important and historic bill for the state. Instead of discussing the bill, the front row decided to block the veterans bill from being heard in committee.

The response from the veterans community was immediate and it was clear. *Stop playing games with veterans or we will march on the capitol.* The constituents who lobbied for veterans property tax relief were the sons, daughters and wives of veterans, and they were the veteran community at large. They were all asking for status reports and updates from my office. The veteran lobby was well organized, and they were on the move on the Internet and on the telephones.

How could I go back to them and explain that their bill hadn't been considered because the front row stalled the legislation for no apparent reason? These men and women in uniform were reminiscent of my family—my grandfathers, father, brother, nephews—veterans all. These were the men and women who made my service in the legislature possible and my nation's freedoms possible. How could I go back to these individuals and tell them that the front row had threatened me so I would drop the ball? I couldn't.

When I began the draft of the Veterans Property Tax Relief Bill, I brought in attorneys and veterans with personal experience on the issue. It was at Harold Grimes's (USMC and U.S. Army, retired) request that I first wrote the legislation. The stories of disrespect and neglect of our Vietnam veterans was and is not a history I want to see repeated. It was for their cause—their banner—that I went to the wall in my caucus. It was their plea that I carried in my heart and fought to be heard. A sacred prayer of the veterans from the Korean and Vietnam wars was that their dishonor and neglect at the hands of the American government would not be the legacy for the veterans of today, from Iraq and Afghanistan.

Maybe it would have been easier to understand if the debate on veterans property relief had been partisan. But it wasn't. Instead, it was my own party's leadership in the front row, blocking the bill from being heard. The entire veterans community saw dishonor in the actions of my party. In fact, with the war raging in the Middle East, the veterans community saw disgrace as well in the actions of my party. Sadly, so did I.

When I relayed the unhappy news to the veterans groups, they sprang into action. They, as a force, insisted that my party's speaker allow their bill up for a vote. They e-mailed, wrote letters, made phone calls, and tried every way they could to lobby their own state senators and their own assembly members—all to no avail.

I polled members of both parties on the Veterans Affairs Committee and the vast majority were in favor of the Veterans Property Tax Relief Bill. However, the chairman of Veterans Affairs would not budge; his staff was instructed by the front row not to allow it up for a vote. The message was clear: *"Do not let McCormick's bill out of your committee."*

Phone calls by an active veterans citizenry caused the junior speaker to transfer my bill under someone else's name into someone else's committee. These all-too-familiar political tactics were not a match for the veterans community, who were determined to see a bill that would keep veterans in their homes and off the streets passed through committee and written into law. The new committee chairman who was told to sit on the new Veterans Property Tax Exemption Bill was less able to take the heat from the several hundred phone calls he would receive from veterans across the state to bring it up for a vote.

Veterans Rally Behind Terri's 'Combat Disabled Property Tax Exemption.' Pictured are state officers of the Rolling Thunder Veterans Organization.

As luck would have it, the new committee chairman was the same individual with the booming voice that had threatened me for standing up for our sitting Republican governor in his reelection bid in 2001. Five years later, this guy was still following orders from the same junior speaker, only this time, he was standing in the way of passing a veterans property tax exemption for 100 percent combat-disabled veterans coming home from the wars in Iraq and Afghanistan. It was the same cast of characters—a political class occupied seemingly by children who desperately wanted to be somebody. Only this time, they were taking on a group of individuals who'd earned their stripes and could not be intimidated—the veterans of the United States military.

Democrats on the floor of the assembly tried their best to embarrass my party leadership. They called for a "pulling motion," a motion to pull my bill out of the committee that was not allowed to hear it and up to the floor of the legislature for a vote. My side of the aisle grimaced and groaned. Instead of swimming against the political current to do the right thing, the majority of members on my side of the aisle sat motionless and did nothing. They pretended as though nothing unusual was happening, as though they were watching a movie and no one else was in the room. The browbeating by the front had so paralyzed the committee members to stand for their own bills that it was like a scene from the movie *Redemption*. No one felt compelled to stand up and speak what was on his or her mind. There was a hidden agenda to the public: whatever the front row wants, the front row gets.

Veteran and Veterans Advocate Harold Grimes is well known for his integrity leadership in Washington DC and in Madison. He served as Terri's chief advisor on the Combat Disabled Property Tax Exemption

This was a serious matter. I was forced to sit on the floor of the legislature, only to watch my own front row make a mockery of the military service of those men and women who crowded the galleries in the legislature to watch the debate. Wisconsin was the only state in the country not to provide property tax relief for combat-disabled veterans at the 100 percent level. As a daughter of a veteran, a sister of veterans, an aunt of veterans, and believer of service to my country, I was sickened by the games of the front row of my party. Their games denigrated the very spirit of the veterans who fought for their right to govern in this democracy, this United States of America.

A NEW STYLE OF POLITICS

Restoring 'Representative Government' will take Courage.

Based on my experience serving in public office, one interesting phenomenon I've observed in political parties is that there is the political class, and it's an "inside game" and an "outside game" for those of us who serve the public. There are plenty of political bullies in the political class who have built up lifetime political careers by playing

King of the Hill and who have absolutely no intention of solving problems or representing the people back in their district. This is the most difficult concept for party loyalists to understand, yet it is true. It is true that the sharpest political knives are not on the other side of the aisle, but often they are on your own turf. Peer pressure, bullies, pettiness and jealousy do exist beyond the fences of our children's playgrounds.

Additionally, there are a number of ongoing stumbling blocks for a new kind of politics. Partisanship can stymie any progress, should one ruling party hold fast to the party line. Also, the political gender of your elected official can alter significantly any real progress and can slow that progress to a crawl. Lobbyists and special interests have influenced many politicians over the years, and they don't appear to be disappearing any time soon. Likewise, self-serving interests and hidden agendas create the culture in which politics is played. And if that's not enough, there are the power struggles that go on every day among politicians at all levels of government. With all this going on, it's a wonder anything gets accomplished. In order to better understand how to effect change in government, it's important to understand the roadblocks.

2008: WHAT HAS CHANGED?

The American people were witness to a new brand of presidential politics in 2008. We saw presidential candidates come into the election with tremendous amounts of personal wealth, spending millions of dollars on their own political races and striking out with the voters. Mitt Romney was such a candidate, with tremendous personal wealth poured into the Republican primary, yet beaten by Mike Huckabee, a populist former governor who struck a chord with the American people. Money didn't matter; the message did. Voters are becoming better consumers of retail politics. We the people—in 2008, anyway—no longer believed everything that was shown on television ads or in campaign literature. Not even the endorsements of all the connected establishment Republicans swayed the vote for Mitt Romney. John

McCain, instead, emerged as the Republican Party candidate for 2008.

What is the reason for this revolution against money in politics? It would appear that the public is placing less emphasis on political party affiliation and more emphasis on the ideas of the individual candidate. According to MSNBC political analyst Chuck Todd, the 2008 election cycle identified 35 percent of our electorate as registered Independent. What's more, half of Barack Obama's Independent supporters, according to exit polls cited by Todd, were former Bush Republicans from 2004. Republican, Democrat and Independent alike have embraced something more powerful than political party; they have embraced a hope that America can be good again.

Never underestimate the American people to stand forthright against what they perceive as wholesale corruption in our capitals. How else do we explain the rise of Ron Paul, a Republican congressional representative from Texas, whose stature and support spans voters of all ages? Call it a revolution of sorts. The American public has diagnosed a disease that is running rampant in our capitals. It is the "ego disease," reminiscent of Lord Akin's observation of too much power in too few hands. Lord Akin said, "Absolute power corrupts absolutely."

THE NEW POLITICS OF EFFECTIVE GOVERNMENT

Effective government will need three things:

1. It will require a free and appropriate press, one that is unencumbered by media buys and marketing departments. A free press must be engaged in research, issues and fact reporting. Sensational journalism making its way into attack blogs and irrelevant smear campaigns must be held accountable to the same credible journalistic standards as other media.
2. Citizen leadership is needed on every level of governance. A well-educated citizenry has been the cornerstone of our democracy since its inception. Modern marketing ploys require a well-educated voting public who are not easily fooled or "hoodwinked" by political marketers.

3. There is a need for qualified people of character to serve in elective office. Ideally, qualified candidates have experience from the private sector, embrace term limits and chose to return home after public service.

Power, despite what some would have you think, is not reserved for the heavily financed political-machine candidates, who too often sit in the front rows in our state and federal capitols. Real Republican forms of democracies derive from the people who elect representatives to speak and act for them in public office. Leading from the back row—from its seating assignments to controlled behavior by front-row elites—takes us closer to the "belly of the beast" of American politics and the clash between insider and outsider politics. Insiders have their own agenda, usually charged with political moves that are guaranteed to advance their political careers. Outsiders come from the real world and often find themselves tipping the front row insiders so that they can get the peoples' work done.

Effective government is more possible than you may think. It is my hope that by the end of this book, you'll be inspired to demand more of your local, state and national government officials. Change is needed. Change is possible. And change is something you can become a part of.

CHAPTER SUMMARY

The front row of the legislative hall is both a metaphor and literal place of power. Bills can be shut down or moved forward by the "front row" contingent.

A new, effective government requires a free press, citizen leadership and qualified candidates to serve the citizens.

Power always has to be kept in check; power exercised in secret, especially under the cloak of national security, is doubly dangerous.

—William Proxmire

CHAPTER SIX

POPULISTS VS. PUPPETS

MYTH:

Elites are found in the Republican Party
and populists are Democrats.

REALITY:

Populists believe in a government
"of, by and for" the people. Populists can
be found in all political parties.

The real battle is conquering ourselves.

—Clarence Thomas, U.S. Supreme Court Justice,
Commencement Speech, 2008

On Wednesday, Feb. 20, 2008, one day after the Wisconsin presidential primary election, Governor Mike Huckabee, a modern-day populist, made the following statement on national television during an interview by Joe Scarborough:

> *"I was threatened to have my arms and legs broken and to get out of the race. I don't know about you, but if elections don't belong to the people in the Republican Party, the Party will be destroyed. I would like to think that the Republican Party is mature enough, big enough and smart enough that it actually knows that competition breeds excellence and the lack of competition breeds mediocrity."*

POPULISM DEFINED

Populism embodies a faith in the intelligence of people and a faith that the people can and will face adversity and lead themselves forward. It is an abiding principle that is set in our founding documents as a free people. It is as Thomas Jefferson wrote in the Declaration of the Independence, "Government exists for the governed, so that the inalienable rights of the people may be protected." Jefferson goes on to define "government as instituted among men, deriving their just powers from the consent of the governed." If we were to study the Declaration of Independence as adopted by the Continental Congress in Philadelphia on July 4, 1776, and signed by John Hancock as president and by Charles Thomson as secretary, we would solidly understand that government of the people is our collective right as a free nation.

The notion that the voters would like to get past the nonsense of politics and get to solutions to better society is populist thinking. Populist politicians are self-identified public servants who strive to make a difference and an impact on the lives of the people they serve. Populism also implies a healthy skepticism in politicians who would hide from the people or patronize them—especially if those who hide from the public believe only a chosen few have the ability to take care of the public.

ELITISM DEFINED

Elitism can be defined as the belief that a chosen few—the political class—are best suited to make decisions for the majority. The elitists are the experts, and the common man should not be trusted to make decisions concerning his own welfare or what is best for the country. This was recently made very clear by comments from Vice President Dick Cheney when he was interviewed on MSNBC.

Cheney was asked for his response to the recent indication that two-thirds of Americans now oppose remaining in Iraq.

Cheney's succinct retort was "So?"

The Iraq war may be the single most important issue in recent history that significantly differentiates elite and populist thinking. Conversely, Democratic elites may believe that the educational and welfare establishments are more capable of making educational and welfare choices than their lower socioeconomic clients. Political party elites on both sides of the aisle are sharpening the intensity of the economic debate in order to argue that their side is better able to care for the American people. The question is: which party elite will be working to empower people and which party elite will be working to enable people?

THE DEBATE TODAY IN 2008

The political debate today is not between political parties—Republicans, Democrats or Independents. Americans are experiencing a realignment of power, based on public opinion on the issues (public evils) and on the candidates (public trust). This demand for change by the people is resulting in a realignment of party majorities at the polls. Jeffrey Bell's work in 1992 first tracked populist and elitist behaviors in his research at the Manhattan Institute and the JFK Institute of Politics at Harvard. Bell attributes the realignment, or shift, of the public's support between the two political parties as "our democracy's version of revolution."[14]

We have witnessed the public's revolution against the Republican political majority most recently in 2006, with the congressional midterm elections. The need for solutions rather than bickering and stalemate has resulted in a horizontal politic that has profoundly changed the political landscape. Voters lost faith in the Republican Party to deliver the conservative agenda that it had promised. With the exponential spending of the 108th Congress, as well as its growing numbers of Republican scandals, the voters punctuated their disdain by voting the Republicans out of power in 2006. Candidates like James Webb of West Virginia, former cabinet appointee of Ronald Reagan, successfully ran as a Democratic, toppling a Republican stronghold for the United States Senate. Webb's campaign was not about party; it was about public service.

How did this populist phenomenon take shape? In my estimation, the people woke up and quite simply recognized that the emperor had no clothes. Voters looked beyond the political campaign propaganda and into the land of show-me politics. Candidates known to be fresh, bright and full of new ideas were welcomed onto the political stage. The new billboards posted outside our state and national capitols now read: *Truth Seekers and Problem Solvers Welcome. No One Else Need Apply.*

The party labels of the past were not only proven to be obsolete, but they also proved to be fraught with empty promises and few results. The public was left holding the tab for political parties run amuck, building cold war—like silos, entrenched in their own personal agendas. The do-nothing Congress of the past was and is no longer acceptable. The public was hit squarely in the jaw on bread-and-butter issues—the energy crisis, the housing crisis, the mortgage crisis and the Wall Street crisis all have convinced the voting public that something has got to give! The voting public is now awake, engaged and on a mission to take their government back.

Voters in 2006 and 2008 looked across political party lines and into the faces of the candidates themselves. The populist revolution has begun. Thanks to the Internet, voters are able to self-educate on candidate speak and compare it to candidate action. No longer are retail campaigns able to pull the wool over the eyes of the American voter. As a result, the political battle today has keyed up with the new Internet and technology media, which may very well put print journalism out of business.

The United States Constitution was written by both populists and elitists. Founders who thrived on the notion of self-government were checked by those who saw the need for electoral colleges. Elitists and populists exist in all political parties, in all countries throughout the world. However, it is far more likely to have an elite-run government during times of voter apathy, just as it is more likely to have a populist-elected government during times of voter engagement and participation.

THE POPULIST EFFECT

American history has repeated itself with a revolving cycle of leadership between elitist and populist presidents and political leaders. As Jeffrey Bell notes, "Throughout history the presence of elites appears to be universal. Civilization is a society which generates elites."[15] In fact, throughout most of American history political equality was so insignificant that the debate between elitism and populism didn't matter. It is only with this great experiment in American politics that the light of populism has shifted the power of governance from one political party to the other. After the Nixon resignation; after the Jimmy Carter Iran hostage crisis; after the Clinton disgrace; and now after the indictments and felonies throughout the Republican Party, the torch of populism has passed and along with it, the mantle of majority party power in our state and federal capitols.

Time and again, as Jefferson predicted, a revolution has been led by the people who have demanded change in the behavior of the men and women they elect to represent them. The mystique that is the American public is quite simple. Americans would like the same work ethic, honesty and sense of fairness shown by politicians that they show in their own daily lives. The American people have come to expect the same opportunities for themselves and their families in education, the economy and national security. It is the American legacy that grants all of us our inalienable rights to life, liberty and the pursuit of happiness that we have all come to know and rely upon.

Each and every day, the people in our great nation lead from the back row. They lead in providing American-made products with pride and hard work. They lead by volunteering as firefighters in their small towns. They lead by showing up in their churches and giving a helping hand when someone is in need. This is what the people expect of politicians. Populism is the political ideology that says *demos cratia*, from the Greek, "people rule."

MACHIAVELLIAN ELITIST STRATEGIES

It was not surprising that the American Founding Fathers found the European courts as filled with elitist games of intrigue and power. Under Machiavelli's political philosophy, politics is no longer the quest to do what is good or right; it, instead, is the pursuit of total control and power. Political good will and a moral sense of leadership is considered weak in this system. Machiavelli writes that it is necessary for a young successful "prince" to learn how to *not* be good and to be able to break promises, to lie, cheat and steal.

Machiavelli pronounced that two tools were necessary to command men's behavior and thus to control humanity: the pen and the sword—or propaganda and arms. Toward this end, he believed that man is inherently selfish, and that all goods are taken at another's expense, and man behaves only by use of force. If man is inherently selfish, then only fear can effectively control him. As an example, Machiavellian wrote in 1494 that the Latin virtues meant power. Niccolo Machiavelli was explicit that one achieves power through wretchedness, cruelty and fraud.

THE ELITIST PUPPET CULTURE

If power is placed in the hands of the few, they maintain power by coercing a pseudo loyalty from a group of individuals who consider themselves lieutenants. These loyal followers. or Machiavelli lieutenants, are recruited because of their weakness and vulnerabilities, which makes them easier to control.[16] These lieutenants then are the carriers of information to their leader, as well as the purveyors of threats to those who question authority. In a free society, this notion of physical and emotional servitude to a party leader due to fear is inconceivable, yet I was informed of its existence by a well-respected lobbyist in 2004. I will refer to these lieutenants for their respective party machines as puppets.

The puppets, spies and other cast of characters from Machiavelli's *The Prince* function in our legislative bodies around this country and mirror a dark sameness. That sameness does not value loyalty from the lens of a populist or public servant; it does not recognize the greater good. Rather, these lieutenants and puppets form a secret bond, operating out of a fear of retaliation and punishment by their political class handlers.

One gray day in Madison at my capitol office brought this point home. Jared, my chief of staff for two years at this time, had been my mock-trial student several years prior to his employment as my research analyst at the state capitol. He was gifted in his ability to not only research policy issues but also in his ability to size up situations and people. His danger meter was going off that day as I picked up the phone.

"Representative, can you take this phone call from the insurance lobby?" Jared hesitantly inquired.

"Absolutely," I said, "This man is going to need to talk to us about the All Sums legislation that the paper companies are trying to push through the House Insurance Committee."

After speaking with the insurance lobbyist, I explained to Jared that this man had some information for me that he could not tell me over the phone or in our offices. "Jared, I need to go across the street to meet this guy," I began.

"In this rain? Can you trust this guy?" Jared inquired with more than an element of concern in his voice.

With less than a convincing tone, I responded, "I believe so. Besides, what do we have to lose? This guy is still talking to us."

The current ban on our legislative office from all lobbyists was a move to keep any support of my ideas or my run for Congress from finding legs. I was curious about what this man had to say—after all, he was courageous enough to break this ban.

"Don't worry, Jared, I will be all right," I said, brushing off the apparent intrigue in the clandestine meeting.

Near the intersection of North Pinckney and East Washington, I found my contact, dressed in a trench coat, ducking under a canopy while carrying a large black umbrella. We looked like a scene from *The Spy Who Came in from the Cold*, a novel written about the cold war. As I approached him, I couldn't help but think … *what next?*

The meeting came on the heels of a much-heated controversy between the paper companies lobby and the insurance companies. The rub was that the Fox River, over decades of paper-making, had been polluted with blue carbon paper. The result was a river so polluted that it had nearly been designated as a Superfund site more than once.

As I walked near the figure who had telephoned my legislative office, I wondered what was so important that this man could not just walk into my office and tell me what was on his mind. The conversation to follow would explain all of that. This man respected me enough to tell me the truth … and for that I am still thankful.

He began as soon as we made eye contact. "Terri, I have to tell you how it works around here. You have too much to offer not to know the truth." The lobbyist went on to tell his story. "It begins with the staffers, Terri. They recruit these staffers when they are young; they get something on them, 'vetting them.' They hold these secrets over their heads and threaten their jobs and their families to keep them in line."

The political games being played by the political class involved deals that not only held up the solutions to a dangerous pollution problem but also games that held the United States Constitution itself hostage. The Fox River had been slated as a possible Superfund site, but the paper companies insisted that they had a better way, and that was to form a nonprofit corporation to jointly share in the burden of cleaning up the river. They hired their own experts and their own engineers but somehow didn't complete the process. Perhaps it had something to do with the continual buyouts and sellouts of paper companies to foreign corporations. It just hadn't gotten done.

It was now time for the paper companies to deliver on a decade of promises to get the river cleaned up. Unfortunately, the tab for cleaning up the Fox River rose in direct proportion to the years of delay. An alternative source of funding, or so the paper companies thought, was to go after the insurance companies. A well-crafted plan to sue Lloyd's of London, which would then sue all Wisconsin insurance companies, was hatched. It came in the form of a bill called the "All Sums Bill."

The problem with "All Sums" was twofold: first, the costs of dredging, transporting polluted sludge and land-filling kept changing. And second, the United States operates under something called the Constitution, which is solidly placed on the theory of contract law.

Although legislators understood the pain of those representatives of the Fox River area and the need to assist the paper companies, it became difficult to justify the violation of contract law and the insurance companies who had already taken on the risk of insuring paper companies and paying out for the Fox River cleanup. The question became "What is the junior speaker to do?" And, "Who should pay more for the cleanup?"

The answer was "winners and losers." There were winners, designated by the junior speaker, with corresponding pressure applied by the caucus whips to influence our votes. Remember that six-foot-ten buddy who resembled Herman Munster in our caucus? He shined in his attempts to intimidate on this issue. The winners were decidedly the paper companies this time, which meant that the losers would be the insurance companies. This required the legislature vote on a bill to sue Lloyd's of London, and thereby, Lloyd's of London would sue all of our insurance companies for money.

How did the junior speaker determine the winner on this deal?

The insurance lobby made several observations over this transaction, as lobbyists are prone to do. First we need to ask who stood against the illogical and unconstitutional reopening of contracts after they had already been paid out? The answer would be that I did... as did a very few others in my caucus. My argument was that we could not violate the Constitution, which was based on contract law. Frankly, this is a tough issue but winners and losers should not have been a roll-of-the-dice answer.

This insurance lobbyist gave me the straight skinny—my caucus was controlled by its staffers, who leaned on their legislative bosses to fall in line. How did they do that? It became all about threats, fear and intimidation. A common threat was, "If you don't weigh in on this for us, we won't help you with your next election and we will make sure you have a primary." This winner/loser debate would have other consequences even more directly linked to quid-pro-quo politics.

Modern-day fear and intimidation appears to be Machiavellian leadership, according to this confession by one courageous lobbyist who dared to tell the truth. It all made sense; I had seen it in practice.

POPULISTS VS. PUPPETS

The eternal struggle between free and bought, people and party elites, oppressed and dictators can be shown throughout world history. It is the politics of fear that has been attributed to Machiavelli and his mastery of puppet-styled politics. The father of modern politics, as Machiavelli (1496–1527) is known, created an amoral philosophy that negates virtue and the moral essence of leadership. Machiavelli redefines virtue as totalitarian control. He was the first to define all political goals around the "complete control of men's minds and bodies," through the use of propaganda and military might. Machiavelli believed that the internal makeup of all mankind is selfishness and fear. His definition of virtue was totalitarian control.

Populism and the principles that founded the United States of America are the direct opposite of "control by a few." Perhaps this is why our Founding Fathers detested the spies and political games that sprang from the political intrigue in the European courts. The royals lived under an illusion of power, in the eyes of our founders. Real power for Americans has always been in the freedoms and liberties of a free people who self-govern. The expectation of a free and open society, then, is that the individual has value and inalienable rights that cannot be taken away by government.

Our Bill of Rights and Constitution are populist contracts, drafted at a time when self-government was a dream to be fought for. They became beacons of light to the world that decried the elitist politics of fear. It is our American Constitution that calls for a government system of checks and balances in order to protect the rights of the individual and the governance of the majority. And it is through the creation of co-equal branches of government—executive, legislative and judicial—that our rights as a free people are protected from tyranny. It is the U.S. Constitution that serves as a lasting contract with the American people. And it is through this contract that populism lives, often despite political parties.

THE SMALL BUSINESS REGULATION REFORM ACT OF 2004: AN EXAMPLE OF POPULISM VS. PUPPETS

Front-row puppets who rule with what is tantamount to fall-in-line dictums will no doubt never understand the integrity principles of populist thinking. Puppets are far more adept at the Machiavellian rule of fear and punishment. That is why the American voter needs to continually self-educate on the issues and the candidates. The following account is intended to illustrate the struggle between populism and elitist thinking in the lawmaking process.

I was committed to the Small Business Regulation Reform Act, as I was myself a small-business person. As an education consultant in private business, I not only needed to keep up my certifications and stay ahead of the research, but I also needed to wade through the bureaucracy of paperwork and regulations required by state and federal government. It was my compassion for small-restaurant owners and other small-business owners that I tapped into how I could help them cut through the red tape that held them back. The American economy is dependent on the survival and growth of small business; in fact, 80 percent of all new jobs arise from small business.

There were too many laws in the Wisconsin state legislature that were passed for self-promotion and interest-group gratification, both of which had little to do with helping small business stay in business or create more jobs. The Small Business Regulation Reform Act required the state of Wisconsin and our administration to tag all business-related bills with an economic impact statement. That meant that for every bill drafted that affected small business, a financial impact statement needed to accompany it. Lawmakers were now made aware of their actions and economic impact on small business. The Small Business Regulation Reform Act was groundbreaking, gaining the notice of the Small Business Administration (SBA) in Washington DC. In fact, my office received a letter directly from the head of the SBA, thanking me for my leadership in getting this reform through committee and up for consideration. What was the problem, then? My name—McCormick—was on the bill. Once again, it became a problem that my own name appeared on my work, and it was being recognized by the Small Business Administration in Washington.

I had been here before. Without a "most favored puppet" status from the front row, my work was destined for the trash bin—or more likely, the desk drawer of some lifer politician who would resurrect my work after I had gone.

The Small Business Regulation Reform Act seemed doomed—that is, until pressure from the White House came to bear on my junior speaker and majority leader. It appeared that President Bush was expected to attend a 2004 political rally for his reelection bid. More to the point, the White House became interested in economic development models that could be used to lift the credibility of the president's domestic policy. The Small Business Regulation Reform Bill was evidently one reform that the White House saw as just such a national model.

The SBA had been kept apprised of the progress of my bill by the National Federation of Independent Business (NFIB). Both groups were becoming more and more anxious about the stall on the bill's progress, as created by the junior speaker. This bill provided a collaborative network of small-business owners around the state that would, for the first time, require financial impact statements on politicians' bills and regulations that adversely affected small business.

This was a novel approach to governing—to require the politicians to think before they legislated against the growth of small business and the jobs that they were creating. The National Federation of Independent Business was pushing this business regulation reform as a must-have policy for business growth, and the SBA and NFIB were willing partners in a coalition that extended from Madison to Washington to get it passed.

It was when my research assistant Jennifer Streblow phoned me on my cell that I began to understand the importance and immediacy of our proposal. Streblow was more than a bit perplexed and rattled as she gave me the news. "I thought someone was playing a joke on me," she said, her voice rising in excitement. "But he was serious. He said it was the White House calling for Representative McCormick, and he wanted to know when our Small Business Regulation Reform Bill was up for a vote." As she relayed the phone call to me, I wondered how the junior speaker was going to squash this one.

I have to admit, I was more than a little stunned at the magnitude of the support for the reform. All I could manage to say was, "Great, maybe now the speaker will stop sitting on the bill!"

Streblow responded this time in a strained yet urgent tone. "You don't understand; the White House said that bill had *better* get up for a vote today! The president wants to use it in a speech tomorrow in Milwaukee."

When I arrived at my seat in the back row of the caucus room, I expected the usual flack. Instead, I was met by Majority Leader Mick Foti. "Terri, the White House called my office," he said, straining to control his excitement.

I responded, "I know; they have been pressuring me to get my bill up for a vote. What do I do about the junior speaker?" I asked for Foti's help in breaking the blockade that the speaker had on all of my work.

"We have to get that bill up for a vote; the White House called me," he said again in disbelief.

This time the political muscle was on my side, or so it appeared. It may have had to come from the White House but evidently, that's what it took to break the junior speaker's embargo on my work. Later that day on the legislative floor, without notice, my Small Business Regulation Reform Bill was brought up for a vote. Unfortunately, the Democrats could see a problem with my political party. It was unusual for the Republican front row to support my work. Who knew? It didn't take an act of God, but it did take an act from the White House. The bill sailed through the first two readings, but its third reading was delayed by the Democrats' front row, who sensed the significance of the legislation. Usually, the junior speaker stalled and prevented all of "McCormick's" bills from a vote.

The president would need to use another example of excellence in economic development and business reform in his speech in Milwaukee the next day. It would appear that those issues were not a priority for the junior speaker, who was on a quest to "be somebody."

Bill Smith, President of the National Federation of Independent Business and the business community attend the bill signing for the 'Small Business Regulation Reform Act.'

OLD STYLE POLITICS AND MACHIAVELLIAN CONTROL

The easiest way to control the behavior of someone serving in office is to employ his or her staffers to run the political campaigns. This is how the old-style politic was run before I came to the capitol. This is an easy control mechanism when the leadership of the majority and minority parties have the ability to hire, fire and remove staff at will—or altogether, if they do not maintain loyalty to the leadership in the front row. I quickly realized that I needed to hire members of the press, or "outsiders," if I were to build a counterforce against the culture of control.

That's right—staffers are hired by the head of their political party and placed into legislative offices in order to report back to their front rows. Political spying is a part of the puppet culture, all the way up the food chain to the leadership in both political parties. Both political parties have studied this playbook. Transparency and the Internet is the only way to break the cycle. No doubt tremendous pressure was placed on my staff for being independent thinkers. My last chief of staff reported that the chief clerk threatened him for using a Gannett news service to save money in getting out my legislative newsletters. Why? It saved money. No doubt it was because the front row couldn't control my message or timing!

Step aside, old company stores and union thugs of the past; step forward, political whips bent on keeping the rank-and-file in line. For the most part, this is a group of twentysomething and thirtysomething political staffers, recruited by their party leaders for the express purpose of guaranteeing control over the system. It is not about party ideology, ethics, morality or even interest-group politics, as much as it's about clicking your heels, raising your arm to the sky and saluting those who played the games to get them to the front row.

LOCAL ELECTIONS AND PUPPET INFLUENCE

If you believe you are immune from Machiavellian influences in local politics, think twice. Whether you're a voter or a candidate, Machiavellian influences are at all levels of politics. Local elections are run by the people, right? Not necessarily. Shadow political parties are often used by county, state and federal party machines to keep an eye on what is going on at the grassroots level. After all, political parties want to make sure the "right" person is recruited to run for political office. In fact, young campaign workers are sometimes recruited as "soldiers" who are taught the ways of the party machine, so that when they are ready, they may be recruited up the party ladder.

So what's to become of these young campaign workers who do what they are told and play whatever tricks they are advised to play? They are promoted up the staffer ranks, of course, to a full-time staff position in our state and federal capitols. What is the lesson learned by these twentysomething campaign workers? Too often, it is *all is fair in love, war and politics*. Most profoundly, these young campaign workers learn that politics is only a game, and they all work for the head politico in office—the speaker, majority leader or minority leaders of their respective parties. "Controlled staffers" do not work for their assigned legislators, and they certainly do not for the voters back in the district.

How do we fight back? Citizen-run campaigns must become the norm in our local, state and federal elections, if we are to counter machine candidates. We the people need to get involved on every level. We must get out of our armchairs, turn off our televisions and radios and put down our biased newspapers. We must stop surfing the Internet to read the blogs that are written, far too often, by "wack jobs of hate and negative ideas."[17] The only way we can make a difference is to personally get involved.

Citizen activists make all the difference in entering voter lists, mailing out literature, taking phone calls and going door-to-door with candidates. The only way to ensure that local governments serve the people is for we the people to step up and volunteer our time and talent on local elections. Our representative democracy comes alive when we make our own choices, support integrity leaders and make well-informed decisions about our political leaders.

POPULIST REFORM LEADERS IN AMERICAN HISTORY

There are periods in our nation's history that are marked by populist reform and public opinion. Thomas Jefferson's grassroots political party is one such period, with the transition in 1789 of the Democratic-Republicans from the more elitist Federalist Party.

Abraham Lincoln was the champion of populism during the 1860s and the Civil War, as the radical Republican. Lincoln radically insisted on equal rights for all men. Teddy Roosevelt ushered in the third wave of populism between 1900 and 1920, during the progressive era, with the nation's first presidential primaries, as opposed to party-boss appointment. Teddy Roosevelt loosened the grip of the money changers with anti-trust laws, referendums and recalls.

The next populist wave can be traced to the 1960s civil rights movement, beginning under John F. Kennedy and Robert Kennedy.

Changes such as the Voting Rights Act of 1965, and California's Proposition 13 in 1978 are two such reforms brought about by changes in popular opinion. Populist leadership in politics requires not only a compassion for the people and understanding of public opinion, but at its core, it also requires the belief in the will of the people. Great populist leaders in wartime were Lincoln, Wilson, Roosevelt, and Churchill, who all have been described throughout history as eloquent speakers, both in their content as well as their style. All of these leaders had, at their core, a belief in self-government and a rejection on all levels to dictatorial systems of their wartime enemies.

POPULISM BEGINS WITH THE GRASSROOTS

Grassroots are "we the people." There are leaders among us who are leading right from where they are. Brown County, the largest county in my congressional district, just experienced a GOP revolution when the residents of that county took back their own party's political governing body. It wasn't easy—the people organized themselves, wrote their own bylaws and recruited leaders from within. Most important, they recruited those leaders based on ability and merit. Professionalism and accountability to the people of their own county became the norm. Anything has become possible once again, as the people create their own destiny and run their own governments.

CHAPTER SUMMARY

- Elitist and populist modes of politics have diametrically opposed goals, tactics and methods of working.
- Transparency in office is a viable, noble and achievable goal; various strategies for transparency are worth implementing.

Some responsibility rests upon the conduct of our own affairs.

—Winston Churchill, March 26, 1936,
Preparing for the German Threat

CHAPTER SEVEN

CAMPAIGNS, DIRTY TRICKS & ELECTION ENGINEERING

MYTH:

Free elections and campaigns are
guaranteed by the Constitution.

REALITY:

Elections are guaranteed, but that won't
stop the power-hungry
from trying to manipulate the system.

*There is so much lying in the world, especially in politics, that telling the
truth can easily shock people to the point of being scandalous.*

—**Craig Crawford (*The Politics of Life*, 2007)**

Truth tellers get caught.

—*Oscar Wilde*

Campaigning is tough business. It takes someone with a lot of inner strength, a lot of community connections and a bit of money to make a solid run for office. Those of us who run "grassroots campaigns" understand just how difficult the road is for those who play by the rules. Yet there exists a breed of politician who does not follow the same road. This chapter is not about political corruption as an ending. Rather, it openly discusses old-style politics as a beginning, reveals the tactics of dirty campaigns and offers voters a strategy to determine a good candidate. It's an appeal to all of us to do something about it!

STAKEHOLDER POLITIC

The political class would have you believe that it is all about ideology—left/right or liberal/conservative—but is it? What if I told you that the political class in both major political parties is only interested in reelection in a quest for power and control? What if I told you that political elections are all about energizing their respective bases by evoking emotional-social issues to signal a particular voting response. Wake up, America, lest we all turn into Pavlovian voting dogs.

Modern interest group politics posed by the political class in both the Democrat and Republican parties represent a stakeholder politic that serves two purposes. First, it provides the campaign cash needed to guarantee the majority party's position in power. And second, it guarantees access to government for interest groups invested in one political class' line of thinking over the other. The voters, in many instances, are just obstacles that need to be charged up, like a battery, and then spun in a cylinder, so to speak.

Are there checks and balances to curtail possible abuse of power in public office? Yes, there are constitutional checks and balances, and there are public servants who freely self-limit their terms and walk away from power. Former representative Joe Scarborough (R-Fla.) commented on MSNBC's *Morning Joe* on April 1, 2008, "Good government needs two things: term limits and the healthy friction that comes with the constitutional separation of powers between the legislative, executive and judicial branches."

There is no question: healthy and open debate is preferred to top-down vertical stakeholder standoffs. Silo or vertical politics has resulted in political rancor freezing legislatures across this country. Democrat and Republican unwillingness to put the public's interests first is an old political culture that must be transformed to a new culture of solving problems.

Politics, in its simplest form, is the distribution of scarce resources. It may represent dollars or gasoline, and it involves two sets of diametrically opposed people engaged in intellectual battle. It may involve interest groups and politicians working to solve great problems for the public's behalf. In the old-style politic, it was reminiscent of a sixth-grade dance, with one group lining up on one side of the room, and the other group on the other side.

DEMOCRATIC VOTING BLOCKS

Democrats are, in large part, supported by voting blocks of women, minorities and trade and professional union members. From a social perspective, Democrats tend to be pro-choice, pro-environment and pro-government programs. Democrats typically favor a *noblesse oblige* philosophy, supporting the case that "nobles" (or people of means) must provide for the less fortunate. Southern Democrats throughout the 1800s carried this philosophy from their plantation economies into the Civil War. President John F. Kennedy altered these attitudes in the 1960s.

REPUBLICAN VOTING BLOCKS

Republicans are generally supported by a voting block consisting of older white men and, to a lesser extent, women and minorities. The Republican groups who tend to be fiscally conservative are farmers, builders, realtors and business groups. Social conservative groups who are more likely to be Republican are pro-gun rights, pro-family, pro-life and pro-military. The origins of the Republican Party date back to the Civil War and the party's first president, Abraham Lincoln. The Republican platform's main objective at that time was to preserve the

Union against the secession of Southern Democrats and plantation owners.

POPULIST POLITICS

Republican origins embrace the populist agenda of "we the people" and "people-run government" with guaranteed rights and responsibilities under the U.S. Constitution. The Radical Republican platform expanded the Bill of Rights and opportunities to all Americans under Abraham Lincoln. Populists and rugged individualists believe in their own ability to raise themselves up and out of poverty. It is the American way! From our nation's first immigrants to the courageous leaders who have dared to take on world despots and dictators, populists tend to vote for the person, not a political party. The self-made grandfathers of modern-day Republicans, as well as our Founding Fathers, would have cringed at the notion of a select group of elites, or neocons, thinking and making decisions for the people.

ELITIST POLITICS

A speech given by George W. Bush in the spring of 2008 gave an interesting view of populism and populist politics. When describing the difficulties of the American economy just weeks before he was to leave office, Bush warned that "populism is a misguided philosophy." This Republican president spoke before the New York Business Club to defend his economic policy of using a select group of individuals in his administration, who knew best.

A brand of elitist entitlement is attributed to the political class in both political parties and will usually land you in the minority. Imagine the speaker in Congress and the majority leader in the Senate as orchestra conductors. Their respective voting blocks are the orchestra. The style of music played is determined by coalition groups that surround the political parties in each house of government. Let's assume for a moment that Machiavelli is right and that politics is the art of elitist leverage, using deceptive games, fear/intimidation and ultimate control over all people at all times. One can vividly imagine the dissonance in the chords of dirty tricks and election engineering, as the front row lieutenants are forced to carry out orders from the top, like puppets on a string.

ELITIST AND POPULIST POLITICAL CAMPAIGNS CONTRASTED

Political campaigns determine which political orchestra is elected into public office. Elitist-run campaigns control everything from message, organization and money (MOM), from the top/down, through the use of lieutenants and foot soldiers, performing on cue from political play books. They prefer a "plug-and-play candidate," and they prefer staff-run offices.

Populist-run campaigns are unpredictable and, as such, genuine. They cannot be controlled or contrived and are dependent on the talent and abilities of the candidate. They stem from citizen leaders and interest groups served by the candidate, through established relationships from the grassroots. Populist leaders are solution-oriented and manage their own offices.

The question we all should ask ourselves is, "In whose interests shall I serve?" If your answer is "the people" for the greater good, you are a populist. If your answer is "Politics is a business, I work for my party bosses and friends," you are on a path of elitism and cronyism.

Elitist	Populist
Machiavellian	We the People
Control Mechanisms	Faith in the Process
Lieutenants & Foot Soldiers	Visionary Leaders to Solve Problems
Elite Elections	**Populist Elections**
Mt. Madison/Washington	Grassroots
Top down & Rank/File	Ground up & Person/Person
Data & Numbers (MOM)	Establish Relationships

Contact Voters 4 times	Purpose/Call to service
Retail Politics with Playbooks	Of, By and For the People
"Plug & Play"	"One of Us!"
Staff-run offices	Citizen-lead organization

DIRTY TRICKS AND ELECTION ENGINEERING

The fifteen tactics outlined below reveal a few strategies used in old-style political campaigning. It is hoped that you will take these as examples of politics at its worst and either become a voice for change or a more informed voter.

Perception is reality in the political arena. In fact, politics pulls directly from the strategies of marketing and intellectual warfare in equal proportions. If human beings were as easily manipulated as some in politics would like to believe, all it would take for a candidate to win would be to touch voters four times! That would include a hand shake, a card in the mail, a radio ad and a knock on the door by a volunteer. If that is indeed the case, we as voters must be aware of the forms of political messages so that we may better discern fact from fiction.

TACTIC NO. 1: CREATE AN ILLUSION OF THE PERFECT CANDIDATE

The perfect family, perfect spouse and neighbors are all a first step in creating the right image on political campaign literature. Your first campaign piece is a bio piece that shows off your family and your personal and professional accomplishments. However, politics is like a Hollywood movie set—some sets are barren, with only a few pictures scattered on the wall. Others have the depth and breadth of the horses, the ranch, and the farmhouse, complete with family and livestock. It is up to the voter to determine if the candidate lives where he says he lives, has the background he is claiming and has actually served as the church bell choir director back home. If we don't do our homework to expose imposters before they rise to power, shame on us.

TACTIC NO. 2: STRAW MAN POLITICS (SHOW ME WHO TO BLAME SO THAT I KNOW WHO NOT TO VOTE FOR!)

Straw man politics is the most commonly used tactic in political campaigns. If you need someone to hate and someone to blame in order to rally your base, straw man politics is the strategy to use. This tactic, like all political diversions, is intended to keep voters' eyes off the ball. The last thing a candidate wants is for the voters to realize that his/her opponent is better qualified and has better ideas on the issues at hand. Instead, straw man politics is intended to be used as a tool to demonize your opponent.

TACTIC NO. 3: CREATE A CRISIS (WITHOUT A CRISIS, WE CAN'T MOTIVATE THE VOTERS!)

Most famous is the phrase "Wag the dog," made popular in Joe Klein's *Primary Colors*. This is a classic fear-mongering strategy that paints a scenario of an inevitable war or national crisis. This create-a-crisis tactic is used to motivate voters by telling them the other guy will make it worse. It uses the emotion of fear to conjure up an unknown threat or enemy. The thought behind this strategy is to make people fearful so one candidate can be seen as the "only" person who can solve the crisis. The Hillary Clinton ad, "Who would you want to answer the telephone at 3:00 in the morning in the White House?" is a prime example. Obviously, you would want the heroine of the movie to answer the phone because she has the experience.

This crisis strategy is used as a perception builder. The reality is that most politicians do not want to solve your problems. Think about it: if all problems were solved, there would be no need to hire campaign fund-raisers, pay graphic artists, print literature, pay political pollsters, hire opposition researchers or orchestrate elaborate political machines.

Without problems, how would we excite and disturb the base of our respective political parties? Republicans must have big spenders and anti-gun people to vote against—or else. Democrats must have war-mongering fat cats that want to exploit everyday citizens—or else.

TACTIC NO. 4: PERSONAL SMEAR CAMPAIGN (EFFECTIVE WHEN USED IN ESTABLISHED NETWORKS)

This campaign strategy is most effective against a member of your own political party. The proverbial whisper campaign is subtle, effective and difficult to trace. It hinges on the claim that one knows his/her party competition best and the competition is flawed. Be wary of political parties and other such clubs that demand blind obedience to the party line. As proverbial sheep to the slaughter, so, too, are those who do not think for themselves, particularly when asked to follow blindly against one of their own.

John McCain was the victim of a malicious smear campaign in his presidential primary bid in 2000. How do we know? George W. Bush's communication director came clean on this topic in a recently published book. On page 149 of Joe Klein's book *Politics Lost*, Mark McKinnon, then communications director for George W. Bush, was quoted shortly after Bush's defeat in New Hampshire at the hands of John McCain:

> *"What followed, in South Carolina, was one of the most disgraceful campaigns I've ever witnessed. Bush and his minions did a clandestine demolition job on John McCain. Rumors about McCain's mental stability swirled through the state—it was said that he had been brainwashed during the six years he had been imprisoned and tortured by the North Vietnamese; it was said that his wife, Cindy, was a drug addict (she had used painkillers for a time); it was said that he was the father of a mixed-race child (the McCains adopted daughter who came from Bangladesh). There were no fingerprints on any of the dirt, but it was funny how these sorts of rumors always seemed to float about in campaigns run by Bush's chief strategist, Karl Rove. Rove*

used this tactic against incumbent governor Ann Richards with claims she was a lesbian."

I can tell you from experience, this particular smear campaign made it to Wisconsin. A political insider close to the Bush 2000 campaign repeated these same statements to me. What was my reaction? "That is ridiculous; knock it off."

TACTIC NO. 5: NEGATIVE CAMPAIGN ADS (WHY NEGATIVE CAMPAIGNING? BECAUSE IT WORKS!)

The vast majority of Americans tire of attack politics, yet attack politics changes people's voting behaviors. Here is an example. How many times have you heard that people just don't care to vote for either candidate? When both candidates beat each other up in television and radio ads, someone has just lost votes. If you have an unpopular candidate who cannot compete on the field of ideas, the strategy is to attack the opponent in hope of raising his/her negatives.

The manipulation of public perception is a complicated one—and it works. There is a demographic of trusting, loyal and supportive voters who are best served by one political ideology over the other. When one candidate cannot compete through honest and clear policy statements, the old-style politics reverts to throwing the dirt. Voters become confused, believing in the end that there is no difference between the candidates. Smear campaigns may serve to keep people from voting all together. Caution: the smear campaign against your own party member may boomerang. If the least popular candidate is weak and happens to win a party primary, it is likely that he/she will lose the general election.

TACTIC NO. 6: SUPPRESSING THE VOTE (A COMMON TACTIC FOR THOSE WITH HIGH NEGATIVES)

The unlikable candidate is more likely to run a negative campaign, in hopes of driving his opponent's negatives up as high as his. In 2008, I watched a local judicial race with great interest. Negative ads were used to distort the candidate's record. In this case, the negative ads were intended to suppress the vote and discourage voter trust and confidence in the incumbent judge. The malicious attacks backfired when the incumbent judge went on the airwaves, asking people to go vote. She didn't tell voters how to vote, but she did tell the public that her opponent was trying to get them to stay home. "Don't let the negative ads win and drive you away from the polls."

What were the results? The voters were awake. And the incumbent judge won with a three-to-one margin. Remember, the only candidates who win when the voters stay home are the bullies who wield the mud of negative campaigns. The only candidates who like to wrestle in the mud are the pigs. So what's a voter to do? Pay attention to the issues and the facts, and don't be diverted from your constitutional right to vote.

TACTIC NO. 7: CARICATURE POLITICS (SENATOR OBAMA IN NATIVE AFRICAN ATTIRE)

The tactic of painting an image of a turban and long African robe is effective when it appears with false information: "He is a Muslim; his middle name is Hussein." Humor creates a track to long-term memory, even though it may be malicious and distort the truth, as this example does. It combines the tactics of name-calling, suppressing the vote and distorting the truth in one powerful picture. As is often the case, a picture paints a thousand words. A false picture distorts a thousand truths.

TACTIC NO. 8: FLIP-FLOPPING THE NEGATIVE ADS INTO THE TRUTH

One of my favorite types of character ads is when there is truth in the statement and the character created is designed to accentuate the truth. This is all a matter of perspective, but using a long nose and calling someone Pinocchio is effective when a politician is often caught changing his or her story and deceiving the people. A caution with this political tool: going negative will anger potential supporters, and you may lose them with this form of negative campaigning. In many states, you will lose votes by disrespecting your opponent. I would not recommend its use.

TACTIC NO. 9: SPIN CITY AND THE POWER OF ANONYMITY (THE POWER OF 527S AND INTEREST-GROUP SPENDING)

In the political ad world, consumers of politics should do continual fact checks before believing whatever they see in print. (As a matter of fact, be skeptical of everything that appears in all print and consider the source.) The deceptive world of politics requires that we all do our own research and fact checking. The "527" groups are political action committees with the ability to spend unlimited dollars on political campaigns, with no ability to trace where the dollars are coming from (thank you, senators Russ Feingold and John McCain). Donors behind these groups are seldom revealed or tracked and often include corporations and other political action committees. The Wisconsin Democracy Campaign reported that there were only seventeen individuals behind the millions of dollars of "issue advertising" in elections in the state of Wisconsin alone. Political shadow groups like 527s, are usually named something benign, such as Citizens Action Committee, Greater Wisconsin Committee or Save Our Families Committee. Examples of 527s exist on both sides of the political aisle, destroying candidates' reputations, livelihoods and political careers under the cloak of anonymity.

TACTIC NO. 10: POLITICAL CHECKMATE (THE PARALYSIS OF BOTH POLITICAL PARTIES)

Extreme partisanship is known as "silo" or "vertical" politics. It was described by both 2008 Republican and Democratic presidential candidates Mike Huckabee and Barack Obama in the same way. They agreed that it is a top-down, high-partisan form of politics that has pitted the two political parties completely against each other. There is no compromise; there is only win/lose debates. In a political silo, there is no place for problem solvers. Problem solvers are traitors who are disloyal to their party leaders, who are doing what they are told. Vertical interests lie in maintaining top-down silos of power and finding fault with the other political party. After a decade and more of finger-pointing and rancor-filled debate, it is now time for the people's work to get done. The American people, in a unified voice all over this country, have awakened, and they have voted this kind of political animal out of public office.

TACTIC NO. 11: STAGING A RÉSUMÉ (IS IT FRAUD, OR IS IT ACTING?)

This tactic is used more than voters would like to believe. Remember the Hollywood movie-set tactics of creating a phony life as it relates to résumés and job performance in order to sell a political candidate. In the bid for Congress in 2006, my primary opponent used a real company as a set for his television motion picture–like political ad. The staging of an entire company came complete with an unwitting cast of company employees, who had never heard of the candidate before the day of production.

Testimony and endorsements presented by employees were scripted by no one the employees knew or had ever met. What was worse, the employees were led to believe that they were being filmed to promote their own company and their own CEO, who happened to have the same first name as my primary opponent. This elaborate scam to create a résumé ended up being a blatant attempt to defraud the public. The scandal came to light when one of the manufacturing employees leaked his story to the press. It then became clear that employees of companies don't like playing the stooge in a political film script. The American gut check is evidently still very much alive and well.

TACTIC NO. 12: SMOKE-AND-MIRRORS PRESS (PRESS PEOPLE WHO BLUR REALITY ARE NOT JOURNALISTS!)

The "fourth branch of government," according to George Washington's letters and diaries, is a free and appropriate press. In fact, our nation's first president believed we would not need political parties, if only we had an effective press. Unfortunately, the world of advertising and media monopolies are a modern reality. Large amounts of campaign cash are targeted toward television, radio and the print medium. The quality of news reporting becomes dependent on the cash, rather than the qualifications, platforms and ideas of the candidates.

Further, the media is erupting with the advent of radio "shock jocks" who are in the entertainment business, rather than the news business. Radio talk, spin-based on political and advertising bottom lines, is the result. Radio spin-talkers too often have become pseudo journalists, ginning up their fictional accounts and passing it off to the public as news. Rush Limbaugh provided a classic example of this interesting blend of entertainer-turned-pseudo-journalist in his remarks shortly after the 2006 midyear Republican congressional losses. "I'm glad they all lost. ... Now I don't have to carry water for them anymore."

Modern technology and the downturn of the print industry have revealed yet another information source, the Internet blogger. Internet bloggers are often anonymous or, worse, closely aligned with a political party in a purposeful attempt to fabricate and manipulate the news. The creep of Internet blogging onto the pages of our newspaper editorials and news stories is a trend that, if not reversed, could permanently lower the credibility of newspaper journalism entirely.

The solution to all of these challenges is us—you and me! Today, more than at any time in our nation's history, the people have the opportunity to turn off the noise and research their own issues, candidates and political parties. The American people now have the wherewithal to demand the news from credible sources from all mass media forms. Whether you get your news from television, radio, Internet blogging or electronic news media, being informed is up to you. The quality of our government depends on it.

Let's focus on the skills you may need to debunk and fumigate political rhetoric and personal agendas in various forms of media:

1. *Print medium.* Consider the source. Please look at a news story with an eye to ensuring that the basics—who, what, where, when, why—are there. You may be shocked and surprised to find that many journalists do not cover basic elements of the story. Fewer use the required two sources of information when writing their stories. Be sure that source information is quoted so that you may "consider the source." Finally, if the news story editorializes or uses shock news, know that you are about to read a biased article.

2. *Television news.* Use the television station's Web site to verify all news with credible sources and the same rules as above. The rule of thumb of most news stories, particularly on television, is "If it bleeds, it leads" on the evening news. The thirty-second sound bite is considered too long for a television news program. Be wary of the news anchors who do not read credible news stories in a professional tone but who instead present the news with an "Aw, shucks, that shouldn't of happened; that was mean" demeanor. Real journalists on television speak with appropriate syntax and diction, and they read well-researched and sourced news stories to their viewers. Watch the comedy channel if you want to be entertained.

3. *Radio news.* Real news on the radio should not be confused with "shock jocks." When a talk-show announcer or radio newsperson is a journalist, he or she will share sources, credit those sources and have the ability to understand complex issues. He or she will be so clear in the intent to report the news in a credible, reliable and meaningful way that you will understand the who, what, where, when and why of the story. A shock jock's job, on the other hand, is to sway you and sometimes manipulate your way of thinking. Don't be fooled or suckered into believing that shock jocks are giving you an unbiased news story. These entertainers on the radio have a personal or professional agenda.

4. *Blogs and Internet stories.* Use credible news sources if you are researching the news on the Internet: Reuters, *Wall Street*

Journal, New York Times, major news publications and research institutes would be my first pass. Local network news may work for a local slant on the news, but be sure that the local journalists understand the difference between opinion and credible journalism. On the very bottom of the journalistic totem poll is the blogger. This is not a worthy source for your news. Bloggers are in the opinion business, with no apparent ethics or professionalism required. Often, bloggers vent from the shadows and attack others for sheer enjoyment. On rare occasions, you may find a blogger who has credible things to say, but overall, stick with Reuters or the *Wall Street Journal* as credible news sources.

Remember to consider the source of the information, and when it doubt, please use the Society for Professional Journalists Code of Ethics as your guide (it can be found at www.spj.org/ethicscode.asp). Journalists must abide by the same conflict of interest and ethics codes as public officials. Personal bias and personal agendas are not acceptable. Marketing departments should not reward political candidates during election time with dollars to buy air time. Pay-for-play politics can pollute our free and appropriate press, just as assuredly as it pollutes public policy.

TACTIC NO. 13: ELECTION ENGINEERING (GROOMING THE CANDIDATE)

This form of campaign engineering happens pervasively in both political parties. A Republican county chairman expressed "the lack of moxie" some candidates demonstrate in an election. Groomed candidates and natural leaders that rise on their own merits frame the leadership debate between elitist and populist-bound candidates. The elite stance is based on the assumption by these "groomers" that hand-chosen candidates are the candidates for whom the public will vote. To quote a former Republican state party chairman, "Leadership needs to take a big step back and see if these groomed candidates can handle the competition."

TACTIC NO. 14: BOYCOTT WOMEN FROM POLITICS

Two women Republican Senate and House candidates, Rep. Katherine Harris and Rep. Deborah Pryce, faced a wall of running against the party-groomed candidates. Katherine Harris was a sitting congresswoman, running for the U.S. Senate in 2006. Her party members said publicly, "If she cares about her party, she'll be out [of the race] in a month." Congressional leader Rep. Deborah Pryce's own party spoke out against her, saying, "She's not been a strong spokeswoman" for the party's agenda. What's amusing about this banter is that both women are strong within their party. They are outspoken advocates for their districts. They also have proven to be tough to beat.

On my January 2006 visit to Washington, I met with a Ms. Block, who represented a law and lobby firm that was described as a "professional company." It was my scheduling assistant's understanding that Ms. Block was someone to see, in that she helped Republican women running for Congress. She described herself as a principal in the law firm that represented Fannie Mae, the U.S. Chamber of Commerce, Pharma and Pfizer to mention a few. Block's background consisted of a BA from a Southern university, as well as experience with Bush–Cheney 2000, staff assistant with the Reagan White House, and various other government affairs positions.

As a senior partner, Ms. Block explained that she led a "value-in-electing-women political action committee," which had been formed by Newt Gingrich to "keep women busy on social planning while the men in Congress debated the issues."

Okay … I was being told by a woman with a bachelor's degree, posing as a senior partner in a law firm in Washington, that congressional women in the GOP needed to be kept busy instead of being bored with the real stuff. I listened in disbelief, incredulous that I was hearing this in the year 2006.

As our conversation continued, I pulled a packet of information from my briefcase; it contained my curriculum vitae and education credentials, as well as several pages of major policy initiatives I had written and led. The small-business regulation reform was supported with a letter and personal note from the president of the U.S. Small Business Administration in Washington, an appointee of the Bush administration.

Ms. Block's response to my packet was quick, succinct and emphatic: "Well, we can't help you. You need to be for abortion under all circumstances and then we will give you all the money you need. Unless you change your policy position for abortion, we can't help you." She offered a slight smile and then added, "Maybe you should talk to Senator Kay Bailey Hutchinson. You seem to be the kind of Republican that she is."

TACTIC NO. 15: YOU SCRATCH MY BACK, AND I WILL BUY YOURS

Old-style politics is as basic as the bullies on the playground in grammar school. When enough of them get together, they form gangs (associations). When such an association takes matters into its own political hands, it creates a "shopping list" for their state and federal legislatures. The next step then is the membership shake-down for contributions. Front-row leaders in both political parties argue before their supportive associations that money is needed in large quantities in order to put people in public office who will deliver their shopping list. **Long's *Almanac of Political Corruption Book*** (2007) discusses this particular tactic at length.

Political bosses were once thought of as having an antiquated role in American history. They were driven to extinction by the likes of Wisconsin governor and U.S. senator "Fighting" Bob La Follette and President Teddy Roosevelt in the early 1900s. The political corruption of these party boss elites, or "money grubbers," as Roosevelt called them, was countered by progressive independents, who were the populists of their time, standing on the side of the people. Roosevelt's actions in office were to usher in anti-trust laws and labor laws that reformed working conditions in the nation's factories.

Sound familiar, one hundred years later?

CHANGE FOR LEADERS AND CITIZENS

All of these tactics create an atmosphere of cronyism and favoritism. When races are not run ethically and dirty tricks monopolize the scene, don't underestimate voters' ability to spread that word using modern technology. Blogs have become the public's voice in the political process.

When used by credible people, however, who attach their names and political purpose, blogs can represent citizen leadership. Kerry Thomas is such a citizen leader. His blog article is reprinted in its entirety, below:

When the GOP Get Behind Closed Doors
Kerry Thomas (Republican), January 15, 2006

It's that time of year. Time to pull the boots out of the closet and put 'em on. It's getting pretty deep around here. No, not the snow. I'm talking about the Republican rhetoric and double speak. Like most storms, this one started innocuously enough. Just a simple e-mail sent out by a local Republican leader to his favorite supporters.

But this year's Republican candidates have more to be concerned about than just their Democrat opponents. This year's Republican candidates also have to watch out for their own party officials and what they're up to behind closed doors. When I objected to the few picking the candidates for the majority of republicans, the Republican 8th Congressional District Chairman had a few interesting comments. "Leaders have to be activists as I are the most informed." [That's not a typo—that's how he wrote it.] "I have a good idea of who is a good candidate and who is not because of past training and experience."

When I pointed out that this sounded like an elitist attitude, all he could respond with was "Are you a Democrat plant? You certainly sound like it, complaining

that we are a party of elitists. That's the Democrat line."
It might be, but it's also becoming more and more clear.
GOP "leaders" like this one seems to think Republican
candidates should be selected by (as he puts it) "our best
informed Republicans."

Republican "leaders" are maneuvering behind the
scenes to position their anointed candidates at the head
of the field. All while insisting to the rest of us that the
official Party line of neutrality and equal opportunity must
be observed. I guess some of our candidates are just more
equal than others."

To confirm what you may already suspect, it's all about control. It doesn't matter how stellar a candidate's record or how much a candidate has done for the community. If the elite club wants you, you're in. If the club doesn't want you, you're no different than a salmon swimming upstream. Your efforts will not be recognized, supported or rewarded. In fact, you can bet your efforts will be misconstrued and used against you as a judgment. If you're not loyal to the pecking order already established, there will be roadblocks. Support comes only for those who respect and obey the club.

WHAT'S THE ALTERNATIVE?

Open debates in front of citizen audiences, with the press holding a big flashlight, is one alternative. Interest groups are a part of the process; there is no need to block them out. But when interest groups are abused by front rows in a "pay up or else" directive from those who want more power, there is a problem. A better use of interest-group politics would be to truly educate their members on the track records and experience of the candidates, and do something guaranteed by the Constitution: let the voters decide.

The price paid for voter manipulation and a blatant disregard for fair play is high. It leads to voter distrust and it leads to great minority-building strategies at the hands of the party elites. Just look in your history books—for every elitist who was found out, a populist president or congressional representative followed. The *New York Times* Sunday edition on April 6, 2008, blamed John Kerry's political loss in 2000 on the fact that he was an "elite."

NEGATIVE WORKS: WHAT THE RESEARCH SAYS

Political strategists closely examine opponents' messages, and then the club concocts and neatly packages what's known as a negative campaign approach. You've seen them—the candidate puts out a commercial or a brochure that shows the opposition in a negative light. It gets ugly as a candidate's character is assassinated, warranted or not. One rather famous encounter was between George W. Bush and John McCain in the 2000 presidential campaign. Bush's camp struck first, with the message that McCain's campaign was "crawling with lobbyists." McCain fought back with a rebuttal that accused Bush, saying he "twists the truth like Clinton."

Negative campaigning is not used to mobilize voters from one party or another but to demobilize them. The goal is not to prove the candidate is more worthy but that the opponent is less worthy. Yet a study conducted by researchers at the University of California–Irvine concluded that the attempts to demobilize a population from voting were not effective. The research points out that in most cases, the study subjects did not remember the negative messages. The research also indicated that those who were more likely to remember the ads were also more likely to vote, and that negative campaigning actually stimulated voter participation.

In 2000, Howard Dean and Richard Gephardt were expected to win in Iowa, but their negative campaigning cost them dearly—both lost to John Kerry and John Edwards, who opted to avoid negative campaigning. Surprisingly, the results of negative campaigning can backfire. A study conducted by researchers at the University of Missouri concluded that negative campaigns reflect just as badly on the author of the message as they do on the target. In one study sample, nearly 59 percent of respondents said that negative campaign messages made them react negatively to the candidate sponsoring the ads. That same study group found that just over 59 percent felt negatively toward the target of those ads.[18]

Despite that, negative campaigning manages to shift the focus of the campaign from the candidate's position to the opponent's weaknesses. A "successful" negative campaign can haunt the target for years beyond the current campaign. It can also cause long-term damage to the reputation of the sponsor of those messages.

IT'S THE PEOPLE'S TURN

Instead of trying to change what status-quo politicians think, I propose we change our own approach to government. We all are needed in this call for populist reforms in our government. All of us can show up and campaign for people of character. We can put up yard signs, make phone calls or contribute five dollars. It is our government and our political process—if we take it back!

The first step is to elect representatives of the people. Try the Candidate Scorecard below.

VOTER'S SURVIVAL GUIDE TO GOOD CANDIDATES
Candidate Scorecard: Finding the Candidate's Passion,
Purpose, Sincerity and Spontaneity

The Integrity Candidate	The Troubled Politician
Positive Points:	*Negative Points:*
Experience and Track Record	Dirty Tricks
Integrity and Character	Lies and Exaggerations
Ideas, Skill Sets and Solutions	Scandals and Legal Troubles
Supported by Small Donors	Money and Corruption
Strategies for Good Government	Playbook to Keep the Status Quo

---

CHAPTER SUMMARY

- The stakeholder politic model is the one in charge right now.

- Dirty tricks and election engineering has profound negative impact on today's political climate.
- Change is needed for citizens, for leaders, and for the press.

When Benjamin Franklin left Constitution Hall he was asked,
What kind of government did you give us?
What was his answer?
A republic, if we can keep it!

CHAPTER EIGHT

FRIENDLY FIRE

MYTH:

Political party members are brethren
fighting for the same cause.

REALITY:

Dysfunctional party leaders run government like a cash enterprise,
while their own members are left to clean up the mess.

*If you stand up and be counted, from time to time you may get yourself
knocked down. But remember this: A man flattened by an opponent can
get up again. A man flattened by conformity stays down for good.*

—Tomas Watson, Jr., CEO of IBM

PARTY POLITICS: SYMPTOMS OF A BROKEN SYSTEM

In August of 2006, I scheduled a series of listening sessions and meetings with citizens and local officials on the northern edge of the congressional district. There should have been push back and resistance, given the fact that my primary opponent was from this area of the state and had represented these people for nearly two decades. The welcome and openness of local officials and community members came with a distinct message of warning:

"Will you represent us, or will you represent the fat cats that put you in office?"

"Are you going to retaliate against us if we don't agree with everything you do?"

Profound sadness came over me as I visited and toured the economic condition of the Marinette, Peshtigo and surrounding areas. These citizens and constituents of my primary opponent had been ignored and, worse, repressed over the course of eighteen years with what can only be described as slum-lord representation.

City and county officials spoke in hushed tones as they told me, "My city has suffered because I don't support your primary opponent. I have never voted for a Republican, but you give me hope that the people in this region will not suffer any longer if you get elected."

It came as no surprise, given conversations like these, when I received anonymous packages in the mail. One was delivered in January 2006 and another in August 2006. The packages contained a collection of newspaper clippings from the 1987 era, nearly twenty years earlier, with a recurring theme: that I learn exactly who my primary opponent was and what his background was. There were a variety of sources listed: *Green Bay Press-Gazette*, November 30, 1989, and April 1990; *Milwaukee Sentinel*, November 27, 1990 and April 23, 1989; as well as stories from the *Wisconsin Corporate Report*, February 1988 and the *Eagle-Star*, Oconto Bureau, September 27, 1989. Most curious was a copy of a letter from my primary opponent himself, dated September 1989, to the "Legal Counsel of the Wisconsin State Elections Board."

The topic of all of the information was the first election of the junior speaker when he ran for his first state house seat in 1987. This very new and very young staffer had been hand-picked by the GOP establishment to run in a special election for Wisconsin's Eighty-ninth Assembly District seat. Well aware of the fact that a twenty-three-year-old capitol staff with little real-world or life experience faced long odds in a state assembly race, the Republican Assembly Campaign Committee and the Republican Party of Wisconsin spent nearly $19,000 on that race, a tremendous amount of money at that time for a state house seat.[19]

There were some problems, however. The news stories revealed that the candidate had apparently failed to report more than $10,000 in in-kind campaign contributions from two Republican organizations.[20] Wisconsin also had a law at that time, that limited 65 percent of a candidate's contributions from committees, such as political parties or political action committees. The law was intended to promote the influence of individuals over large organizations in the election process. The candidate had exceeded this limit by $7,607.[21]

In what amounted to a slap on the wrist, the State Elections Board ruled to fine this person six hundred dollars. The board voted four to three to reject a staff recommendation of a nearly two-thousand-dollar fine, concluding that the violations were the honest oversights of a political novice. Instead of admitting that this was an honest mistake, accepting responsibility, paying the fine and moving on, the candidate decided to fight the ruling—all the way up to the U.S. Supreme Court, which of course rejected his argument. His argument wasn't that the State Elections Board's ruling was wrong. Instead, he claimed that Wisconsin's law limiting contributions from political parties was unfair and unconstitutional. His attorney made the case to the State Elections Board that "he would not have been able to win the election without the intervention of the state Republican Party."

It all began to make sense as things came into perspective. My opponent never would have been in the House in the first place without the approval and financial backing of the GOP establishment. Now, after nearly twenty years of "carrying water" and "paying his dues," they were running the same playbook to try to get him to Washington. The playbook consisted of preprimary endorsements from GOP leaders, $5,000 contributions from Republican congressmen like the speaker and majority leader of the U.S. House,[22] large donations from special-interest groups and political action committees, and the stump speeches from the vice president and president of the United States.

I had always believed that the way to run a campaign was door-to-door, voter to voter. In the case of this mysterious package, someone had taken the time to send me these newspaper clippings. That individual wanted me to know that my congressional primary opponent had a different style than I had. From these newspaper accounts, it was as though he was from a different political party—one of entitlement and elitism. This was surely a candidate who was running for political office to "be somebody."

The desperation on the faces of the local officials I had met, as well as the stories they told, all came into perspective. The people had not poured money into the chosen candidate in their state house seat, so it was the people who suffered the consequences. In effect, they had been denied representation in their own state legislature through the manipulation of party players and big shots. And it was the people who would feel the impact of lost opportunities in jobs and support for families and children who happened to reside in a district owned and bought by one of the political machines.

POLITICAL INSIDERS AND OUTSIDERS

The notion that mountains of cash are necessary to win an election is bad news for the public. After all, that cash has to come from somewhere and, as the previous story illustrates, most career politicians would rather take the easy route, relying on large sums from special-interest groups, lobbyists, political action committees and political parties. When a candidate seeks the help of powerful groups to win an election and climb to the front row ... well let's just say that most of these groups are hoping for something in return.

The distinction between the front-row political insider and the back-row political outsider is just as wide as the difference between the ideologies of the two major political parties. Unfortunately for those of us who are Republican, we must take responsibility for the GOP majority's actions in 2006—that of quadrupling the nation's debt, record numbers of earmarks, and holding the record for fewest days in session. The do-nothing Congress was a by-product of the stalemate of silo politics. Congress did little at that time to hold back taxes, reduce the deficit or stave off the impending economic collapse and banking crisis.

During my time in the Wisconsin legislature, I witnessed numerous examples of this kind of behavior. Particularly troubling was the practice of holding campaign fund-raisers at the same time the state budget was written. Legislative leaders took the opportunity to fill their campaign accounts as they debated who would ultimately become the winners and losers of the budget process. Think of the state budget as an anticipated Christmas or holiday gift. The more anticipation a legislator could create around the excitement of a specific gift, the more control he or she could potentially demand on the lobbyists and individuals expecting a specific holiday gift.

According to the Wisconsin Democracy Campaign, the Wisconsin governor and the legislature took in over two million dollars during the first six months of 2007, while they were writing and debating the budget. Is it a coincidence that spending is on the rise yet again? Some examples are more egregious than others.

HOW MONEY CANDIDATES BUILD A BASE

Two groups with long-standing reputations for heavy activity in Wisconsin's political process are the transportation and road construction lobbies.[23] In a number of locations, Wisconsin's highway system hasn't been able to handle the increased traffic caused by population growth. The harsh winters can also take their toll on road conditions. This situation has led to numerous battles over the transportation portion of the state budget and has created a fierce competition among road builders for hundreds of millions of dollars in government contracts. Politicians are quite good at taking advantage of this type of situation.

The relationship between party leaders and road builders in Wisconsin is so notorious that it prompted an academic study at the University of Michigan in 2003.[24] Dr. Roland Zullo analyzed ten years' worth of campaign donations and government contracts. He was curious to see if there was any relationship between contributions from road builders and contracts awarded by former governors. His results were suspicious, to say the least.

Dr. Zullo's study actually found that 86.3 percent of road construction firms performing work for the state during the period of time being investigated did not make any campaign contributions to former governors. At first, this appears reassuring. After all, nearly nine of ten contractors don't make financial donations to try to influence the political process in some way. That's a good thing, right? Yes ... until you look at the size of their contracts. The average contract awarded to these firms was worth $870,000.[25]

The construction firms that chose to donate money to the governors, on the other hand, did a little bit better. The remaining 13.7 percent of government contractors all made at least one political donation to the executive branch. These donations averaged out to $4,267 for each contracting firm. Would you care to guess how much the average contract awarded to these firms was worth? Would $20,600,000 sound high? That's right. Statistically speaking, by forking over a mere $5,000 in campaign cash, a firm could increase the size of their contract by nearly $20 million.[26]

It's easy to point the finger at the big, bad corporations, but isn't that just a good business decision? Business does not set the political agenda, nor does it schedule bills for votes or appropriate funds. Business is, however, forced to play by the rules given to them by the party leaders that you and I elect for government office. Could this be a coincidence? Absolutely. That is why Dr. Zullo researched the timing of the donations in his doctoral thesis. He wanted to see if contracting firms were more likely to donate money during the months surrounding important budget votes or contract awards. Sure enough, for large contractors the timing of contract awards explained 60 percent of the campaign donations.[27]

These types of issues are certainly complex, and you are free to draw your own conclusions. Are large firms better equipped to handle large construction projects? Maybe. Do they have more resources to show their appreciation in the form of a campaign donation following a large contract award? Probably. All I know is that I was in the assembly when the former speaker approved $800 million in new highway projects, within weeks of attending a fund-raiser hosted by Wisconsin road builders and contractors.[28]

Just so you don't get the impression that this type of activity is limited to one particular political party over the other, be aware that overspending on transportation has continued under Republican and Democratic governors alike. The 2005 Wisconsin budget proposed by the governor sought to increase spending for new road projects by $64.3 million, to a total of $384.8 million over the budget period.[29] At that point, according to the Wisconsin Democracy Campaign, people and interest groups connected to road builders had already contributed $389,367 to the Democratic governor since the beginning of his career.[30]

Furthermore, the totals from the 2005 budget listed above didn't even include the $184 million in interest being charged to the taxpayers, *just to pay off the loans for previous projects.*[31] As it turns out, a 2003 state audit revealed that since 1987, Wisconsin politicians approved eight new major highway projects, worth $824 million, *that were not even requested by officials from the state Department of Transportation.*[32]

Overspending has no political affiliation. Interest groups contribute money to politicians with the power and influence to support their cause. Patrick Stevens, a lobbyist for the Wisconsin Transportation Builders Association, was recently quoted in the *Milwaukee Journal-Sentinel* as saying, "We are not partisan political activists. There is no such thing as a Democratic road or a Republican road. There are just Wisconsin roads."[33]

EXAMPLE ONE: THE ALL SUMS/FAIR CLAIM ACT OF 2005

One example of this spending pattern was the fierce battle that took place a few years back between lobbyists for the insurance and paper industries over 2005 House Assembly Bill 222. This piece of legislation was affectionately known as either "All Sums" or the "Fair Claims Act," depending upon whose spin you were buying. Unfortunately, I mean "buying," literally.

According to the Wisconsin Democracy Campaign, paper manufacturer Georgia Pacific spent $337,547 on lobbying during the first half of 2005, while the assembly was debating the bill. The Wisconsin Insurance Alliance spent $400,697. Compare those amounts to the $60,000 that each group spent in the first half of 2003.[34]

The dispute centered on the cleanup of the heavily polluted Fox River in northeastern Wisconsin. In the 1950s and '60s, paper companies began dumping waste in the river that contained chemicals that were later linked to cancer. Though this type of pollution was legal at the time, a number of paper companies eventually entered into an agreement with the federal government to pay for the cleanup of the river. The cost of this process was estimated at anywhere from $300 million to $600 million, possibly higher.[35]

With such staggering costs, the paper companies obviously had an interest in trying to get their insurance companies to pay for as much of the bill as possible. A previous court ruling had determined that environmental damages were covered under general liability insurance policies, meaning that a number of insurance companies were going to be on the hook for at least a portion of the cleanup costs. The Wisconsin Insurance Alliance acknowledged and accepted this fact. The problem was that many of the paper companies had changed ownership and switched insurance policies so many times over the forty-plus years in question that the process of determining exactly who was responsible for exactly what percentage of a half-billion-dollar liability was an absolute legal nightmare.[36]

So the stage was set for a showdown between two heavyweight political-interest groups with hundreds of millions of dollars at stake. As a member of the House Insurance Committee at the time, I had an excellent view for the fight! Bill 222 would have altered the definition of "all sums" in the books, effectively allowing the paper companies to pick one insurer, sue it for the entire cost of the cleanup, and fight it out later. In other words, it retroactively changed the definition of a contract to allow the paper companies to file a class-action lawsuit against the insurance companies.

This was a dangerous road to travel. Contracts are the basis for the United States Constitution and are critical to the health of our economic system. It seemed clear that this was a matter best left to our legal system. If the legislature intervened to change the rules of the game, it would create a dangerous precedent.

With so much money at stake, both the paper company lobby and the insurance lobby based their arguments on either the public trust or economic development. Both sides claimed that they were only concerned about cleaning up the river as quickly as possible and keeping jobs in northeast Wisconsin. Quite frankly, both groups were willing to use every trick in the book to make their case, ranging from disinformation campaigns (each side consistently accused the other of distorting the facts) to campaign contributions.

In fact, political action committee (PAC) groups representing both the paper and insurance industries donated a total of $9,500 to the house speaker *within ten days* of Bill 222's public hearing.[37] You may recall that the speaker decides which bills receive committee hearings and ultimately reach the assembly floor for a vote. It is not surprising that these two groups would attempt to get on the speaker's good side. In that the speaker was running for Congress, it's probably not a coincidence that these donations appeared in his congressional campaign account. If they were being honest with you, a few representatives would probably tell you they felt a bit of pressure from the leadership offices to vote in favor of the bill.

This scenario does illustrate something interesting about the nature of campaign donations, however. When thinking about government corruption, many people envision a quid pro quo arrangement. This would involve special-interest groups writing checks in exchange for specific favors, usually votes or support on certain legislation. This, of course, is highly illegal. And while it would be naïve to suggest this never happens, I suspect the situation described above is probably much more common. We'll call this one "playing both sides of the fence."

Both the insurance and paper company lobbyists contributed large amounts of money during this debate. One cannot make the case that money was the reason the bill eventually passed the house assembly by a vote of 49–44. Was money the reason that the bill came up for a vote in the first place? Bill 222 died in the Senate, which refused to bring it up for a vote, presumably because the issue was so complex and contentious. The Senate likely did not want to vote on a bill on which they couldn't reach a consensus and gain the votes needed to pass it. Why did the house assembly take up the issue? Could it have been the case that someone saw an opportunity to pit two powerful interest groups with deep pockets against each other? You can draw your own conclusions. However, hundreds of millions of dollars in liability payments were at stake. The serious problem of the Fox River cleanup is an ongoing issue, even at this writing.

It's simple and convenient to blame corporations and lobbyists for trying to influence the political process. By bringing this particular bill up for a vote, however, assembly leadership was, for reasons unknown, trying to pick the winners and losers in a private dispute. The paper companies had been preselected as the winners in this fight, while the insurance companies were designated the losers. The reality is that it's hard to blame these groups for taking the steps they did with such high stakes. Until we have a government that is more focused on solving problems than creating them, we can probably continue to expect more of the same.

EXAMPLE TWO: PAYING DIRTY COPS

The previous example demonstrates that in the game of intellectual tackle football that is politics, it can be difficult to determine people's motives. This is especially true when an issue is complex or when a lawmaker can hide behind excuses like "saving jobs" or "protecting the environment," as was the case during the All Sums debate. But when in doubt, "follow the money" seems to be standard political advice. Sometimes, though, politicians just can't help making their intentions a bit too obvious.

Of the common stereotypes about Republicans, being "pro-taxpayer" and "fiscally conservative" would probably be somewhere near the top of the list. You might assume that Republicans would favor business groups over unions, which have primarily supported Democrats over the years. Since both of these are reasonable assumptions, you would probably guess that Republicans would support a piece of legislation designed to ensure that taxpayers aren't paying the salaries of police officers who were fired after being charged with crimes. But you would be wrong.

Wisconsin has a law that allows Milwaukee police officers who have been fired to keep collecting full salary and benefits until all of their appeals are exhausted.[38] According to the *Milwaukee Journal-Sentinel*, the law is unique to Milwaukee, and there is no other provision similar to it anywhere in the country. The situation was highlighted by the case of a Milwaukee police officer who was fired after being charged with such felonies as substantial battery, calling in a bomb threat, bail jumping and attempting to purchase a submachine gun. In August 2006, the *Journal-Sentinel* reported that he had been receiving his full salary and benefits package for over fifteen months since his initial arrest.[39]

Three other officers were charged with crimes and fired in February 2006, and since the appeals process can take years to complete, paying officers who have been fired adds up to a considerable cost to the taxpayers. A state representative from Milwaukee introduced a bill to end this practice.[40] It seemed like a straightforward piece of legislation that taxpayers could get behind—save tax dollars by refusing to pay employees fired for cause.

There was just one problem: the Milwaukee Police Union had made a $5,000 donation to the house speaker's congressional campaign account on June 10, 2005.[41] And remember, the speaker decides which bills make it to the floor for votes. Despite the fact that the bill passed the Republican-controlled House Assembly Committee on Corrections and the Courts by an overwhelming 8–1 margin, the house speaker refused to allow the bill up for a vote by the full assembly.

Not surprisingly, both the speaker and representatives for the police union denied any relationship between the donation and the death of the bill. Plenty of people had their suspicions, however. Patrick Curley, chief of staff for Milwaukee mayor Tom Barrett, was quoted by the *Journal-Sentinel* as saying: "[This speaker] is putting the interest of the Milwaukee police union ahead of the interests of Milwaukee property-tax payers."[42]

When it comes to campaign contributions and political favors, a variation of the classic "chicken and egg" dilemma is raised. Do interest groups donate money beforehand, with the expectation of receiving something in return? Or do they make campaign donations following favorable outcomes, as a show of appreciation? Either way, this type of activity makes it appear that something suspicious is occurring and further erodes public confidence in government. It also makes it rather difficult for government leaders to say no to anyone. But they usually manage to come out on top, as they fill their campaign coffers with the cash to fight their next election battle. The loser is the taxpayer.

EXAMPLE THREE: CAPCO, 2003

One of the best examples of government failure was something I happened to come upon during my second term in the House. Depending on your personal level of cynicism, the CAPCO (short for "capital companies") program was, at best, an example of extraordinary incompetence, costing the taxpayers millions of dollars. At worst, it was a scam demonstrating government corruption at its finest.

In politics, you know you have discovered something highly questionable when colleagues in your own party start to threaten a primary challenge in your next election. Translation: you are making the party leaders nervous, and you better start following orders from the front row, or they will try to replace you with someone who will.

At the time, I was unsure exactly what I had done to warrant this kind of a threat. As chair of the Committee on Economic Development, I had been working on legislation designed to improve capital investment in Wisconsin.[43] Our state had long been a national leader in creating ideas and patents. We lagged well behind most other states, however, when it came to finding the investment dollars needed to turn those ideas into businesses and, ultimately, new jobs.

Wisconsin had passed legislation in 1998, designed to accomplish a way to find investment dollars.[44] Known as CAPCO, the program was modeled after similar legislation created in Louisiana in the 1980s and later expanded to other states, such as Florida and New York.[45] The idea behind the program was to offer tax credits to insurance companies, encouraging them to invest some of their considerable case reserves into funds set up by certified capital companies. The companies, in turn, were supposed to invest the money from these funds into small start-up business ventures. It was anticipated that these investments, administered by the capital companies, would generate a surplus of revenue, guaranteeing a return for the insurance companies, CAPCO, and the state of Wisconsin, in the form of thousands of new jobs and additional tax revenue.[46] Everybody wins, right? Wrong. When the tables are skewed, no one wins—certainly not the taxpayer.

I had been approached by several economic experts and business leaders who informed me that this program was not doing what it was designed to do. Seeing a problem in need of a solution, we jumped in and got to work. I held numerous meetings to begin crafting a model and writing a bill to promote capital investment, while guaranteeing a higher rate of return on this investment for the taxpayers. Our bill was designed to promote a more free-market–oriented method of distributing venture capital funds, along with greater levels of oversight and tighter benchmarks for success.

On September 18, 2003, I introduced House Assembly Bill 524. The bill was part of a series of economic development legislation we introduced that year, known as the "Blueprint for Change." The package was designed to stimulate the economy and create jobs through mechanisms such as capital investment, small-business regulation reform and reducing the tax burden.

The capital investment bill began to move quickly through the legislative process, passing the Committee on Economic Development unanimously on September 29 and the Joint Committee on Finance by a 12–4 vote the next day.[47] Several prominent business groups, including Wisconsin Manufacturers and Commerce, registered their support. As the bill worked its way to the assembly floor, however, pressure to kill the proposal began to rise. The lobbyists were out in force, raising questions that something was amiss. My attempt to reform the CAPCO program was halted on October 2, when House Assembly Bill 524 was "laid on the table," which is legislative speak for "Something came up and we're not going to deal with this right now." Some mysterious force was conspiring to kill my bill.

It was only a matter of time before the truth was revealed. The sudden turn of events had made people curious. State Senator Robert Cowles, a Republican from near Green Bay, had requested an investigation from the state audit bureau, the results of which triggered a report from the *Milwaukee Journal-Sentinel*.

The results were so incredible that they truly are difficult to believe. Bruce Murphy, in his article for the *Milwaukee Journal Sentinel*, quotes experts who summed it up:

> *"It's a crummy deal for the taxpayers," said Julia Sass Rubin, a Rutgers University professor of public policy, who has spent five years researching these kind of subsidies and helped defeat a similar proposal in Rhode Island. "It's a scam," said Colorado State Treasurer Mike Coffman, speaking of a*

*similar bill passed in Colorado. "I don't think there's anyone
who thinks this is a good deal for Colorado, with the exception
of those companies who lined their own pockets."*[48]

According to the state audit,[49] three firms had been certified by the
Department of Commerce to receive funds: Advantage Capital, Bank
One and Wilshire Investors, which are located in New Orleans; Baton
Rouge, Louisiana; and New York City, respectively. After the first five
years of the program, these firms had only invested $20.7 million out
of the $50 million in subsidies they had received from the state to help
start-up businesses. Yet by 2002, CAPCOs had already managed to
withdraw $18.9 million to spend on "administrative fees."[50]

It was bad enough that these capital companies were spending
nearly as much on their own administrative expenses as they were
on the businesses they were supposed to be helping but, as it turns
out, the vast majority of that money (90 percent) was spent outside
Wisconsin. CAPCOs had taken a $50 million subsidy from the state of
Wisconsin and managed to ship almost half of it to their headquarters
in Louisiana and New York.[51]

You may wonder what Wisconsin received in return for this
expense. After all, the CAPCO program was created to create jobs,
so it might all be justifiable if the economy was jump-started, creating
tens of thousands of new jobs for the state. So how many new jobs did
the State Audit Bureau count? A grand total of 157. Some economists
estimated that Wisconsin was getting back in investments less than
forty cents for every dollar that it spent on tax subsidies.[52]

If there was any consolation, it was that Wisconsin wasn't the only
state to fall for the scam. By 2003, seven states had combined to provide
a total of $1.6 billion in tax subsidies to capital companies.[53] How did
Wisconsin get so deep into this mess, even after a 1999 study by the
state of Louisiana called its own program "expensive and inefficient"
and concluded that "the greatest and most immediate beneficiaries
of the CAPCO program are [capital] companies and their owners"?
Many wondered if the $210,000 in campaign contributions spread
over ten years from Bank One, which owned Stonehenge Capital in

Louisiana, had anything to do with it.[54] Or maybe state senator Glen Grothman (R-West Bend) was on to something when he was quoted by the *Milwaukee Journal Sentinel* as saying, "I think most do not understand the legislation and are accepting its merits on the say-so of established lobbyists."[55]

Either way, what is clear is that when the original CAPCO bill passed, Wisconsin had a bipartisan government. Republicans controlled the governor's mansion and the state assembly. Democrats ruled the state senate. Lobbyists gave money to both political parties. Both Democrats and Republicans voted to approve the CAPCO bill. And a few years later, the leaders in charge of both the state senate and the assembly at the time would be indicted for felony corruption charges. It is hard to imagine an example that more clearly illustrates that the divide is not between left and right, but between the front row and the back row.

WINNERS AND LOSERS ARE THE CITIZENS

Of course, the real losers of this process were the citizens of Wisconsin, who continued to see their tax burdens mount, along with the runaway spending and corporate giveaways. You see, when your method of operation is to use the prospect of government funds and contracts to leverage campaign donations, there is an unintended consequence: *it becomes very hard to say no to anyone.* Legislators become afraid to make tough choices, which might alienate any of their supporters, and spending continues its gradual climb.

This vicious cycle prompted me to write the following editorial, which appeared in the *Appleton Post-Crescent* in May 2006:

Time for Truthful Talk on Taxes

Wisconsin residents don't need a reminder that we are among the highest taxed people in the nation—we experience it every time we cash our paychecks or fill up our gas tanks. But if we are going to talk about taxpayer protection and revenue controls, we need to discuss the reasons for our high spending levels in Madison.

Consider:

- Current legislative leaders raised $765,893 for their campaigns in 2008 while the budget was being debated and passed.

- Campaign contributions have more than tripled over the last twelve years. Not surprisingly, state spending from the general fund doubled over the last six years.

- On the same day the legislature killed an ethics reform bill, it changed the assembly calendar, allowing solicitation from lobbyists just in time for this fall's elections.

- Last session, the legislature passed $800 million in unapproved highway projects within weeks of a fund-raiser hosted by state road builders.

- Special-interest tax breaks now cost every Wisconsinite over $1,000 each.

Look at just a few examples from Wisconsin's budget, and it becomes clear that if we truly want to protect taxpayers, we need to change the behavior of politicians and lobbyists, and end 'politics as usual.'

Here are a few solutions: Ban fund-raising during the state budget process. Ensure every bill gets a fair hearing and up or down vote. Finally, create a Government Accountability Board—Senate Bill 1—to enforce the laws that are already on the books.

There is still time to hold a special session to clean up our act. I urge you to contact the assembly leadership and ask for an extraordinary session on ethics reforms and SB 1. Wisconsin taxpayers literally can't afford to wait much longer.

Terri McCormick
State Representative
56th Assembly District

Old-Style Politics	Change
$$$$	**PEOPLE**
Horse Trading/ Deals	Open Meetings/ Transparency
Fall in Line Politics	Independent Thought/ Ideas
Retail Politics: Attack, Attack, Attack-	Honest Debate Based on Merit
Control from the Top/ Plug-and-Play Puppets	Ethical & Open Forums

In March 2006, the Republican-controlled U.S. Senate voted to raise the debt ceiling to nearly $9 trillion. Senators quickly passed a record $2.8 trillion budget.

CHAPTER SUMMARY

- In addition to cross-party attacks, "friendly fire" from one's own political party can have marked effects on a political career.
- Money candidates build a base of followers through campaign contributions, kickbacks, and pay-for-play strategies to pay off supporters.
- The losers in this scenario are the citizens that the politicos are supposed to serve.

As Karl Rove left the White House on his last day in 2008, he was asked,

What do you blame on the losses in the 2006 midyear elections?
He said, *Corruption and overspending.*

PART THREE

CHANGING
THE WAY
THINGS ARE

CHAPTER NINE

RUN YOUR OWN CAMPAIGN

MYTH:

You have to be a millionaire to
run for political office.

REALITY:

Anyone can run for office, but you will
need the courage of your convictions.

"I have accepted a seat in the [Massachusetts] House of
Representatives, and thereby have consented to my own ruin,
to your ruin, and the ruin of our children. I give you this warning,
that you may prepare your mind for your fate."

—John Adams to Abigail Adams, May 1770

CAMPAIGN LESSONS FROM AN IRISH PUB

In November 2002, shortly after my reelection to the state house in Wisconsin, I made an official visit to the Irish Parliament. As the just recently appointed chair of the Economic Development Committee, I accepted Speaker Rory O'Hanlon's invitation to meet to discuss economic development. The Irish speaker would share Ireland's success story in economic development, and I would share my success stories in education reform and dyslexia research. Jennifer, my chief of staff in the state legislative office, scheduled the official visits and travel arrangements, understanding that coming after my mother's death just a few months earlier, I could use the short respite.

This was my first pilgrimage to Ireland. My mother often talked about one day going home to her parents' country, but as fate would have it, she never had the opportunity. In my mind, I believed that if I could visit her homeland and listen to the sounds of Irish music, I could begin to let her go. My going home—if only to honor my mother's memory—was important to me.

While flying over the Atlantic, there were problems with a passenger on the plane, and my already tight schedule at Parliament became even tighter. Arriving several hours behind schedule, it was a relief to see a familiar face—Donna Kemp—at the Dublin airport, waiting to put me in a cab and take me to my hotel. Donna was my roommate in college at the University of Windsor and was now a top-level professional with the International Red Cross. She had finished an assignment in Afghanistan and was now taking advanced coursework at the university in Dublin.

After we scurried through customs, we quickly secured a Dublin cab.

Looking fit and well-traveled, Donna's smile broke through the years that separated us. "Terri, it is so good to see you! How are you? How are the kids?" she got out all at once.

While at Windsor, I had studied foreign policy and international relations; Donna was in the postgraduate social work program at the same university. She and I had recognized each other as friends from my first day on campus.

"Donna, I cannot thank you enough for being here at the airport. A man suffered a heart attack on the flight, and we were rerouted back to Newfoundland over the Atlantic," I said in a worn-out voice.

As luck would have it, I had only twenty minutes to pull myself together at my hotel, situated across from Trinity College, just two short blocks from Leinster House (the Irish Parliament) where I was to meet with Speaker Rory O'Hanlon.

O'Hanlon's staff had researched my background and my family's name, which made my official visit possible. McCormick is a name well thought of in Eire—maybe not as well thought of in Northern Ireland. Representative government meant life itself to my family and, not surprisingly, to the people of Ireland. As I took the brisk walk to meet with the speaker, I began to feel a sense of humble pride in the opportunity to meet the leaders of my family's heritage. My paperwork was in order for the visit, so briefcase in hand and in a fresh change of clothes, I had the energy I needed for my visit.

I approached the gates in an enthusiastic and determined way to make my meetings at the Parliament Building.

"Yes, Representative McCormick, we were expecting you," one of the security guards said, looking at a clipboard of acceptable names to be escorted into Leinster House.

As I walked on the cobblestone walkway to the Parliament, I began to reflect on the Irish Revolution and the lives that would be sacrificed for Ireland's representative democracy. The ornate tapestries and paintings that marked the majesty of the grand halls and walls were both awe inspiring and humbling.

My security guard took me to an area where I was to wait before I would be introduced to the speaker; there I would be faced with a bit of Irish and American history. On the wall of the great hall was a large tapestry presented to the Irish government by John F. Kennedy. It was given to Ireland to commemorate the sacrifice of Irish American soldiers in the United States Civil War.

"Do you recognize any names on that tapestry?" asked the rather tall and hearty guard. As he pointed at the names, a few seemed to jump off the page.

"Yes, actually, I have been told stories about my great-grandfathers, and I see names that could be them—William Boyle and Lincoln McCormick." My heart found its way to my throat as I choked back a tear in my mother's memory. How proud she would have been to have had the opportunity to see this.

We then walked the long hallway, past the rows of portraits of prime ministers and speakers of the Irish Parliament, on our way to Speaker Rory O'Hanlon's office. I was simply trying to drink in the moment that seemed to be overwhelming me with personal significance.

Speaker O'Hanlon was waiting for me in his office as I greeted his two aides who were seated just inside the entryway to his office suite.

"Speaker O'Hanlon, it is such a privilege to meet you and to have this opportunity to share ideas with you," I managed to calmly say.

As we began our conversation, I admired his poise and graciousness, particularly as I probably appeared to be yet another Irish American politician coming home to Ireland.

I was there to find answers to Ireland's economic success story. It had been considered a second-tier economic nation less than ten years earlier, and now it was the leader of technology and economic development in the European Union.

I smiled when I asked the speaker, "What is the secret to your success in lifting Ireland from a developing nation up to the number one nation in the European Union in just ten years?"

Speaker O'Hanlon met my eyes with a smile and steely determination as he shared his success. "It was quite simple, really. First, you need cheap money to encourage investment. Second, you need to attract talent, as we did by removing all taxes from musicians, artists and writers in Dublin. And finally you must untangle cumbersome bureaucracies that choke the growth out of business."

Rory O'Hanlon, the speaker of the Irish Parliament, had confirmed the draft on my legislative desk back in the Wisconsin state capitol for something called the "Blueprint for Change."

And Rory O'Hanlon gave me more than a confirmation of my new legislative policies; he gave me a part of my family's history that I was missing. From the tapestry commemorating Irish Americans who had fought in the Civil War to the warmth and support in his smile, it felt as though I understood who my parents were for the first time. Many emotions flooded over me as I took in Irish music at the Royal Symphony Hall. The dramatic murals prominently placed on gallery walls embraced Ireland's melancholy past in such a way that I could understand from where I'd come. The stories artfully designed on the murals at the National Art Gallery painted a tragic history, one of struggle, slavery and injustice.

I grew, in that moment and time in Ireland, to better understand my parents' impatience for injustice. And through them, I was now able to understand my own passion for public service. It was finally now time to say good-bye.

My visit was historic, if not professionally, then for me personally. The two became one and the same. But as profound as the experiences and realizations were; I was about to be taught a significant lesson from taxi cab driver on my way back to the airport and America.

It was through a conversation in a rearview mirror in a taxi cab that my driver would foreshadow the next four years of my service in public office.

With a confident and in a bold Irish brogue, my driver began his first round of questions: "So, you're a woman traveling alone to Ireland, are ya? What is it that you do? Do ya work outside the home?"

I hesitated for a moment before answering his questions. After all, I was provided bodyguards at Leinster House because President Bush had declared war on the IRA. I thought to myself, *Be careful; be very careful.*

I could tell immediately that my response to his questions didn't sit well with the young lad. when I answered, "I am a public servant."

The pace in the conversation picked up immediately as he quipped, "A politician, are ya? Oh ... my ... gosh! My garsh!" I felt as though an apology for my occupation was in order, but before I say anything, he went on, "They exchange brown paper bags filled with money in Ireland for votes! Ah-h, my gosh!" Again, I thought to somehow apologize for my profession, but before I could speak, he offered his final words—words that still sting my heart. "Let me tell ya something," he said in that lovely Irish accent. "My brother owns a whole chain of pubs in Boston and if you ever want to go legitimate, I can come to America and help you open up your own pub!"

In the tradition of old-style politics, my Irish cab driver may have been right. But if you are someone who truly wants to make a difference, running for public office is a sacrifice, particularly if you choose to change the status quo. Just as assuredly, however, if you are running with the wrong intentions, it is only a game. There is a strategy to every campaign. If you want to make a difference, the honesty tour must begin with you.

BEFORE YOU RUN

Before you announce your intentions to run, ask yourself, "What are my values and the skills I can bring to public office?" Your core values are your convictions that cannot be compromised. You will need a strong personal mission and vision from which to lead. Speaking skills, participating in debates, holding town-hall meetings and meeting one-on-one with your constituents can be learned. Courage, conviction and compassion cannot be learned.

The issues in whatever office you are running for will be complex, and you'll need to come up with creative solutions. You will also need to do research on your district and the people whose hearts and minds you hope to win. When you decide that you have what it takes to run for office, you will need a support network. Candidates literally run from one event to another—debates, parades, county fairs, knocking on doors, town-hall meetings.

There is little time for much else but campaigning, and many times you will need to be in two places at once. You will need the support of family and friends. They will need to know that you are the same person going into the silly season of campaigning as you will be coming out. In addition to having a family that is on board with the campaign, you will need friends—and you'll soon know who your friends are. Your friends will be there with you in good times and in bad; they will be there with you on hot summer days, walking in parades, and they will be there with you, win or lose, on election night.

PUTTING YOUR TEAM TOGETHER

To do well in any election, you need to assemble a strong team:

- A competent and trusted treasurer to keep the books balanced and who knows campaign finance laws
- A campaign manager who keeps staff and volunteers on task and moving toward goals
- A scheduler who keeps track of the busy candidate's schedule, pushes to get on the calendars of groups who would likely support you, puts together town-hall meetings and figures out how to overcome scheduling you in two places at once
- Field coordinators with excessive amounts of energy, who can engage volunteers in strategic grassroots efforts
- A communications director who is skilled at crafting messages, obtaining earned media and organizing editorial board meetings
- Campaign chairs who keep you on task while offering ideas and support

MONEY

It's inevitable: to run a campaign, you will need some money. But don't let your campaign be about money. As Teddy Roosevelt said, "Who will decide this race—the people or the money?" While all candidates need money to print brochures, buy signs, and get the word out, those who focus only on raising money will have missed the point. The true focus of a campaign is the desire to serve the people. Money is necessary, but lack of it is no indication that your campaign is doomed. Wisconsin governor Lee Sherman Dreyfus, who was outspent by more than ten to one, went on to win his primary contest by nearly 70 percent of the vote. *Powerful ideas can—and should—win elections*. Realistically, you cannot be drowned out by the noise of the other campaigns. You will need to be able to deliver your message to the voters, so a little advice about funding is in order.

Rule of thumb: In a congressional race, past history has suggested that you may need $250,000 to reach an audience of 600,000 voters;

this covers staff and radio/print/television advertising and coverage. That is not, however, the usual game plan of some politicians—in 2006, one of my opponents spent nearly $2.5 million hammering away at opponents in negative television and print ads.

I prefer the grassroots method to connect directly with voters and earn their support. This is much more labor intensive, but it works. Barack Obama has mastered fund-raising with the grassroots approach. He raised record amounts of campaign dollars with an average contribution of $109. Ron Paul did the same thing in his populist Internet campaign for president.

SAMPLE COSTS OF CAMPAIGNS IN WISCONSIN

- Presidential campaign: $500 million
- United States Senate: $3–5 million
- Congress: $500,000
- Governor: $3–5 million
- State senate: $100,000 to campaign across 100,000 people
- State house: $50,000, with 56,000 people represented
- School board: $2,500
- City council: $2,500
- County board: $2,500
- (These figures are based on average campaign dollars spent in 2006.)

DELIVER THE MESSAGE

Throughout your campaign, you'll need to speak in a consistent voice and with a clear message. This message needs to convince voters to get out to the polls and vote for you. Make sure your message conveys exactly what you want it to. Don't let the voters guess what you are saying. It is important to align your message to the needs of your constituents. For example, a message like "Kennedy will slash wasteful spending" is concise, while aligned with voter needs. Taxpayers need the government to lower taxes. Then next step in building your platform will be to determine just how you are going to accomplish this goal, and show it with action points.

Your message should also show how you are the most qualified candidate to fight for the people. No one truly wants to know your personal story unless they can see how you can make a difference for them. Avoid using the word "I." Instead, place the emphasis on voters—after all, you are campaigning to represent them.

Consider this: if you were given the following messages, which person would you vote for?

1. "I promise I will fight for your rights when you elect me into office. I know what is best for you and will make sure I get to the top so that I make things happen."
2. "Know that you will have a champion in Congress who will not forget who put her in office in the first place."

It's important that you gain the public trust. Whether your message is on the radio, television, literature or on your Web site, it needs to be clear and it needs to be consistent. This will keep the voters focused on your message. Even the best ideas must be communicated clearly, with a sincerity of purpose and mission.

STRATEGIES AND TACTICS

Campaigning is about making a personal connection with the voter. A solid plan requires an integrated approach to send your message to constituents; it's also an opportunity for voters to voice their concerns. Begin by identifying who your voters are and visiting with them. The next journey, then, is to engage these voters in their homes, at events, through direct mail, and in debates and forums. To end your journey with victory, you need to win the voters' trust—and then their votes.

Here are five strategic areas on which to focus in an affective ground campaign:

- Find out who votes in primary and in general elections.
- Motivate new voters and get them to the polls.
- Use a map to make a strategic plan to go door-to-door.

- Have a strong supporter or family member at your side every step of the way.
- *Earn the voters' trust* and you will earn their votes.

You will need volunteers to gather lists from towns, cities, villages and counties. Computer databases will need to be maintained and updated on a regular basis. Some counties and towns will have this information readily available, and some will not. Be prepared to handwrite voter files and then data enter them on Excel spreadsheets.

After you put together your voter information, you will need to obtain detailed ward maps from local government clerks. Organize the voter lists by street and by precincts, and go visit your voters, one neighborhood and subdivision at a time. You will need volunteers to walk with you and keep your efforts high. It will be a long process, but it will be a rewarding one. During your door-to-door campaign is where grassroots campaigns are won.

KNOCKING ON DOORS

The more local the public office, the more important it is to visit the voters, one door at a time. This "ground campaign" is the most important campaign you can run. Voters want to see you, hear you and test you, face-to-face, if possible. Having the candidate or a volunteer knocking on doors is the best way to open a line of communication. "Doing doors" is a strategic operation, and you will need a plan.

DIRECT MAIL

Once you have all the primary or general election voters' names and addresses, you'll have a powerful tool. One way to get your message out is through direct mail. To a certain extent, the more you touch voters, the more likely they will be to remember you and possibly vote for you.

If you cannot walk to every area in your voting district, by all means send direct mail. But remember, no method of campaigning takes the place of the candidate herself/himself. If your core values match up with the core values of the voters (and voting groups), you are more likely to earn their trust and their support. Be sincere! Voters know when they are being pandered to and when they are seeing the "real deal"!

TELEPHONE POLLING

It has been said that the easiest way to plan a campaign is to identify the voters who vote frequently. Use a database to collect the names of your voters and include their addresses and phone numbers. Then, see where your voters stand on the major issues of the day and note their stance. Telephone polling on these major issues will help you to create a list of voters who support your candidacy. Make note of your supporters through polling, walking door-to-door or reaching out to interest groups that share your views. Count your votes and finally, turn your supporters out to the polls to go vote! The voter-turnout strategies that your campaign designs are essential in winning a campaign. If you can't turn out your voters on election day, you will not win your election.

MEET AND GREET: CATFISH DAYS, DAIRY BREAKFASTS, COUNTY FAIRS AND PARADES

There is no better way to reach large numbers of voters in an interactive way than to go to area events. In Wisconsin, one of the unique opportunities a candidate has to meet with voters and support farmers is at county dairy breakfasts. Dairy breakfasts bring families and community members to a local farm for food and fun. To make an impact at events like this, you need to be ready to meet and listen to voters and create some fun on your own.

One way to get your name out at events is by giving out balloons and stickers. When kids see colorful balloons (with your logo on them), they will have to have them. No matter how many giveaways you do, you are the most important part of working events. Don't just shake hands; learn about your constituents and their concerns and then tell them what you stand for. Come to parades or events with a large group of volunteers who are wearing campaign shirts and supportive smiles. This reinforces your name recognition and the fact that you have support.

MESSAGING OUTSIDE THE BOX: THE NEW MEDIA

Old-style politics relies on television, radio and direct mail. This may not be as effective as it once was. Between 2006 and 2007, network television lost 2.5 million viewers. Voters are getting news and entertainment from more sources than ever—iPods, the Internet and cell phones are but a few new forms of communication.

The fact that advertising and posting online messages is cost effective is one reason to make use of the new technology that is available. One of the most important pieces of your campaign is your Web site. This is where voters tune in to get a closer look at your message, views and background. Keep it simple but entertaining. Include pictures from local events, news releases, endorsements and a television commercial, if you have one.

To keep voters engaged, change your postings on your Web site frequently and be sure to include in-depth views and your track record on the issues. I posted links to my white papers and voting records on my positions on ethics, spending reform, tax reform, the Iraq War, energy, immigration, health care and economic development. If you have held public office before you can also include a background on the bills or resolutions that you have worked on in office.

The Web site is also your opportunity to collect information from potential supporters. Make it easy for people to request a yard sign or to volunteer to knock on doors or hold an event. Also, be sure to insert an easy link for site users to donate money in a secure area online. To drive traffic to the Web site and get our message out online, we placed animated banner ads on the two largest local newspaper Web sites. Traffic increased on our Web site, and the banner ad was a cost-effective alternative to a static ad in the newspaper. Fund-raising ads in national and state magazines will generate traffic to your Web site as well.

Some of the younger campaign staff and volunteers may choose to set up a universal group for supporters to join on Facebook, a popular social networking site. This is a way to get the word out among young voters and send messages to group members to remind them to vote on election day. Groups and profiles on social networking pages have become increasingly important to voters in the 18–40 age demographic. Placing catchy ads on YouTube is also an important tool to garner support. The 2008 presidential candidates all took advantage of the new media available on the Internet.

Ron Paul, a Texas congressman and grassroots presidential candidate, gained a large following among young voters with Web technology. He established a profile on Facebook, with links to his Web site and other social networking sites. Ron Paul gained a successful presence on MySpace, garnering more than 130,000 friends as of early 2008. A blog, a count of the world debt, a song and other personal information was effectively used to keep supporters engaged and active. The Paul campaign also used YouTube, Flickr, Meetup and other networking sites to engage supporters.

To succeed in capturing young voters in the future, it will become increasingly important to take your message to where they are and to speak in their language. As technology and media evolve, you will need to examine this expanding medium and take advantage of the new trends.

PUBLIC DEBATES

You can not fool the American public. Unless you are a candidate with strong self-identified convictions and a strength of character that can not be shaken, you likely will find public debate an exercise in anxiety and emotional torture. Understanding the issues, the facts and logical arguments for your debate topic is only a beginning. To begin, go back to your core—your personal honesty tour—with the following values: *passion, purpose, sincerity and spontaneity.*

Terri debates on the floor of the Wisconsin House Assembly Floor.

PREPARING FOR A DEBATE: PASSION AND PURPOSE

Begin with a bit of soul searching. What convictions hold you—you know, the ones that hold on to you, not that you hold on to them. These are your core values that you base your judgment and all decisions around. These values give you your purpose and your passion to serve. Think back on your early childhood memories of education and what was important to you in that setting. Think back to your family and your faith; certainly, there are core convictions that hold you at your core.

An example of this conviction is President Obama's pledge to not accept political action dollars from lobby organizations. That pledge resonated with a core value of integrity of purpose. It demonstrated that Obama chose to be the voters' president, not the special interests.' As he organized Internet social networking opportunities and booked tours around the country, Obama put his life on the line for the world to see. The full disclosure of his life, from childhood to adulthood, demonstrated an honesty tour. The voters responded to the honesty and integrity displayed in the pages of his book and in action throughout his campaign. The rest of the story spoke for itself—Republicans, Democrats and Independents alike put their faith in a man who was willing to put his core values into action.

SINCERITY AND SPONTANEITY

Next are your debate issues themselves. Diagram your research in a pro-and-con format, with research backing up both sides. Only through this exercise of looking at problems through two viewpoints will you be able to find the solutions that the voters so desperately need. Using your values, mentioned above, identify your own positions on the issues. If the topic of economic development comes up, ask yourself what your convictions are and then apply your reasoning and research to seek possible solutions. Visionary leadership is necessary if you hope to win the voters' hearts and minds.

In order to debate with more than hot air, you will need to research all major issues that could possibly come up in your debate. Then, so that you don't appear to be a flag blowing in the wind—or worse, a bobble-head—you will need to take a stand on various issues, based on your convictions. This technique of grounding your principles in the issues of the day will lead to a sincere approach to solving problems for the people you hope to serve.

Spontaneity is the last of the four major attributes of a candidate in a debate or in front of voters and the press. If you have been programmed like a Manchurian candidate (as if there's a computer chip in your brain), you will not be able to be spontaneous. If you have been scripted every step of every way on every issue, you will not do well in debates—or in a campaign, for that matter.

Well-qualified candidates with a sense of passion, purpose, sincerity and spontaneity embrace debates and any public forum. The "plug-and-play" candidates that have been scripted by some party elite sales team and run for office as a career move will run from debates. Schedule as many debates as you need in order to meet and know the voters.

Here is a candidate debate checklist—a helpful summary of how to be ready for a debate:

1. Opening statement is clear, providing a basic philosophy, reasoning; stances clarified
2. Argument is clear, with a clear stance on the issue
3. Testimonials, statistics, examples are provided
4. Argument is logically constructed to simplify complex ideas
5. Evidence and conclusions are linked; causal reasoning
6. Communications skills are sharp and clear; the audience is listening
7. Responses provided to opponent's arguments
8. Direct, clear, insightful and direct questioning of your opponent, if called for
9. Character is demonstrated through a caring nature and background of telling the truth
10. Closing statement is consistent with the remarks that have been said throughout

CANDIDATE TOOLBOX

It's important to remember what you are running for. Evaluate the checklist below if you're ready to run for office and hope to assume office at the end of your campaign. These are the skills you'll need and the points you should remember when you get elected.

Your Personal Checklist, Before Running for Office:

1. Have confidence that the timing is right.
2. Know yourself and what you bring to the table.
3. Possess the passion to serve.
4. Have a purpose for yourself in public office.

5. Be determined and know that failure is not an option.
6. Surround yourself with a strong support network and make time for them.
7. Keep your family and inner circle close; – a "No new friends" rule might be needed.
8. Focus your campaign strategy on the voters.

What You Will Need:

1. The ability to think and communicate, clearly and concisely
2. A qualified treasurer
3. Patience, patience and patience
4. The power pause
5. Professionalism in appearance and demeanor
6. Punctuality; arrive early and leave on time
7. Study, study, study … and study
8. The ability to coordinate your staff; remember, the candidate is accountable!
9. Stamina; this will come from your passion and purpose; sleep wherever you can.

Important Points to Remember in Politics:

1. The people you will serve with are human—and so are you.
2. Never stop learning—you cannot "fake" wisdom.
3. Reserve time for yourself and your family.
4. Always be accountable to your core values.
5. Your boss is your constituency. You represent them. They live in your district and so should you.
6. Make a difference for the people who elected you, not for those who promise to get you reelected.
7. You swore to uphold and defend the Constitution. Read it and remember it.
8. Carry a book written by Winston Churchill. You will need the courage.
9. Stay grounded in your family and core beliefs. Listen to them and do the right thing, no matter what.

CHAPTER SUMMARY

- Reform is needed for worthy leadership in action.
- Transparency in office is a core ideal for good reform.
- A policy plan should be formulated before implementation; there are a number of factors to consider and steps to take.

It is always the right time to do the right thing.

—Reverend Dr. Martin Luther King, Jr.

THE HONESTY TOUR CAMPAIGN

CHAPTER TEN

REFORM FOR ALL: LEADERSHIP IN ACTION

MYTH:

Reform takes years and is nearly impossible to achieve.

REALITY:

Reform can happen anywhere, anytime, given the presence of a plan and good people to think outside the box!

Law and liberty cannot rationally become the objects of our love, unless they first become the objects of our knowledge.

—James Wilson,
Of the Study of the Law in the United States, circa 1790

What's in a label today? As demonstrated previously, Democrat and Republican interests often overlap. While the country seems to be polarized along party lines, the fact is that elite-run political rancor is thriving in both political parties' vertical silos. What is the impact of political party polarization? *Inertia*! Many politicians become entrenched in their own party's politics and caught up in partisan top-down silos, the result of which is entrenched political parties and a paralyzed political system. Whether the motivation is misplaced loyalty or a skewed sense of survival due to leadership pressure, legislation stalls and the people lose. Bills that could fix some of our more pressing problems are waiting for politicians to end the debate over who gets credit. The process grinds to a halt, and a vote that would take a week or two of debate is now stalled for months or even years.

My policy plans call for ways to bypass these roadblocks through building strong coalitions. Politicians listen to and understand large groups of noisy, informed constituents who vote. When you back up these constituents with experts and facts, you will break the log jam. The front row may not like it and it may not be their agenda, but most politicians cannot deny the obvious and will eventually step aside, so as not to look like an obstacle. (I have seen the exception ...)

There will be opposition to any approach that is new and that goes against business as usual. The point to remember is this: innovation requires you to think ahead of the curve. Put on a flak jacket and keep walking. As Einstein once said, "Today's problems were caused by yesterday's solutions. We need a new way of thinking to solve the problems of tomorrow."

TRANSPARENCY: A CORE IDEAL

Legislators, change agents and citizen leaders, I can tell you from experience that when you enter the world of politics as an integrity leader, as a leader of a social change in the legislature, or as the head of a new policy movement, it will be easy to get lost in the swarm of activity. When you're in the thick of "the way things are done," it's difficult to adhere to your core values. Yet in order to be an effective agent for change, you must find and maintain a balance. Running a transparent office will help find that crucial balance. Here are some tips on how to manage transparency:

TRANSPARENCY AT A POPULIST OFFICE

Transparency is an essential tool for populists serving in public office. Openness and a broad beacon of light are essential in serving as a populist. The only counterforce to fear and threats by the puppets is the use of faith and a belief that there is something out there much greater than you. For me, it was a belief in my convictions, that I was put in office to find solutions for the people back home. It was my faith in the Constitution and market-driven competition. George Washington once said that this nation would not need political parties if only we had a free and appropriate press. I was banking on the press—or rather, on journalists who emerge from the press.

Tip No. 1: In setting up a populist office, the first rule of thumb is to hire staff that are free-thinkers and have a background with the press. I have had wonderful staff throughout my years in the state capitol. My office staff was intentionally chosen from "outside" of the pool of workers that had taken an oath of loyalty to the front-row leaders and fall–in-line lieutenants. There was only one time that I regretted my hiring decisions and that was when I failed to recruit from the journalist corps. Print journalists understand the need for transparency and are conscientious under a deadline. Journalists look at issues from both sides and all sides in order to get at the truth. Television journalists understand the merit of bold statements and press conferences. Radio journalists understand the importance of serving constituents.

Tip No. 2: The second rule of thumb in achieving a transparent office is to "sunshine" all of your press releases and all of your legislative work on a fully accessible Web site. In my case, there was a twofold reason for having a transparent website: first, predatory legislators became much more honest about my ideas when they were out there for the world to see, with specific dates and testimonials from my constituents. Second, my constituents and the press back home had a means to keep tabs on my progress and provide input for future improvement on bills that we could work on together. I considered my work the people's work.

Tip No. 3: Always put your constituents first by holding office hours and share with them how to reach you, if needed. My being accessible and ready to take criticism as well as praise built the kind of trust that I relied on when I was under "friendly fire" from my own political party. Providing the integrity needed to follow through on legislative promises and providing updates to the people back home is essential in maintaining trust and earning your reelection.

I was not a puppet; I was comfortable operating in the light of day in full view of the press and the public. The darkened rooms and secret deals, complete with the Machiavellian spy networks reporting up to the speaker or the minority party leaders, was not a part of the way I did business. For that, I had a tremendous amount of freedom of thought, expression and action on the part of the constituents who elected me to office.

A SUCCESSFUL POLICY PLAN

The first step in building a successful policy plan is to identify those goals you are attempting to reach. Examine the motives behind those goals—are you hoping to get a charter school law passed as a private citizen, a veterans bill passed in order to help the veterans in your community to afford a better retirement, or trying to get a health-care bill passed as a legislator because the physicians group that is lobbying for its passage is one of your largest campaign contributors? What are your motives for seeing legislation enacted? Are you hoping to save your small-business trucking firm by supporting an innovative new energy policy that will convert large truck engines to natural gas?

Furthermore, before taking up the cause of any movement or any political candidate as a citizen leader, examine what that candidate has done—to get a glimpse of what that candidate is capable of doing. Is he there to help you enact legislation that will save your part of the country's 10,000 jobs, or is she there for the preelection photo opportunity that will certainly boost her campaign? That's not to say that you can't work with a politician whose allegiances swing widely with the wind. Just be prepared to go it alone as a citizen leader when the going gets tough.

Concentrate instead on building a strong policy model. My outline below is targeted to legislators in public office, *but it can also be used by citizen leaders and reformers to build a movement for change.* The new energy revolution PickensPlan is one such citizen-led revolution that has the power of over one million citizens across the country urging Congress for change in our energy infrastructure.

The policy model shown below outlines, from start to finish, how to create and implement those policies that you feel passionately about. Using the six-step policy model below, you can develop a strong plan that may result in your being instrumental in creating change.

1. From Plan to Passage

It all starts with an idea. There's a problem; there needs to be a solution. The first step is to generate ideas and identify your stakeholders. Who are the people most able to help you sell your point to the legislating bodies? Who holds expertise in this area? Who has a stake in how this shakes out? Those are the people you want to approach first. Tell them about the problem you've identified. Enlist their help in creating a plan of action. Get stakeholder buy-in and participation in reaching the goal.

Identify patterns and possible solutions. Look at how similar legislation was enacted. Look at the voting records of key political party members. Could these people be an integral part of your plan, or would you be better going it alone? Discuss various solutions to the problem. What solution would be more acceptable to the political parties? Why? What solutions would be tough sells? What political hot potatoes should you avoid? Which ones should you pick up and run with? How will the plan be implemented, once it is enacted into law? Also, discuss what will happen if the plan fails.

Once your stakeholders are on board and you've identified both your problems and a number of solutions, you can begin to collect data and research. Your position will be much stronger if you use irrefutable facts and logical arguments to make a strong case for resolving the problem. Look to the economic indicators and forecasts to give you general information on how the problem is affecting the population, and which segments of that population are most affected by the problem. Search for associations, organizations or coalitions that may already have formed around the problem you're trying to solve. In many cases, these groups will have obtained data and research. By sharing information with these groups, you will form a stronger coalition and will succeed in enlisting their help and their buy-in with your plan.

2. Experts, Goals and Targets

Once you complete those steps, you're ready to search for experts and expert private-sector research. Turn to those who have extensive experience in areas that connect to your problem and the possible solutions. Because these experts come from the private sector, their words will hold much more weight than if you sought out the expert advice and research of career politicians, particularly those in the same party.

Now is also the time to look at the problem in terms of national and state and local impact. How are the national trends measuring against state trends? Are more people affected in your region than nationwide? If so, perhaps your plan should be limited to a state legislature. If the problem is nationwide, such as the workers compensation crisis, then your battlefield is on a federal level.

Still, you should consider regional and community advocacy in order to get your message out to a concentrated group of people. A grassroots effort at educating the public on the problem is often a good way to start a movement toward change. Often, if a change is confined to a state level, chances of reaching the goal are increased. And many times, other states will use your legislation efforts as a model for change in their own states.

That brings me to another area—legislation already in place in one or more of the other forty-nine states. In many cases, the battle you're about to take on has already been fought and won in another state. Before doubling your efforts, take the time to research legislation on that particular subject that may have been enacted in other states. Associations, organizations and coalition groups often have this information.

3. Build a Support Team

To get a law enacted, you will need plenty of professional support, whether as a legislator or a social reformer and citizen leader. These are the people who will dot your i's and cross your t's, making sure you have the latest information, the dollars to continue the strategic plan, the research to support your position and the legal support to make sure you're doing things right.

If you are a citizen leader of a social reform movement, you will need individuals to organize others to action through social networks or community organizations. Policy savvy wouldn't hurt—read below for some examples of how best to structure your ideas for solid public policy.

At some point, whether you are working as a citizen leader or a legislator, you will need the help of a legislative council or bill drafter to help you fashion a bill that reflects your movement or supports what you hope to accomplish. The attorneys in legislative councils can keep you abreast of the ins and outs of putting together legislation. Also, you will need fiscal support—quite simply, dollars. Some of your stakeholders should be ones who will buy in to your plan. While they have a voice in policy plans, they may not be the only individuals involved in key support of your bill's passage. The advantage of having a diverse group of supporters from all demographics, communities and interests involved in public policy is that the politics of money or pay-for-play politics has less of a chance of preventing your movement or your bill from succeeding.

The importance of facts and logic in putting together a message to support your movement is critical. Use economic indicators and private-sector measures for key pieces of your policy plan. Draw clear contrasts between those families, children and individuals who could be helped with policy changes. Show how your legislation will affect a demographic or group of individuals, economically and socially. Finally, make sure you have the expertise or the staff to help you research all pertinent information and provide you with winning statistics.

Legislators trust that there are experts in the private sector with experience and policy ideas. Citizen leaders trust that there are key supporters, advocates and experts in the legislature who are willing to help, should they both share the same core values and vision for public policy. Objectivity and a will to find the middle ground will reduce the politics and eliminate roadblocks much faster than the old politics of partisan silos and turf-building.

4. Short-Range Gains vs. Long-Term Solutions

This may sound like a no-brainer, but when planning a policy model, you must consider both the near future and the long term. The fact that you were able to halt the nuclear power plant from dumping waste into your backyard until an inquiry is conducted is a far cry from getting the plant to clean up the toxic waste and pay for damages and health-related illnesses. Take time to identify those short-term goals and which long-term solutions you're working toward. Also, determine where the decision making in your coalition will come from. Are you going to meet as a committee on every aspect of the issue? Are you going to appoint a panel to decide on these issues? Is one person making these decisions? At what level in the organization will decisions be made? What about branches of your coalition—what decision-making power will they have? How does that interact with the overall decision-making body?

What are the implications of the policy model you're building? What econometric measures can you apply to determine the policy's impact? In other words, if you are successful in getting the power plant to clean up the toxic waste and pay for medical bills associated with that waste, how will that affect the community? Will jobs be gained or lost? Will the company move from the area as a result? Will taxes go up as a direct result? Understand exactly how your policy will affect the economics of the region or the nation. It makes it easier to defend or to choose a different path if you have projections of the economy as a direct result of your policy.

Also, consider the political implications of your policy model. How will your policy affect those in office? If office holders choose to take up the banner of your cause, what benefit can they see from it? You will not change the behaviors of politicians, yet you still need to enlist their help with your cause from time to time. Politicians are motivated by self-serving interests. It would behoove you to pay attention to those interests and to give the politician the idea of what return on his investment he might see. Define also her political safety net—how will this policy protect her, should your idea fail? What assurances will he have that this won't damage his political reputation?

5. Partners in the Process

Even the strongest of coalitions needs to partner with objective outside sources. There are a number of possible partnerships—first, the press. Turn to trade publications that would have an interest in your particular plan model. Also, newspapers may reach a larger audience base, though their interest may only be fleeting. Concentrate on reaching news organizations that can help get the word out to those who would be most affected by your policy.

Use different forms of technology. Find Internet-based venues to spread the word. Many groups and subgroups within your policy's interest area would want to know about something that could directly or indirectly affect their members or readers. Make sure you court those people accordingly.

Your efforts should have two goals—to get the word out and to bring the issue to the forefront politically. Too often, issues become stuck in hidden caucuses or in meetings held privately. By generating interest in the private sector, you can work toward "sunshining" the process, or making the public's right to know a precedent over the secrecy.

6. Securing the Vote

Once you've created a buzz and have enlightened key stakeholders and coalition partners to your policy, you can then concentrate on getting to the yes vote. Use your partners and your coalition members, both public and private, to get the message to politicians. Secure support for your efforts from *both* political parties. If two opposing sides are somehow seeing things in the same way, your chances of seeing your policy succeed have multiplied exponentially.

Now is the time for leadership in the policy push, not "followership." Encourage all members of the coalition to lead the charge—not just expecting the lead to come from you or someone else. The more people leading dialogue and action, the stronger your policy becomes in the eyes of the public—and in the minds of the legislators.

7. Measure Your Success

The most often overlooked area of policy modeling is the measurement. If you don't measure the results of your efforts, you cannot know if this model will be effective for you in the future. While things may have turned out well, mistakes were made. That's a given. Look at the process in stages. What was successful immediately? What wasn't? How did you turn it around? What would you do differently? How can your steps be refined to bring about better or faster results?

In truth, your policy should be measured as you complete each step. If you continuously monitor the progress, you can more easily adapt the model to accommodate any surprises.

IT WORKS

Now that you know how to build a policy model, you can begin to see how it works. Or can you? Perhaps a few examples from my own policy-modeling efforts will help. For instance, I built a blueprint for job growth in Wisconsin. By using a simple model, I was able to identify reform areas, create a mission statement, define the objective, locate other areas of concern and put together an action plan for job growth. This same strategy was used with education, taxes, health care, court reform and agricultural growth.

The beauty of this plan is that it can work in every level of government. It can also work in the private sector, helping to identify goals and strategies. Follow below as we put the plan into action with my health-care cost reform package. Citizen leaders in small business, local government partners, and taxpayers alike advocated as a part of the "new we" that made prescription drug purchasing pools possible in the state.

The pages that immediately follow are examples of a health-care reform that passed into law. The actual policy template used is included as well as—interest group statements of need, a mission statement with goals for the task force, a sample media advisory for public listening sessions, an overview of the health-care reform package and finally, the press release and administrative announcement on the Badger RX cost savings of $25 million the first year.

CHAPTER SUMMARY

- Transparency is a core ideal.
- With a strategic plan in place, a policy model based on goals, support, votes and measurement can meet with success.

If you do good, people will accuse you of selfish ulterior motives;
do good anyway.
The good you do today may be forgotten tomorrow; do it anyway.
People who need help may attack you if you help them; help them anyway.

—Mother Teresa

Representative Terri McCormick
56th Assembly District

Phone (608) 266-7500 • Toll Free: 1-888-534-0056 • E-mail Phone: (608) 266-7500 • Toll Free: 1-888-534-0056

Policy Model Template

From Idea to Passage

1. Generating ideas and identifying important stakeholders
    Patterns and Solutions
    Data and Research
    Economic Indicators and Forecasts versus Standard Accounting

2. Finding the experts and identifying goals and targets
    The Wise Men and Women—Private-Sector Experts
    National Trends versus State Needs
    Regional and Community Advocacy within the State Context

3. Pulling in the legal and support staff
    Legislative Council Support
    Fiscal Support
    Economic Indicators and Private-Sector Measures
    Private-Sector Attorneys

4. Short-range gains versus long-term solutions, or policy versus politics
    Branch and Root Decision Making
    Policy Implications with Econometric Models
    Political Implications—How to define the Safety Net

5. Building coalition partners & transparency in the process
    The Message and the Art of Technology
    The Press as Partner
    Trade Publications—and Communications

6. Getting the majority to yes & securing the votes
    One Vote at a Time
    Coalitions within Both Political Parties
    Leadership versus Fall-in-Line Follow-ship

Representative Terri McCormick   **Chair Health-Care Cost Reforms**

CONSTITUENT-INITIATED LEGISLATION
Counties, Cities, Towns, Villages, School Boards

URGENCY (If asked to identify the top 1 or 2 items that are most on the minds of constituents… I'll bet most of you would say health insurance issues.)

WHO BENEFITS?

✓ Local government need—number one spike in budgets

✓ Bipartisan task force
   Thank members on task force
     Representative Huebsch
     Representative Meyer
     Representative Stone
     (Highlight thanks to Bonnie/Insurance and Greg/Health)

✓ Recommendations encourage competition-fair market practices

✓ Shadow ETF (DEPARTMENT OF EMPLOYEE TRUST FUNDS) -mirror state

✓ Experience ratings

✓ 2 provisions that affect employees directly

   o ETF as a benchmark
   o Unilateral switch—3 assumptions
     1. Substantially similar provisions
     2. Guaranteed windfall

    3. Substantially similar language protected

✓ Quality measures for health care

✓ Refer to handouts—provided as a nutshell to summarize Web site

✓ Hope that this piece will be a contribution to those who will continue to work to solve problems on the health and insurance committees

✓ Thank leadership

Additional Anecdotes. time permitting:

1. Quintessential GOOD government in action—an idea initiated by the people, who worked locally and partnered with legislators, to craft a solution. (shows responsiveness, HEARING constituent concern)
2. Success story: Menasha—competitive health insurance resulted in higher salaries

Terri McCormick
WISCONSIN STATE REPRESENTATIVE

MISSION STATEMENT
Task Force on Local Government Health Partnerships:
A Brief Overview

A. **Mission**: Lowering the cost of health insurance for local governments

1. Explore new health insurance partnerships opportunities for local governments
2. Improve the market to compete with lower insurance prices

B. Public Hearings and Executive Sessions

1. *May 29, 2002: Local boards*
2. June 26, 2002: Department of Employee Trust Funds and the Commissioner of Insurance office as well as local boards who use the Wisconsin Public Employer's Group Health Insurance Program (WPEGHIP) administered by the ETF
3. *July 24, 2002: Insurance companies*
4. *August 21, 2002: Health care providers*
5. *September 25, 2002: Executive Session-moved recommendations forward*
6. *October 23, 2002: Executive Session-voted drafts forward to be introduced next session*

C. Task Force Drafts: Approved October 23, 2002

1. Total Compensation Packages: Providing More Options for Quality Choices:
   ✓ Provides a definition of a total comprehensive compensation plan, requiring both salary and health insurance costs to be considered in the bargaining process

    ✓   Examines the feasibility of using the Wisconsin Public Employer's Group Health Insurance Program as a non-bargainable, meaning those governments who opt to participate in the program would not have to bargain their health insurance

    ✓   Allows a local government unit to change health insurance carriers, without the consent of a bargaining unit, as long as benefits and providers are maintained

2.   Strengthening Fair Market Practices: Opening Bids and Experience Ratings:

    ✓   Allows local governments the opportunity to have access to their health insurance experience ratings

    ✓   Requires bids received by local governments to be posted on the state's Internet site

3.   Supporting Aggressive Reforms for Local Governments: Improvements for the WPEGHIP: (Many of these are already being implemented by the Department of Employee Trust Funds.)

    ✓   Creates program awareness for statewide buying pool

    ✓   Creates a system of tiers with varying co-pays and deductibles

    ✓   Creates a competitive prescription drug management program

    ✓   Promotes demographic sensitive products such as long-term care

4.   Empowering Consumer Choice: Providing Charge and Quality Data

    ✓   Encourages consumers to become more active participants in their own health care choices by offering charge and quality information available online (This recommendation was not drafted because it is already available in its beginning stages through a Web site unveiled by Governor McCallum in September (www.dhfs.state.wi.us/healthcarecosts.))

D. Other: Health insurance reform package (compilation of approved drafts) introduced as AB 304

1.   For more information on the task force (including the drafts in their entirety), please go to http://www.legis.state.wi.us/assembly/asm56/news/

MEDIA ADVISORY

MCCORMICK TO HOLD LISTENING SESSION FOR TASK FORCE

Task force set to investigate health insurance costs for local government

FOR IMMEDIATE RELEASE   **CONTACT: Rep. Terri McCormick**
May 16, 2002   **PHONE:** (608) 266-7500

APPLETON- Representative Terri McCormick (R-Appleton) will hold a listening session to hear local government leaders thoughts and concerns regarding a speaker's task force to investigate local health insurance costs tomorrow. Representative McCormick has been named to chair the task force that will potentially save local governments, and taxpayers millions of dollars through the practice of shared services and collaboration. **The listening session will take place tomorrow, May 17, 2002, at 11:00 a.m. at the Appleton Public Library, 225 North Oneida Street.**

The newly formed task force on health insurance will explore the opportunities of shared local government health insurance pools. It will be meeting monthly beginning in May 2002 and anticipates providing its preliminary findings by October 1, 2002.

###

Representative Terri McCormick
56th Assembly District

2005 McCormick Heath Care Reform Package: A Brief Overview

Initiatives included in legislation:

Total Compensation Packages: Providing More Options for Quality Choices:

✓ Provides a definition of a total comprehensive compensation plan, requiring both salary and health insurance costs to be considered in the bargaining process

✓ Examines the feasibility of using the Wisconsin Public Employer's Group Health Insurance Program as a non-bargainable, meaning those governments who opt to participate in the program would not have to bargain their health insurance

✓ Allows a local government unit to change health insurance carriers, without the consent of a bargaining unit, as long as benefits and providers are maintained

Strengthening Fair-Market Practices: Opening Bids and Experience Ratings:

✓ Strengthens current law, allowing local governments the opportunity to have access to their health insurance experience ratings as well as providing a uniform form for the process and posting those experience ratings on the state's Internet site operated by the Department of Administration.

✓ Requires bids received by local governments to be posted on the state's Internet site operated by the Department of Administration.

Supporting Aggressive Reforms for Local Governments: Improvements for the WPEGHIP:
(Many of these are already being implemented by the Department of Employee Trust Funds.)

- ✓ Recommends program awareness for statewide buying pool
- ✓ Recommends a system of tiers with varying co-pays and deductibles
- ✓ Recommends a competitive prescription drug management program
- ✓ Recommends promoting demographic sensitive products such as long-term care

For More Information about the McCormick Health Insurance Reforms, Visit: http://www.legis.state.wi.us/assembly/asm56/news/Health%20Care%20 Reform.htm *(Note to readers: Link no longer active)*

CHAIR, COMMITTEE ON ECONOMIC DEVELOPMENT
VICE-CHAIR, COMMITTEE ON JUDICIARY
COMMITTEE ON PUBLIC HEALTH
COMMITTEE ON INSURANCE

TERRI MCCORMICK

WISCONSIN STATE EPRESENTATIVE 56TH ASSEMBLY DISTRICT

MEDIA ADVISORY
McCormick to Hold Press Conference on
Heath Care Reform Package

FOR IMMEDIATE RELEASE CONTACT: Rep. Terri McCormick
June 8, 2005 608-266-7500

Madison – State Representative Terri McCormick (R-Appleton) will address the urgency of the health care cost crisis in Wisconsin at a press conference Thursday, June 9, at 10:00 a.m., in the Assembly Parlor at the State Capitol building.

Rep. McCormick is reintroducing five bills making several changes to health insurance plans and other benefits offered to local government employees. The plan was piloted in the last budget cycle for non-represented state employees, resulting in a $25 million savings on prescription drug costs in the first year alone.

The purpose behind these changes is to offer needed flexibility to local governments in negotiating health packages with their employees without diminishing the level of care the employees have negotiated for themselves in past collective bargaining agreements.

McCormick is optimistic her proposals will move quickly through the legislative process now that Governor Doyle and the Joint Finance Committee have committed to combating the health insurance crisis in Wisconsin.

###

Capitol Office: Post Office Box 8953 • Madison, WI 53708-8953
(608)-266-7500 • Toll-Free: (888)534-0056 • Fax: (608)282-3656 • Rep.McCormick@legis.state.wi.us *Home:*
W6140 Long Court • Appleton, WI 54914

801 W Badger Road
PO Box 7931
Madison WI53707-7931

1-877-533-5020 (toll free)
Fax (608) 267-4549
TTY (608) 267-0676
http://etf.wi.gov

STATE OF WISCONSIN

**Department of Employee
Trust Funds**

Eric O. Stanchfield
SECRETARY

June 9, 2005

The Group Insurance Board, along with leadership from the governor and support of the legislature, initiated a pharmacy benefit management system that was incorporated into the state of Wisconsin Group Health Insurance Program and resulted in 2004 savings of more than $25 million.

xxx

You've built the model. You've found people to help you implement it. You've garnered support. And you've faced the opposition. Now you're ready for your action plan—the steps you need to take in order to make your model work best.

The best way to decrease government dependence is to increase the number of jobs available to our citizens. The transformational power of a job can allow all Americans to realize their American dream.

State Representative Terri McCormick, 2004

THE POLICY MODEL PLAN

If you want to develop your own policy plan, here are some suggestions. Start with a written plan. It's important to write down each planned step in the process. Start with your mission statement, your goal, your coalition partners; then move on to the precise methods you will employ in order to make this model happen. A typical policy plan will look like this:

- Mission statement
- Coalition members
- Member experience/skill set
- Demographics
- Population profile
- Policy detractors
- Promotions plan
- Communications objectives
- Communications contact(s)
- Goals
- Contingency plans
- Measuring the results

MISSION STATEMENT

What is your reason for being? Why did you form this coalition? What goal or goals are you trying to reach? Use this section to summarize your policy model and its rationale.

COALITION MEMBERS/EXPERIENCE

Use this section to identify the people and organizations backing your model. Give information on the experience or skill set of each person or group, making sure to spotlight those who have the most experience in the area in question. Make sure you have outlined the duties of each member/group involved so it's clear to those reading your business plan just who is in charge of which area.

DEMOGRAPHICS

Here's where you identify whom you're trying to reach. Which portion of the population will be interested in what you're trying to accomplish? How will your efforts change their lives? Which group of people would best benefit from this plan?

POPULATION PROFILE

It would be wise to delve a bit deeper into your demographic to show who they are and what motivates them. Also, make sure to include profiles from a broader demographic to illustrate the effects of this policy model on the public at large.

POLICY DETRACTORS

Who wants to see you fail? Why? What motivations can be identified? Remember the key motivators—special interests, self-serving interests, political interests and constituent interests. Examine each motivator to understand the mind-set of your detractors. This will serve as the foundation of a plan to alleviate your detractors' objections.

PROMOTIONS PLAN

Just like a publicity plan, your policy model needs some good PR. In this section, identify ways to get the word to your audience. Examine which form of media will work best—in many cases, it will be a combination of two or more media outlets. Who will promote the message? How often? Your timeline should be built within this section.

COMMUNICATIONS OBJECTIVES

In the end, what do you hope to accomplish with your promotions plan? This is strictly your objective for your plan. The goals for your policy model will be listed later.

Communications Contact(s): Who is your main contact or contacts for this policy model and plan? How can people reach these contacts?

GOALS

Different from the objectives, here you will outline the various goals you hope to reach with the policy model. Give short summaries of how you intend to reach those goals.

CONTINGENCY PLAN

Even the best-laid plans don't work. Spell out here what you'll do, should your initial efforts fail. Will you continue? Will you give it up? Will you reevaluate your plan and revise?

MEASURING THE RESULTS

Here's how you'll know if your goals have been met, and if you've used your time and resources efficiently. Identify each key step in the policy model—when were these goals reached, if ever? How close to your target were you? Where did things go awry? How can you improve that in the future? Ideally, you will perform measurements during each phase of both your policy model and the subsequent action plan.

RALLYING SUPPORT

As part of your plan, you should include methods for garnering the support of the public. Find those who are well versed in getting messages to large groups—these are your messengers. What avenues can you take in order to get your messenger in front of these groups? Colleges, universities, city league organizations, etc., can be great places to start. You're only as strong as your support system. Part of the plan should include finding out who can best lend support to your cause. Make good use of your key supporters—court their interests, share information with them, ask for their support.

THE PRESS

I cannot express strongly enough the need to get your message to the public through the media. Newspapers and journals, as well as television and radio, can help you to reach thousands of people. But don't think the press will automatically be interested in your policy model. You have to find an angle—something that will generate interest. Is your policy about to affect a large section of the region? What are the negatives, should your policy fail? Who stands to gain from your policy? Start with statistics, and then build a case for an interview around your subject.

ACCOMPLISH THE GOAL

Armed with both a policy model and an action plan, you're now that much closer to success. Because you've walked through each step of each document, you are armed with terrific information, a sound reason, good people behind you and a solid plan to help you get to your goal. But you're not there yet!

ROADBLOCKS AND LABELS

It's as sure as there are two main political parties that you will face resistance. You know by now the roadblocks—partisan politics, special interests, personal interests, etc. Yet if you've planned correctly, you can overcome most or all of these roadblocks. For instance, partisan politics don't come into play if you've garnered support from both sides for your plan. And you do that by approaching politicians one by one and giving out an honest account of your policy model and what it will mean to that politician's voting contingent.

Special interests can also be overcome by identifying exactly what it would take to please those groups, or what it would take for a politician to vote against those groups' interests. Personal interests, oddly, are the easiest to get beyond. I've often said that a politician only needs a solid reason why the policy should matter to him—so give him one. Show those politicians just how this policy can help to bolster their own popularity or, at the very least, show those politicians why it's unwise for them to continue to ignore the growing popularity of this policy.

The funny thing about labels is how quickly they disappear when you're on to something good. For instance, I was considered a novice until I teamed up with strong veterans groups in an attempt to pass legislation favorable to combat veterans. Then I was smeared as a political hot potato—one with whom my political colleagues were afraid to associate. If you can't shake the labels, shake the people making the labels.

For instance, no one wants to be known as being opposed to job growth. That's why it was easy for me to silence the critics when I introduced my Capital Investment Corporation idea for Wisconsin. I provided a clear-cut plan that was direct, honest and would be applied to the job situation with little effort. By identifying both the problem and the solution in one document, I was able to spell out the plan and identify who in government would be able to help. Some say by giving credit to my political opponents may have hurt me; I say if the policy passes because of it, so be it. The idea is to keep your focus on the goal and to include as many of your political colleagues as you can. The plan, as it was written, can be found below.

Wisconsin Capital Investment Corporation
"Investing in Wisconsin ideas to grow jobs for our state"

The Problem:

The state of Wisconsin in 2001 had been a leader in medical research, manufacturing and the idea industry, but yet we are third from the bottom in the United States in investing in our people and those ideas. At this writing, there were only three capital investment companies operating in the state of Wisconsin with limited to no success in getting investment dollars into the hands of entrepreneurs.

The Solution:

There were two critical pieces missing in investing our ideas:
1. A mechanism for funding that would attract private investors
2. The accountability we need to connect ideas to business development to dollars

These missing links are addressed with the formation of a Capital Investment Corporation that is accountable for infusing the maximum amount of revenue into the economy and growing jobs.

What It Is:

This model for capital investment is a competitive, performance-driven, and market-guided model housed in a Capital Investment Corporation (CIC) that is accountable through tax credits and the oversight of the Wisconsin Leadership Board. The CIC is critical to the model, performing the following:

✓ Work with professors, entrepreneurs, and angel networks to create viable, new economy companies with high-paying, high-growth jobs.

- ✓ Work with the seed and early-stage companies to assist them in obtaining grants, loans, etc., from the Department of Commerce, other governmental agencies, etc.
- ✓ Tee up the companies for angel and early-stage fund managers to take to successive levels of financing, having selected the fund managers with measurable standards and information systems to hold managers accountable.
- ✓ Work with Commerce, the governor and the Wisconsin Economic Leadership Board and the legislature to plan for overall strategies with new legislation and tracking of the overall economic impact and financial results of the program.

The board is also vital to the model as it provides a nonpartisan report mechanism and oversight entity to the corporation. The board is made up of the following members: governor, governor appointee, majority/minority leader of the senate (whichever is a member of the political party opposite of the governor), majority/minority leader of the assembly (whichever is a member of the political party opposite of the governor) appointee, chairperson of the CIC, and the executive director of SWIB.

Why We Need It:

Other models simply aren't working. Wisconsin continues to fall farther behind our Midwest neighbors in venture capital opportunities, encouraging entrepreneurs to look elsewhere for their business locations.

Venture Capital Under Management (Source: Venture Economics 2001)

United States	$209,803,000,000
Minnesota	$3,842,000,000
Wisconsin	$168,000,000

"Wisconsin has a long tradition of entrepreneurs who turned good ideas into great companies, and turned those companies into household names, but if we want to add new names to that roster, we need to attract more capital—especially seed and early stage seed capital-to Wisconsin."

—Governor Jim Doyle

Why is a Capital Investment Corporation a Necessity in Wisconsin?

Accountability ⟶ The CIC answers to the taxpayers of Wisconsin for the tax credits received through an economic leadership board.

Performance Driven ⟶ The CIC only succeeds when business grows in this state, with caps and limitations set.

Ethics Defined ⟶ The CIC may not be a fund manager and has specific safeguards in place so that its goals are to grow jobs through business growth. Its bottom line is to deliver jobs for the state, not grow its bottom line.

How Will the Capital Investment Corporation Work?

✓ The CIC model ensures ethics limitations on itself and on the fund managers. There are limits to the amount of carries as well as the requirement that investments are made in Wisconsin on Wisconsin-based companies with 51 percent of their employees in the state.
✓ The CIC model provides accountability for the fund managers so that one fund manager cannot monopolize the system. This is critical

in that Wisconsin needs to attract more fund managers and not less. It needs to attract more capital and not less, but it must do so in a competitive pro market fashion. Further, the CIC has strict ethical obligations to not be a fund manager itself.

✓ The CIC model can only exist on a performance-driven basis. It must make the connections between ideas, business growth, and investment capital. If these connections and jobs are not grown, the CIC makes no money.

✓ The Leadership Board is the interface piece of government to the free market. It literally holds the CIC accountable for the economy of the state, while holding the tax credits accountable as an investment. This is a critical piece in a continual audit system of how these tax credits are working for the people of the state.

✓ Without the performance-based nature of the CIC, the ethical definitions of the CIC, limits to the carry of competitive fund managers, and the accountability of the CIC and fund managers to the Leadership Board, there is no measurement of results. There is no accountability piece that ensures that the free market is free to openly compete.

The idea worked. The model was crafted with the knowledge of experts in economics and investment. A prominent member of the National Bankers Board took the idea to Secretary Snow in Washington DC, who embraced the idea. Did it see the light of day from the front-row politic in Wisconsin? No, of course not. That is not what is important; once again, the ideas we all have from the private sector are the only way to create outside-the-box solutions for our states and nation.

Mapping Progress

Another way to sell your plan to a tough crowd is to provide a map of how it will be done. In the case of the CIC model, I showed what had been done with the model in other applications. The map I included with the CIC model is below.

REFORM FOR ALL: LEADERSHIP IN ACTION

McCORMICK MAP FOR ECONOMIC DEVELOPMENT IN ACTION

REGULATION REFORM	INVESTMENT CAPITAL	INFRASTRUCTURE TRANSPORTATION
• *Authored and passed legislation to streamline and simplify the processes used by agencies in preparing proposed rules for small businesses*	• **Introduced legislation to provide the tools individuals and corporations need to invest capital in start-up ventures**	• Established new incentives for municipalities to allow the construction of power plants, providing more jobs by improving Wisconsin's energy infrastructure
• Passed the Job Creation Act, clarifying government regulations that discourage businesses from doing business in Wisconsin	• **Authored and passed legislation to restore funding to Wisconsin Manufacturers Extension Partnership to provide technical expertise and hands-on assistance to small and midsize**	• Stabilized the transportation fund, keeping all road construction projects on track for on-time completion and supporting Wisconsin's economic development needs

By instituting a well-designed action plan along with your policy model, you can strengthen the importance of your message. Remember to keep your stakeholders and supporters informed and involved. Don't be afraid to cross party lines in order to find the support your policy needs. Often, it's there—you just have to know how to ask for it.

CONCLUSION

Villainy wears many masks, none as dangerous as the Mask of Virtue.

—Washington Irving, *The Legend of Sleepy Hollow*

The mask of virtue blinds us from the light of truth, creating barriers that cannot be seen by the trusting eye. Words and actions do not coincide and, worse yet, people become separated from their own souls. The beauty of the mask often hides the mastery of manipulation that lies beneath. The pretense of the mask becomes the excuse for doing nothing at all. Finally, masks make it far easier to miss the ethical questions spun around the lonely cause of self-interest.

In today's world we have many forms of masks that relate to ego and greed. The newest addition is the mask of cyberspace. The technological shadows empower the bullies who would be cowards in the light of day. This mask permeates our next generation of would-be leaders. Bloggers operating from the shadows represent the new form of attack ad in American politics and in life itself. Bloggers possess no accountability for their words or for the impact of their assertions.

Masks make it far easier to miss the ethical questions. Soon, legal and illegal are spun on the looms of convenient truths and personal greed. Masks often claim high moral ground but, at the same time, seek the shadows of ill-gotten gain.

SB1—THE BILL THAT CHANGED MY VIEW OF PUBLIC SERVICE

One life lesson motivated me to call for change. It was a journal entry that disturbed me, inspired me, and called upon my heart to put pen to paper for one purpose; to stand tall and change the way things are. It was my last day in the Wisconsin state legislature in 2006.

The agenda of the day did not include SB1, a bill I was leading in the house, the Government Accountability Board. It was a bill resisted by my house colleagues as it was intended to oversee the ethical behavior of all public officials in the state.

It was a day that began as any other. The pledge of allegiance and prayer began the ceremonies. ...

The day became more interesting when the other side of the aisle, the minority party, called for a filibuster of my front row's agenda. The topic of their filibuster was my ethics bill, SB1. My party's front row found themselves in such a knot that they buckled at the mention of ethics. One member tore into my party's speaker for going to the press and lying about his record on ethics reforms.

The speaker was then chastised for his connections to politicians who were then convicted felons. My speaker and primary election opponent folded and agreed to pass a basket full of Democratic bills in exchange for their silence.

There was a trade of a gas-gouging bill, as well as the trade for many others that had never gone before their committee chairs. The Masked Ones stumbled into motion as suddenly these bills were pulled to the floor, one by one, as if by command of the silenced lambs that had all at once become lions.

The reaction was a newly designed agenda that was intended to hush the Democrats' passion in their push for SB1. The mistake of the majority party was in underestimating the bipartisan support across the aisle for clean government, the consequence of which was my ethics bill—SB1 began a life of its own.

The front row huddled like a rookie league lost on the mound. It appeared as though the mischief planned for the day was failing and the playbook was empty. Comically, the huddle continued for some time, with no strategy in sight.

In spite of all this pandering and childish behavior, we had work to do. Sadly, the day wasn't about jobs or health care. This was a day about payback and political intrigue. The rancor escalated between the two political parties, as they became more like two unyielding Little League teams than a legislative body. There, on the last day of the legislature in 2006, before the people's house in the Wisconsin state legislature, there was no debate, no argument, only a protracted game of hide-and-seek.

Throughout the day there were vote tallies circulating in caucus and on the floor. The death penalty was then—and is now—a controversial issue, but one state senator was hell-bent on passing it.

My vote was no. I was asked again and responded, "I don't have any wiggle room on this one."

After the front row realized they did not have the votes, they took up horse trading again. They brought up bills that were killed in closed caucus and made trades for votes with which others could compromise. Those whom the front row could not persuade to change their death penalty vote were asked to "take a walk" (leave the voting floor without casting their vote).

That tactic is usually easy enough to cover up, but one of the women was wearing a bright peach jumpsuit. As she pranced in the chambers right after the vote and pranced back out, it became obvious to the body what was going on. The gasps on the legislative floor were deafening. The vote was an especially serious one. To play games with such a vote wrenched the stomach and pulled on the heart. We were shocked, appalled, and outraged—yet paralyzed.

As I got in my car at 1:30 a.m. and drove back to Appleton from Madison, I just wanted to get the garbage off me—the manipulation, the lying, the backstabbing, the complete ugly mess. The lack of integrity in the people entrusted to serve the public was astonishing.

In contrast, the giddiness of the front-row club was reminiscent of children who must never be allowed to stay home alone. They grinned and snickered that they had won. Machiavelli would have been so proud—these pretenders behind their masks of virtue had passed the death penalty so that our speaker could secure one more name for his political campaign. That was the trade, confirmed by the death penalty author himself to the press and to the public.

The mask of virtue was transparent that day. The body on the legislative floor peered into the face of deception as it challenged the leadership every step of the way. The death penalty passed. The ethics bill failed.

If this scene was not a call for political reform and citizen-led leadership, nothing ever would be. ...

THE IMPORTANCE OF SB1

Without an ethical government based on laws like SB 1, elected officials may one day think they are above the law. In some cases, they already do. How can we, as citizens, believe in our representative government if the laws do not apply equally to each of us? The corruption that landed on our capitol's doorsteps is not new; it is as old as our nation. Personal weakness and fear have turned what should be hallways of opportunity and freedom, into pay-for-play capitols of desperation. The price we will pay as a people is still not known. We are a nation of entrepreneurs, innovators and hard workers. Yet Wall Street has been robbed, jobs are on the decline, and our economy is on the brink of ruin. Corruption and greed were major factors in all of these things.

It is hoped that the consequence of this book will serve as a reminder to all of us that we must all continue to fight for our freedoms, our Constitution. The Constitution reminds us that the only "just power derives from the governed." It is "we the people" who must change our government from its present course. Senate Bill 1, Ethics Reform Wisconsin, was needed because it took steps to guarantee that the Constitution and laws would apply equally to each of us—lawmakers, citizens and journalists alike. "Equal justice under the law" was the constitutional principle that Senate Bill 1 represented. America needs to restore that principle in all of our state houses and U.S. Congress.

SB1: THE REST OF THE STORY

Senate Bill 1; Ethics Reform Calling for a Wisconsin Government Accountability Board, was passed immediately after the losses in the November 2006 elections. Citizen leaders were brought into the process, taking on the role of watchdog and clean-government advocate, so that a true version of government accountability could be passed. We cannot legislate personal ethics. There will be other cases of abuse of power in public office—bribery, conspiracy and collusion. The continual vigilance by citizen leaders, the press, and integrity-driven public servants will be required to preserve our republican form of government.

The Veterans Property Tax Law was never introduced as a bill but quietly was moved into the Veterans Administration Budget by a governor who understood the importance of keeping my promise to those who safeguard our freedoms. As of this writing, those veterans who are disabled in the service of their country are now exempt from Wisconsin's high property taxes.

The Prescription Drug Purchasing Pool package, although not allowed up for a vote, was executive ordered and budget line-itemed by the governor in the Badger RX Prescription Drug Plan. According to the recognition that the Wisconsin governor gave to my office, it saved tax payers $30 million for those individuals under this health-care cost savings plan. It has gone on to be one of only a handful of national models in reducing health-care prescription drug costs.

As for my ten-year-old daughter, who was an innocent bystander during her mother's founding of the public charter school movement in Wisconsin, she has done well for herself. Kellie graduated from medical college with honors in 2009, beginning her own path to leadership and public service.

Kristen, who witnessed the political class' attack against their own sitting governor, graduated from Northwestern University and the Medill School of Journalism, *magna cum laude*. She continues to lead efforts around the world in corporate citizenship and communications.

Without hesitation, both of these young women lead in the tradition of service over self.

Former governor Scott McCallum heads up a private Global Relief Foundation, bringing over $1.5 billion in philanthropic donations and world relief to countries hit with global pandemics and famine. He works with several international organizations, the United Nations among others.

THE NEW WE

Integrity leadership requires that the American public is awake and involved. Deception and corruption is an equal opportunity employer for political parties. Courageous leaders need courageous individuals to stand with them. That is why I ask all of us to get involved in our own political process and our own government. The "business as usual" crowd has mastered a bag of dirty tricks and retail politics. It is up to all of us to change the way things are.

The "new we" can be found in the three pillars of citizenship: a free and appropriate press governed by the Society of Professional Journalists, integrity candidates and legislators who pledge to serve the people of their districts, and citizen leaders and activists who are willing to step forward to volunteer, advocate and stand on their convictions.

The "new we" has read, studied and understands the Constitution.

> *Let every American, every lover of liberty, every well-wisher to his posterity, swear to never violate, in the least particular, the laws of this country and never to tolerate their violation by others. Let every man remember the Constitution and laws and let every American pledge his life, his property, and his sacred honor to support the Declaration of Independence and the Constitution. Let it be taught in schools, seminaries, and in colleges; let it be written in primers, in spelling books and in almanacs ... let it become the political religion of the nation, and, in particular, a reverence for its study.*
> —Abraham Lincoln

For all of us who are interested in being change agents, remember to play it forward. Please do what is right, not what is popular. Think of the greater good and not about going along with the flow. Once you establish yourself in this new pattern of governing, take the time to encourage others to lead in the same manner. It will not be easy—leading never is.

Falling off the horse is not an option—for any of us.

The abuse of power, by whatever label you would like to give it, has significant consequences to the American people. Elitism and its nemesis populism have worn many labels throughout American history and politics: Republican, conservative, neocon, polluter, far right, Democrat, liberal, tree-hugger, and far left. The only protection that the American people have against an abusive and overzealous government, under any label, is the United States Constitution and the principles of integrity and freedom it represents.

As you have been shown throughout this book, the political class that exists in our present-day system of government has no gender, no ethnicity, no creed, no other discerning characteristics. Instead, it is a political animus with an arrogant and careless disregard for all Americans. The political class has only one motivation: a perpetual lust and pursuit of power through whatever means possible. The political animus' greatest personal flaw is the need to be somebody ... anybody.

Through the actions of the political class, the party elites, on both sides of the aisle, "we the people" have been treated like Joe the plumber and, worse, Joe the schmuck. Retail politics has dumbed us down, making us civically complacent and, worse, civically illiterate. The American people have been lulled into believing that the political process is looking out for our interests. Unfortunately, nothing could be further from the truth. Political inaction and stalemate has one intention in mind: to hold up legislation long enough so that a political interest group or individual pays for it to be pushed through.

When we the people expect someone else to take our responsibility of citizenship away from us, we are inviting trouble to walk in our front doors. And it has—today, we have a failed economy, a collapse in the housing and real-estate market, a collapse in the credit market that has impacted homeowners and small-business owners alike. The consequences to the American people are reportedly as bad as they were during the Great Depression, with record job losses, foreclosures on homes and businesses, and continued revelations of corruption in government and on Wall Street.

Know now that nothing will change unless we the people change it. I ask all of us to take responsibility for what our government has become.

MAIN POINTS

The political system is broken. To change the institutional corruption, we will need a citizen-led revolution, such as those during the 2006 and 2008 elections. A new "we the people" must call for new integrity-driven leadership to put the people's house right again. Keep in mind that changing the political party will only change the teams' jerseys on the field; the same institutional games will continue.

From staff-manipulated offices to assigned seating, controlled lieutenants and politicians rise and fall at the whim of the Machiavellian political class. The resulting culture is one of flawed personalities, short on merit and know-how and long on political favors owed. Political interest groups who align with this system of good old boys add to the problem by throwing money into the building of political silos. This does nothing to solve legitimate policy questions—the economy, banking crisis, education, war. The political games and tenure in office do nothing to serve the public and restore our republican form of government.

WHAT'S NEXT?

Three major changes must take place: first, there should be term limits for all legislators to stop the pursuit of power for power's sake. Our Founding Fathers brought talents and resources to public office, sacrificing their lives, possessions and sacred honor for the greater good. We should expect nothing less from our present-day leaders. (Lust for power is a personality flaw and need to be somebody.) Second, we the people need to study and engage in our government through the U.S. Constitution. It is this contract with our government that guarantees our liberties and protects us from dysfunctional and self-serving leaders. Third, we must ensure that the checks and balances of our three branches of government are working, as the U.S. Constitution intended. All three branches of government—executive, legislature, and judiciary—must be co-equal branches that check the power of the others.

There will be another layer of scandal in our government and in our justice system; we must prepare ourselves with a new generation of leaders and leadership. We the people must vote and support courageous candidates who understand that they are running to serve the public and the greater good.

Making an impact in public office does not require a lifetime of seat leather. It is possible to serve the greater good regardless of the length of time in public office. It simply depends on the candidate and politician's policy skills and attitude. I believe in term limits, now more than ever, after having served in government. New ideas and innovation will serve the people best. The power games played in our front rows in our state and federal government serve as a reminder that the Founding Fathers never intended for us to have a standing army of politicians. Rather, they intended that citizen leaders would take their turns serving—and then go home. It is your turn.

As for me, I will continue to work with individuals dedicated to the principles of our nation's founding, that of integrity leadership and public service over self. We the people must remain vigilant in safeguarding the U.S. Constitution and the rights and responsibilities that come with self-government. At this pivotal time in our history, it is up to all of us to change the way things are.

Fear of the abuse of the power of political parties is as great as the abuses by kings. ... Wherever there is an interest and power to do wrong, wrong will generally be done and not less readily by a powerful and interested party than by a powerful and interested prince.

—James Madison, 1788

APPENDIX I

NEWSPAPER ACCOUNTS & EDITORIALS

A Crisis of Conscience
Gannett News Editorial 2/2007
Published in the Appleton Post Crescent
Terri McCormick

Integrity and Hope Must Replace Fear and Despair at Home and Around the World.

The greatest challenge in leadership today is a "Crisis of Conscience" one of American integrity and hope for the future. We have lost our way as a people and as a nation, in a "crisis of conscience." We have further failed to inspire and lead other nations in this global war on terrorism. Greed and corruption have overshadowed political life and public policy makers, as rivaling forces of greed have replaced what once was a nation that stood for "one nation under god, with liberty and justice for all."

So, too, American culture has transformed to the leadership examples from the top. Recent university surveys have indicated, "university students are the most self-centered of all generations of students." San Francisco Bay schools have now declared that "homework stands in the way of downtime and is unnecessary." How are we to compete against ourselves, much less the world's global economy, with such examples of present-day leadership in the U.S.?

The microcosm of U.S. university and U.S. public school students can be extrapolated out to national politics and the world stage. Where there should be skilled diplomats, too often there is cronyism. Where there should be a faith and belief in the democratic process, there are distortions of the facts designed by political strategists and pollsters. And where there were once solutions, there are political divisions punctuated with partisan rancor.

Our national crisis of conscience was answered by the elections of 2006, with a reminder that the strength of this nation rests with the people whose fate this nation rests. *The greatest test of leadership in the U.S. has been and will always be the ability to inspire through vision and ideas.* Leadership today has been denigrated in public office with "masks of virtue" and "masks of integrity" designed to mislead the American public. These masks are among the most dangerous of deceptions; they have darkened the view of public life and they have violated a sacred trust with the people of this country.

As the scandals and convictions of the 109th U.S. Congress revealed to the world, the great American experiment had lost its way. When the Wall came down in Germany, a fractionalized and vulnerable Eastern European Block remained. National identity, economic and social disorder and dislocated alliances were the norm. The former satellites of the USSR and their alliances in the Middle East watched as the United States stumbled as leaders in the world. The United States will always be as strong as our people and the leaders we elect.

As the single remaining super power in the world, the United States, has failed to provide ethical leadership that honors the integrity principles found in the U.S. Constitution. Past paradigms of defined alliances and food-for-oil policies have given way to global economics and the dynamics of terrorism. *We as a nation must learn to lead through hope and inspiration, first within our borders, and then, throughout the world.*

Newspapers editorials and headlines across the state and nation carried a unified voice and call for the end of corruption and the pay-to-play system that paralyzed the political process. The *Milwaukee Journal Sentinel* published an article on January 1, 2006, titled, "To Play, You Paid, Lobbyist Reveals" which gave a detailed account of how the system worked with SBC/Ameritech personal checks of $40,000. Washington's *The Hill*, on January 11, 2006, disclosed an insider corruption story, "The Year of Abramoff," detailing a list of bipartisan corruption, naming political leaders and staff members who took bribes, used public monies for personal use and took illegal campaign contributions. Lavish trips, expensive sports tickets, jobs for spouses, gifts and other kick-backs were exchanged for expensive legislation for his clients at the taxpayer's expense.

A Gannett paper in Wisconsin at that time wrote a series of opinion pieces on the need for ethics reforms. One such article was titled, "When Will We Get Reform in the Capitol?" Representative Stephen Freese was quoted in that opinion piece with the following:

> *"Felony convictions, emerging scandals and voter discontent are shaping up as the 'perfect storm.' We must do our best to improve the public perception of the legislature and Wisconsin government."*

The corruption and pay-for-play culture in Wisconsin was painted on the front pages of many newspapers throughout the 2005 and 2006 legislative session. Making matters complicated for editorial boards in my own backyard was the fact that I was running for United States Congress against the major stumbling block to ethics reform, in a primary in my own political party. The lines separating my candidacy for U.S. Congress and my opponent's were drawn sharply and distinctly by other newspapers throughout the state.

Courageous general managers and editorial boards examined the content of the character of both candidates. One such man of courage was Roger Utnehmer, president and general manager of the *Door County Daily News.*

Bipartisan Corruption Requires Republican Leadership: State Representative Terri McCormick is Providing It.

> *Bi-partisan corruption has tainted Wisconsin government. Five former legislators have been found guilty of violating the public trust. The recent caucus scandal resulted in convictions of three Republicans and two Democrats. That makes both parties an embarrassment to the Wisconsin tradition of clean government. While the corruption is bipartisan, the responsibility to clean up the capitol is clearly that of Republicans who control both the state senate and assembly. Republican leaders have ducked that responsibility and should be ashamed. The conservative* Wisconsin State Journal *in Madison editorialized that the assembly Republican leaders are "blockheads."*

Terri McCormick joins a small group of Republicans who understand Wisconsin voters deserve better than the partisan defense of the corrupt status quo you hear from leaders in her party, like the speaker. Members of the Republican Party would be wise to look to others who support clean government for leadership, men and women of conscience like Terri McCormick and others.

Terri McCormick, by making ethics in government a point of difference with her primary opponent for Congress, stands head and shoulders above Republicans who ignore the smell of scandal, bipartisan corruption and government for sale to the highest bidder.

Terri McCormick is a woman of conscience, an independent thinker who puts the public ahead of petty partisanship. We need more people like her in the Republican Party ... and the U.S. Congress.

Roger Utnehmer
President and GM
Door County Daily News

My hometown newspaper declined comment in endorsing a candidate. Citizen accounts of the congressional race during the 2006 election spoke for them:

Party's Choice Doesn't Make Voter's Decision. *I guess that by the normal definition, I would be considered a chauvinist; however, I do admire capable women. I'm also a Republican and resent what the national Republican Party has done to my right to select a candidate to represent me in Congress. I resent the fact that the National Republican Party felt that it was more capable of choosing who should replace Mark Green to represent me and announce that it was backing someone before the primary.*

Terri McCormick is a very capable legislator. I was in politics and, with that background have watched Terri McCormick over the years represent us in Madison. She did a great job. In all fairness I feel Terri McCormick deserves a fair chance to run for the seat in Congress but we should start on a level playing field. Although the Republican Party chose to usurp my opportunity to choose, I will, and do, back Terri McCormick. She can do the job.

Tony Rosecky

Another citizen excerpt was written by a known GOP political insider with a "love 'em or leave 'em" theme:

When ostensibly Republican McCormick supporters attack President Bush, Vice President Cheney, Tom DeLay and the National Republican Congressional Committee, they don't seem happy with anyone in the Republican Party. If they dislike the GOP leadership figures so much and faithfully echo Democrats' attacks, perhaps their goals and agenda would be better served in another political party.

Appendix II

Policy Templates: Additional Notes

While the plans I've laid forth are key in working with the current political climate, that doesn't mean we shouldn't be working toward solutions for the American people. However, to expect to do so in a year, two years, or even four years will not happen unless we take steps to restore citizens/voters on every level of governance, private and public sectors alike. It took centuries for us to get entrenched in partisan politics. That can't be undone overnight, but with all of us working toward a more transparent community, state and nation, we will make the changes we need with the checks and balances we all deserve.

It's all about developing relationships for the purpose of solving the major problems and issues of the day. We live in an evolving global economic environment; truth seekers and problem seekers are critical if we are to transform the way things are. In order to do that, we should all first train ourselves to look at people without the veil of party affiliation on a more horizontal plain. Reform begins within ourselves.

LOCAL GOVERNANCE

Become involved in local government, but don't let personal feelings and party affiliations cloud your judgment. Stick with the facts. Successful people understand how to separate emotion from decision making. If you don't like the person suggesting a radical, positive change, you can still support the idea, if it's a sound one. Remember, change in attitude begins with you. If you're willing to look beyond someone's political affiliation in order to create positive change, you set the pace for others to follow.

If you think local government is small potatoes and that the real change happens higher up the food chain, think again. All policy and, therefore, politics is local, beginning with the small nonprofit to the county board. First, decide if you believe that change is needed and that you have a passion to lead on the issues. You don't have to have clout or money or financial backers. You need a solid idea and the ability to utilize your own personal assets and those of others to bring that idea to fruition.

COLLABORATIVE DECISION MAKING INSTEAD OF WINNER-LOSER POLITICS

Every region has assets; every individual does as well. We can't be all things to all people, but we can gather the talents and skills necessary to bring about effective change. Collaborative efforts hold more clout than one voice against the throngs of naysayers. While all efforts start with one person and one idea, real change comes from knowing how to inspire and motivate others to help your ideas to grow into plans, and your plans to grow into action.

How much more involved would your neighborhood and your community be if you asked for their support on an issue close to their hearts? Suppose you're lobbying for a stop light to be installed on a busy corner where school children walk to school. Parents in that neighborhood would be the first you would approach. How about the local school bus company, area schools, school board members, the PTA and local shopkeepers? Isn't community safety in the best interest of us all? Think of anyone who might have a vested interest in the safety issues surrounding that intersection. Those are the people you want to contact about your plan. Why not talk with local road contractors and public safety officers regarding the traffic flow and any research or studies involving the safety of that intersection?

One opposition to your plan that may stall it before it starts is revenue. Even local political figures who have your best interests at heart have their hands tied all too often due to budget constraints. In this case, prepare a feasibility study—how much would it cost the region to ignore the problem? What are some alternative sources of funding? Asking for local politicians' help is one thing—giving them the facts and tools they need to move forward is much better.

ECONOMIC DEVELOPMENT RELATIONSHIP

We all want to live better, and we want our hard-earned dollars to go farther. That's why your ideas should include the "what's in it for me" factor—how will your ideas affect working people who pay taxes. You will need to build a relationship between your community and your ideas. Community support comes from understanding vested interests in the outcome.

It starts with learning who your local government officials are. Go to meetings. Listen. Learn. Form relationships with those who make the decisions in your town or township. Become a volunteer at the local level in your community. Learn what your community's needs are from a volunteer perspective, as well as from those who work in the private sector. Build your knowledge base, your network base, and then become involved in helping others to find solutions. Now ... use this plan as a framework.

INTERREGIONAL TOOLS FOR STATE LEGISLATORS

Legislators want to be known for being proactive and on top of the issues that matter to their constituents. Yet in many cases, local and regional problems don't make themselves known to those who can do something to solve them. Jurisdictional planning that could save taxpayer money often is entangled with political webs formed by local and state decision makers. What could be effective is a liaison between community and government. Too often lobbyists' hands are tied with more narrow interests of their clients. While there are any number of lobbyists serving the public interest, a regional approach to state spending to address the layers upon layers of duplication of local services must be addressed if we are to serve the public's needs and address the taxes paid for these duplications.

Bring your observations and ideas to your state legislators. Invite them to a function you've organized to help raise awareness at the state level. Know exactly what you expect of your legislators and don't be afraid to ask. When you ask, make sure you have used this plan to build the strong network of support that will capture your legislators' attention. And always remember that collaboration and personal relationships work much more effectively than "gotcha politics."

Suggest or provide your legislators with easy ways to communicate with your region. Volunteer to create and maintain a monthly blog for the legislators. Help with sending informational e-mails to area voters.

Create and maintain a newsletter for the legislators' districts. Sell the legislators on the value of maintaining face time with the voting public. Understand that in some ways, you are working as a politician would—you want something, he wants something; work together for the common good. Don't forget that lobbyists are already in place, and you may have groups out there that already share your common goal. Most lobbyists are honorable and effective experts. Do not hesitate to call on them and ask how they may want to help.

CREATING A BLUEPRINT FOR CHANGE

Reaching your goal is as simple as creating a blueprint. Your action plan will map out your entire plan. On that diagram or action plan, you'll identify ways to approach each area of change. How? Create a culture that is open for the change you are making, and build a strong coalition of public- and private-sector partners. These partners will lend voice and research to your idea and will become allies in the journey toward your goals. You will then be building reform through strong alliances. Through alliances, change is created. If you've follow the plan in this book, you will have one path of action. This is not the only way. Think outside the box and create your own plan for solving the problems and issues in your neighborhood, community, state and nation. That is what citizen leadership is all about.

BENEFITS OF COLLABORATION

Do not discount the benefits of building a strong alliance with others. In my personal experience, I've found that more legislation passed with fewer roadblocks when I worked with atypical strategic alliances in the planning and implementation of policies. As a new legislator, I was mentored in this regard by a GOP speaker of the house from years past. His advice was to "make friends where [I] could find them." That advice led me to look at public policy through a nonpartisan lens. I kept my core values and convictions, and then sought those individuals from both sides of the aisle as strategic partners in crafting and passing public policy. In chairing the House Economic Development Committee, it soon became evident that jobs and a strong economy to support families was not a partisan interest. My focus, instead, was on the 40,000 small businesses and the near 80 percent of all new jobs they would create in Wisconsin.

In 2004 a bipartisan task force was formed to study the need for better government practices in enforcing small-business regulation. The task force members came from the government administration, governor's office and the business community at large. The result as the passing of the Regulatory Flexibility Act, creating a review board that oversees small-business regulation. The impact of the Flexibility Act has been more compliance through the use of a transparent Web site with information readily available to business owners. The impact of the Flexibility Act on politicians is restraint. No longer are businesses at the whims of a lone legislator who has not thought out his or her proposal without an economic impact study prior to the vote. Taking "gotcha politics" out of the practice of government has built bridges where there were once bureaucratic land mines and a needless partisan divide.

THE SCHEMATIC

As outlined in previous chapters, your blueprint will identify areas of need, identify ways to approach each need and give you sound guidance for creating an atmosphere conducive to change. Building reform is a lot like building a house—you have to lay the foundation before you can construct the walls. Your blueprint is your foundation. The more time and effort you put into planning, the stronger your foundation. Reform is the building you're constructing. By implementing change through following a plan of action, reform stands a better chance of withstanding the political storms that threaten to wipe it out.

CITIZEN LEADERS AND PUBLIC POLICY MAKERS: BLUEPRINT FOR CHANGE MENTORS AND MENTORSHIP

One of the most important alliances you may make in your professional life is with a mentor who holds your values and convictions. Many individuals have taken the time to guide me on my way and from a wide array of political viewpoints. An army colonel and Pentagon employee, a former international peace institute director from Sweden, a former GOP state speaker of the house, a former U.S. Congressional House member, my hometown state representative … and on and on.

Chief Justice Shirley Abrahamson is a mentor of mine whom I hold dear. The justice and I met years earlier at a law education event sponsored by the Director of Courts Office. At that time, I coached a mock trial team, believing that law education is critical to our future leaders. It was not surprising some years later that we were still on the same page of priorities. The Director of Courts Office was a partner with me, ensuring that the Court Interpreter Program was passed for our state. At a time when I should have been celebrating after such a policy win, I was instead planning my departure from the legislature.

I had only five months under my belt and already I knew I did not fit in with status quo politicians. I was receiving a lot of flak from older GOP members to keep quiet and stop thinking up these "new ideas." Pressure was already being applied to make me fall in line. I was told to never speak unless someone from the front row told me I could.

It was at this time that Justice Abrahamson and I ran into each other at a Sheboygan Fest event. She quickly recognized the disappointment in my face when I confessed that I would not be running for a second term in office. I shared what had happened and why I did not belong in public office. The justice, in her quiet, articulate strength, reminded me that I had value—and that my ideas and plans for solutions had purpose. Her game-changing words at this critical time in my career became the basis for everything that I would do in public office.

"Terri, never let anyone tell you that you cannot speak. Never let anyone tell you that you do not have ideas. Your ideas are some of the most important ideas that I have ever heard. Remember, always, that good policy is good politics."

From that pivotal conversation, I never looked back. I focused on visioning out solutions for the problems at hand. By hitching my courage to my convictions and core principles, my courageous staff and supporters would affect the lives and livelihood of the people we served.

We must settle this question now ... whether in a free government the minority has the right to break up the government of the people. If we fail it will go far to prove the incapability of the people to govern themselves.

—Abraham Lincoln, May 7, 1861

PHOTO GALLERY

JESSE BOYLE, FIRST-GENERATION IRISH AMERICAN BUSINESSWOMAN.

Grandma Jesse was Terri's kindred spirit and role model. She graduated from a business college in Little Falls, Minnesota, with such notables as Charles Lindbergh.

BIDDING FAREWELL AND BEST WISHES

Newly sworn-in representative Terri McCormick addresses the
student body at Xavier H.S. in Appleton, WI as long-time students
give their best wishes and farewell to their teacher.

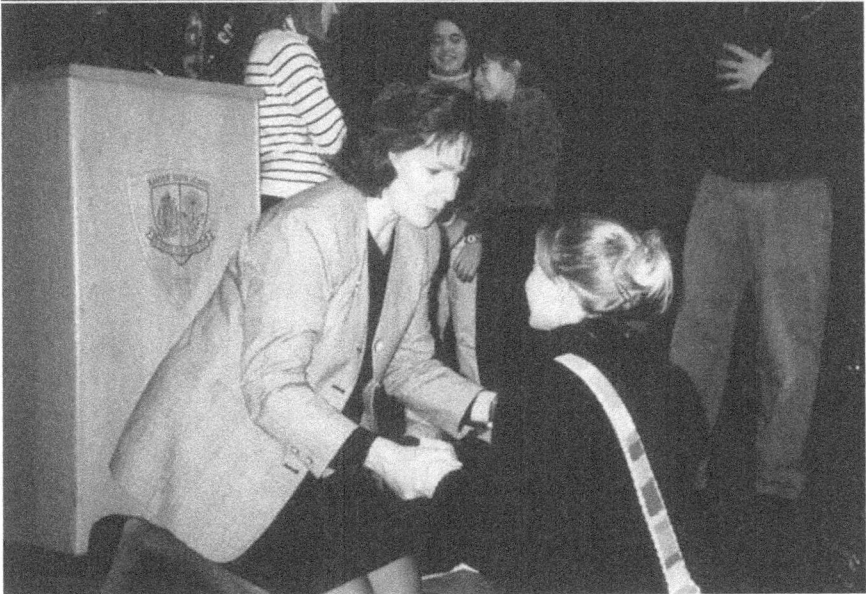

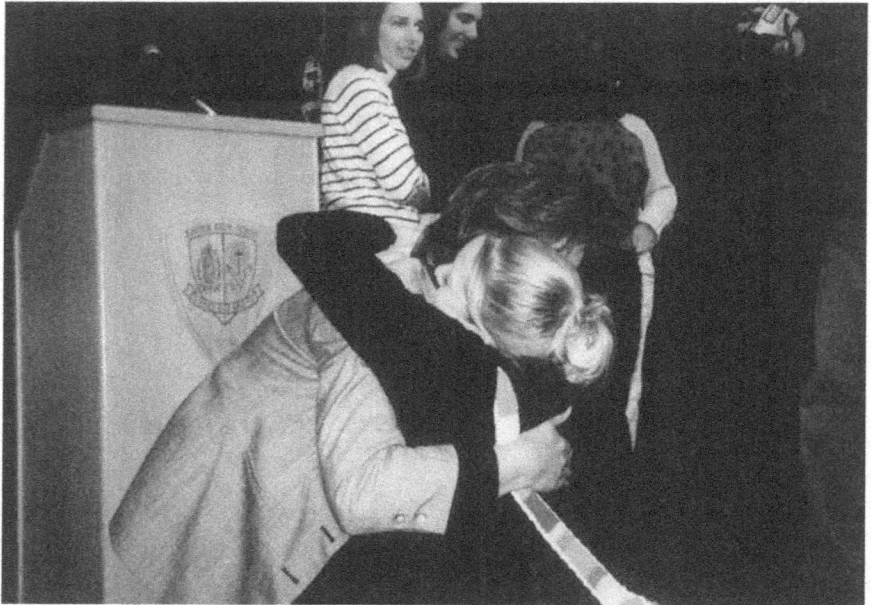

A CALL TO SERVICE AND CITIZEN LEADERSHIP

Citizen Terri McCormick, author and founder of Wisconsin's first Charter School Law, discusses the future of education reform and public charter schools with Governor Tommy Thompson. Pictured with Terri are former governor Tommy Thompson, former United States H.H.S. secretary, and Terri's daughter Kristen.

Terri and Tommy meet in 2000 to discuss education reform.

AN EARLY CALL TO POLICY LEADERSHIP

Terri and the state director of courts look on as the state's first Court Interpreter Program is signed into law just a few months after Terri takes office.

First-term legislator and Chairwoman Terri McCormick and Representative Stone confer during a committee hearing that would establish Wisconsin's first prescription drug purchasing pool.

(Committee on Health Care Cost Partnerships aimed at reducing the costs of healthcare; 2001- 2002.)

ECONOMIC DEVELOPMENT CHAIR

Chair of Economic Development

Author of the Blueprint for Change, Terri's *"Blueprint for Change"*
capital investment policies, small business regulation reform act,
support for WMEP and manufacturing, as well as business law
reforms, ushered in a wave of new job growth in the
2004 Wisconsin economy.

Wisconsin's Manufacturing Leaders join Terri

Breaking the gridlock between the executive and legislative branch, saving the WMEP program in the state of Wisconsin.

THE 2004 ECONOMIC BLUEPRINT FOR CHANGE DELIVERED

Terri receives the first pen, as Governor Doyle signs the Capital Investment Bill into law.

Terri receives the Guardian of Small Business at Tri-City Glass Inc., for her work as the author of the Small Business Regulation Reform in the state.

A PASSION FOR THOSE WHO HAVE SERVED
OUR NATION

Terri and her husband Ken meet with Adrian Cronauer, the subject of *Good Morning Vietnam* and POW-MIA advocate, at an event honoring Wisconsin veterans, servicemen and servicewomen.

Terri congratulates and rallies veterans for their leadership at the Appleton, Wisconsin VFW, for the 2006 Veterans with Disability Property Tax Bill.

A CHAMPION OF JUSTICE FOR ALL

Terri receives the Scales of Justice Award from the State Bar of Wisconsin for her reforms in court finance and legal rights under the U.S. Constitution.

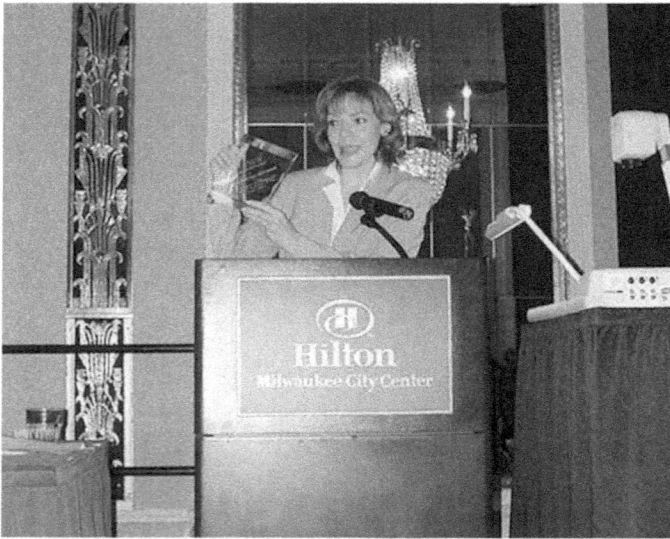

Terri receives the Eisenberg Award from the State Public Defender's Office for her work with the First Court Interpreter Program for the state of Wisconsin.

PUBLIC SERVICE IS A FAMILY TRADITION

Take Your Daughter to Work Day

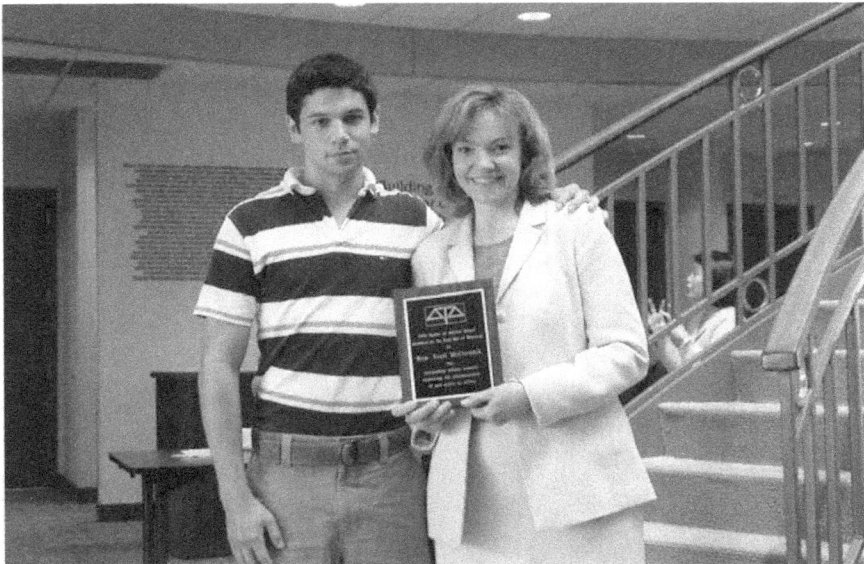

Terri's son, Nathan, looks on with pride at an award ceremony.

EDUCATIONAL OPPORTUNITIES FOR ALL

Terri's passion for education reform is reflected in her face as she greets schoolchildren from throughout Wisconsin.

Terri listens to testimony from charter school and school choice advocates.

HEALTH INSURANCE COSTS IN LOCAL GOVERNMENT

Terri looks on as local government leaders testify before her committee on the burgeoning costs of health insurance and its impact on property taxes in 2002.

Representatives McCormick and Underheim debate
the alternatives to health-care costs.

A PASSION TO SERVE

Terri speaks to the body in 2004 about the
urgency of health-care solutions.

As vice chair of the Judiciary, many constitutionally charged issues came before her committee.

THE HONESTY TOUR CAMPAIGN

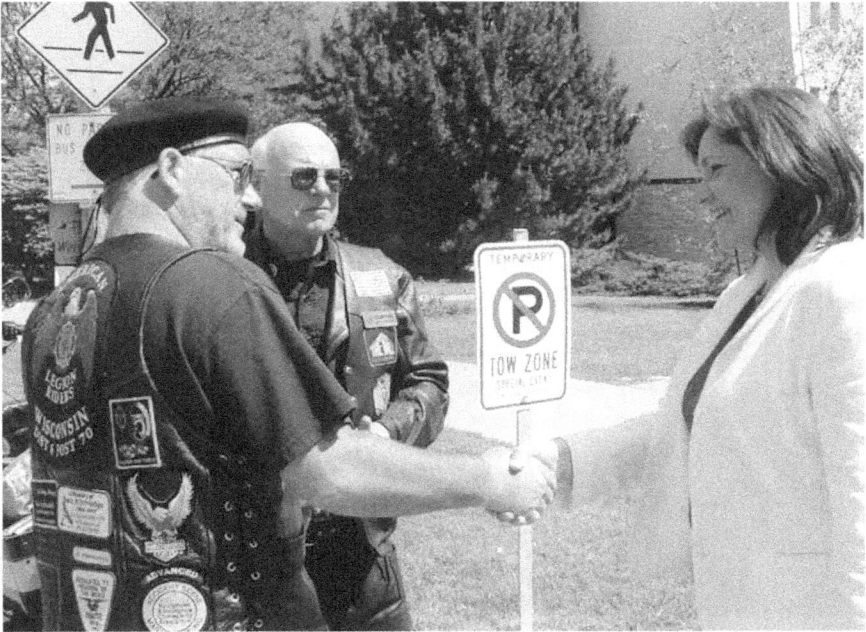

Terri greets members of "Rolling Thunder" veteran's organization thanking them for their dedication and public service.

Campaign staff and volunteers at the Seymour Hamburger parade.

End Notes

Preface

[1] Noonan, Peggy. 2006. "Baseless Confidence," *Wall Street Journal* [www.wsj.com], May 11.

Chapter One

[2] Wisconsin Court System Website, description of the Court Interpreter Program. [http://www.wicourts.gov/services/interpreter/index.htm].

[3] McCormick, Terri. 2003. "Expanding Eligibility for Public Defender Representation AB 616." *Wisconsin Lawyer*, [https://www.wisbar.org/AM/Template.cfm?Section=Wisconsin_Lawyer&template=/CM/ContentDisplay.cfm&contentid=49201], Vol. 76, No. 12, December.

[4] Wisconsin State Legislature. 2005/2006. Wisconsin Senate Bill 1Ethics Reform. [http://www.thewheelerreport.com/releases/Feb06/Feb22/0222mccormickwalkerethics.pdf], February.

[5] Iglesias, David. *In Justice: Inside the Scandal That Rocked the Bush Administration.* Hoboken, NJ: John Wiley & Sons, Inc., 2008.

Chapter Two

[6] U.S. Federal Charter School Support Website. [httphttp://www.uscharterschools.org/pub/uscs_docs/fs/index.htm].

[7] Manhattan-institute.org , Think Tank and Research on Charter Schools. [http://manhattan-institute.org/cgi-bin/search-manhattaninstitute.cgi?ul=http%3A%2F%2Fwww.manhattan-institute.org&q=Charter+Schools].

8   Sowinski, Mary. 1993. "Ten Who Dared," *Wisconsin School News, Inc.* December.
9   Wisconsin Department of Public Education Website and Charter School Resource. [http://dpi.wi.gov/sms/csindex.html].

Chapter Three

10 Montopoli, Brian. 2005. "Jilted. The Bush Brothers Kick Katherine Harris to the Curb," Slate.com. [http://www.slate.com/id/2121746/], June 30.

Chapter Four

11 Kuhn, David Paul. 2008. "GOP Fears Charges of Racism, Sexism," [Politico.com. http://dyn.politico.com/printstory.cfm?uuid=4CD6F8F1-3048-5C12-00DC54CD0B7E61E8], February 24.
12 Johnson, Rebecca. 2008. *Vogue*, February. Web Link to Article, [www.style.com/vogue/feature/090108VFEA/] and [http://www.style.com/vogue/feature/2009/03/altered-state/].
13 Johnson, Rebecca. 2008. *Vogue*, February. Web Link to Article, [www.style.com/vogue/feature/090108VFEA/] and [http://www.style.com/vogue/feature/2009/03/altered-state/].

Chapter Six

14 Bell, Jeffrey. *Populism and Elitism; Politics in the Age of Equality.* Washington DC: Regnery Gateway, 1992. pp. 114.
15 Bell, Jeffrey. *Populism and Elitism; Politics in the Age of Equality.* Washington DC: Regnery Gateway, 1992. pp. 38.
16 Machiavelli, Niccolo. *The Prince.* Translated and edited by Angelo M. Codevilla. New Haven: Yale University Press, 1997.
17 Noonan, Peggy. 2008. Commentary, Morning Joe; MSNBC, July 16. Further commentary found here, [http://townhall.com/blog/g/c14ff059-4746-45b3-aaae-a94ee8865b82].

Chapter Seven

18 Chang, Won Ho, and Park Jae-Jin, and Shim, Wung Wook.
Journal of Mass Communications. 1998. "Effectiveness of Negative
Political Advertising." December. [http://www.scripps.ohiou.edu/
wjmcr/vol02/2-1a.HTM].
19 Associated Press. 1990. "Candidate Vows to Continue Fight for
Campaign Finance Reform." November 27.
20 Shively, Neil H. 1988. "Candidate to Pay $600 for Not Reporting
Donations." *Milwaukee Sentinel.* November 17.
21 Associated Press. 1989. "Candidate Refusing to Pay Fine on
Campaign Donations." September 23.

Chapter Eight

22 Federal Election Commission Reports Online. 2005. [Candidate
For Congress FEC Reports. www.fec.gov. http://search.fec.gov/s
earch?q=2006+WI+8+House+Seat+John+Gard&ie=&site=fecgo
v collection&output=xml no dtd&client=fecgov collection&lr=
&proxystylesheet=fecgov collection&oe].
23 Marley, Patrick. 2006. "Cash Paves Way for Roads." *Milwaukee-
Journal Sentinel.* January 14.
24 Zullo, Roland, PhD. *Campaign Donations and Public-Private
Contracts, Wisconsin 1991-2000.* Ann Arbor, MI: University of
Michigan, 2003.
25 Zullo. 2003.
26 Zullo. 2003.
27 Zullo. 2003.
28 Wisconsin Democracy Campaign. 2003. "Still Fiddling While
Rome Burns," [http://www.wisdc.org/wdc.php September 10].
29 Wisconsin Democracy Campaign. 2005. "Graft Tax 2005: Playing
Peter to Pay Paul." [http://www.wisdc.org/wdc.php], May 27.
30 Wisconsin Democracy Campaign. 2005. May 27.
31 Wisconsin Democracy Campaign. 2005. May 27.
32 Wisconsin State Legislature. Wisconsin Legislative Audit Bureau
Report. 2003. "An Evaluation: Major Highway Program."
November.

33 Marley, Patrick. 2006. "Cash Paves Way for Roads." *Milwaukee Journal-Sentinel*, January 14.

34 Wisconsin Democracy Campaign. 2005. "If You Add Up All the Special Interests, Do They Equal the Public Interest?" [http://www.wisdc.org/wdc.php], August.

35 Wisconsin State Legislature. Wisconsin Assembly Insurance Committee. Assembly Bill 222 Public Hearing Notes, Insurance Committee Clerk.

36 Wisconsin State Legislature. Wisconsin Assembly Insurance Committee. Assembly Bill 222 Public Hearing Notes, Insurance Committee Clerk.

37 Federal Election Commission Reports Online. Candidate for Congress, 2005. FEC reports. [www.fec.gov. http://search.fec.gov/search?q=2006+WI+8+House+Seat+John+Gard&ie=&site=fecgov_collection&output=xml_no_dtd&client=fecgov_collection&lr=&proxystylesheet=fecgov_collection&oe=].

38 Barton, Gina. 2006. "Fired Officer Found Guilty of Bomb Threat." *Milwaukee Journal-Sentinel*, August 15.

39 Barton, Gina and Diedrich, John. 2006. "Fired Officer Faces Federal Gun Charge." *Milwaukee Journal-Sentinel, August 4.*

40 Wisconsin State Legislature. 2005. Wisconsin Assembly Bills 599, 1032. See bill history here, [http://www.legis.state.wi.us/2005/data/AB599hst.html].

41 Federal Election Commission Reports Online. 2005. Candidate for Congress, FEC report. [www.fec.gov. http://search.fec.gov/search?q=2006+WI+8+House+Seat+John+Gard&ie=&site=fecgov_collection&output=xml_no_dtd&client=fecgov_collection&lr=&proxystylesheet=fecgov_collection&oe=].

42 Diedrich, John. 2006. "Police Salary Bill is Arrested." *Milwaukee Journal-Sentinel,* February 28.

43 Wisconsin State Legislature. 2003. Wisconsin Assembly Bill 524. [http://www.legis.state.wi.us/2003/data/AB524hst.html].

44 Wisconsin State Legislature. Creation of CAPCO Investments 1997. Wisconsin Act 215. [http://www.legis.state.wi.us/1997/data/acts/97Act215.pdf].

45   Gillman, Catherine M. and Ross, Anne E. 1999. "Attracting Venture Capital for Business Start-ups." *Wisconsin Lawyer*, May.

46   Gillman, Catherine M. and Ross, Anne E. 1999.

47   Wisconsin State Legislature. 2003. Creation of Capital investment Corporation Model for Competition and Reporting to the AP Jobs Created. [http://www.legis.state.wi.us/2003/data/AB524hst.html].

48   Murphy, Bruce. 2003. "Capital Subsidy Bill Raked - $75 million deal 'scam,' says Colorado critic." *Milwaukee Journal-Sentinel*, December 23.

49   Wisconsin State Legislature. 2003. Wisconsin Legislative Audit Bureau Report. CAPCO Audit. November 12.

50   Wisconsin State Government. Wisconsin Department of Commerce Memo. 2003. WISCONSIN CERTIFIED CAPITAL COMPANY PROGRAM. August 20.

51   Wisconsin State Government. Wisconsin Department of Commerce Memo. August 20, 2003.

52   Murphy, Bruce. 2003. "Critics Question Merits of Economic Development Legislation." *Milwaukee Journal-Sentinel*, November 28.

53   Murphy, Bruce. 2003. "18 States Reject Wisconsin's Venture Capital Program." *Milwaukee Journal-Sentinel*. November 29.

54   Murphy, Bruce. 2003. "Capital Subsidy Bill Raked - $75 million Deal 'Scam' says Colorado Critic." *Milwaukee Journal-Sentinel*, December 23.

55   Murphy, Bruce. 2003. "Critics Question Merits of Economic Development Legislation." *Milwaukee Journal-Sentinel*, November 28.

REFERENCES

Associated Press, "Some Schools Reduce Homework; Some Say Kids Need More Time to Play, Relax."February 26, 2007. http://www.wsbtv.com.

CBS News/Associated Press. "Will Homework Ban Ease Student Stress?" February 27, 2007. http://www.cbsnews.com/stories/2007/02/27/national.

Crary, David. "Study:College Students More Narcissistic."Associated Press. February 27, 2007. http://news.yahoo.com/s/ap/20070227/ap_on_re_us/self_centered_students.

Dorning, Mike. "Polls Grow Gloomier for GOP; Foley Scandal Turns Many Against Hastert." *Chicago Tribune.* October 10, 2006. http://www.chicagotribune.com/news/nationworld/chi-0610100020oct10,1,316318.

Johnson, Mac. "Killing the GOP Brand." *American Thinker.* November 1, 2006. http://www.americanthinker.com/2006/11/killing_the_.

Noonan, Peggy. "Baseless Confidence." *Wall Street Journal.* May 11, 2006. http://www.peggynoonan.com/article.php?article=319.

Noonan, Peggy. "Media Anarchy has Its Downside." *Wall Street Journal.* September 29, 2006. http://www.opinionjournal.com.

Schemo, Diana Jean. "Grades Rise, but Reading Skills Do Not. *The New York Times.* February 23, 2007. http://www.nytimes.com/2007/02/23/education/23tests.

Simon, Richard and Levey, Noam N. "Foley Probe to Focus on Who Knew, When." *Los Angeles Times.* October 10, 2006. http://www. latimes.com/news/nationworld/nation/la-na-foley10oct10,0,1981435.

Sullivan, Andy. "Reform Bill Stalled in Congress." Reuters. July 9, 2006. file://K:\Newsarticles\ReformbillstalledinCongress.htm.